THE GREAT CENTURIES OF PAINTING

COLLECTION PLANNED AND DIRECTED BY

ALBERT SKIRA

TRANSLATED BY STUART GILBERT

★

Library of Congress Catalog Card Number: 58-8335

© by Editions d'Art Albert Skira, 1958

THE GREAT CENTURIES OF PAINTING

ROMANESQUE PAINTING

FROM THE ELEVENTH TO THE THIRTEENTH CENTURY

MURAL PAINTING BY ANDRÉ GRABAR

Member of the Institut de France, Professor at the Collège de France
Member of the Board of Scholars, Dumbarton Oaks, Harvard University

BOOK ILLUMINATION BY CARL NORDENFALK

Chief Curator of Painting and Sculpture at the National Museum, Stockholm

THE studies and reproductions of Romanesque paintings contained in this volume, covering as they do the most characteristic manifestations of this art in every part of Europe, will enable readers to appreciate the rich diversity, lively imagination and resourcefulness of the Romanesque painters, no less than their feeling for monumental composition and dynamic form. The 12th and 13th centuries witnessed a memorable flowering of pictorial art throughout the Western World. Whereas in the 11th century painters' ateliers had been relatively few and far between, there now arose a very great number of flourishing centers of artistic activity, with spheres of influence no longer local, but widespread. Moreover painters now began to give expression to their personalities, both fertilizing their art by careful study of the antique sources and striking out in new directions. Thus not only were the time-honored themes interpreted with greater freedom and boldness but this was also an age of experiments in art of an increasingly complex character.

True, the Romanesque painter continued to exploit the legacy of forms and techniques bequeathed by Late Antiquity and Early Medievaldom. But these were now transmuted and revitalized by the use of an increasingly expressive language and closer observation of nature. So much so that in some works, such as the frescos executed north of the Loire from the mid-12th century on and in 13th-century German miniatures, we find a new interest in pure form, linking up with the Gothic style which was to carry the process a stage further; whilst other works, those of Central Italy for example, point the way directly to that "realistic" painting which was to be the great discovery and the glory of a later age.

★

As regards the present work, a sequel to our *Early Medieval Painting*, we owe much to the good offices and generous aid of the many persons and institutions mentioned in the Foreword of the previous volume, to whom we would once more express our gratitude, as also to Miss Rosalie Green at Princeton and Dr Guglielmo Matthiae in Rome.

We also owe much to all who have given invaluable help in resolving the many technical problems and difficulties that arose in connection with the present work: in particular to the Direction des Monuments Historiques in France; to the Superintendents of Fine Arts and Antiquities in Campania, Latium, Lombardy, Lucania, Piedmont, Puglia, Tuscany, Udine and Venetia; to the Direzione dei Monumenti, Musei e Gallerie Pontificie at the Vatican; to ecclesiastical authorities and curators of libraries in Austria, Belgium, England, France, Germany, Holland, Italy, Spain, Sweden and the United States; to the Académie de Mâcon; to the Scuola Superiore d'Arte Cristiana Beato Angelico at Milan, and to the Chapter of Canterbury Cathedral.

We also tender our warmest thanks to Messrs Otto Demus of Vienna, O. Norn, Director of the Danish Academy at Rome, and Juan Ainaud de Lasarte, Director of the Museums of Catalonia.

GEOGRAPHICAL DISTRIBUTION
OF ROMANESQUE PAINTING

ROMANESQUE PAINTING
FROM THE ELEVENTH TO THE THIRTEENTH CENTURY

★

INTRODUCTION
TO ROMANESQUE PAINTING

I

MURAL PAINTING

ITALY - SPAIN - FRANCE
ENGLAND - GERMANY AND AUSTRIA
SWEDEN AND DENMARK

II

BOOK ILLUMINATION

DURATION AND DIFFUSION OF ROMANESQUE BOOK ILLUMINATION
PRINCIPAL TYPES OF MANUSCRIPTS
ROMANESQUE INITIAL LETTERS
PICTORIAL STYLES IN THE ROMANESQUE MINIATURE

INTRODUCTION
TO ROMANESQUE PAINTING

BY ANDRÉ GRABAR

THE subject of this volume is the medieval painting of Western Europe generally known as "Romanesque." But this term is even vaguer than the term "Gothic," applied to the succeeding period, and stands in need of explanation when, as here, it is used to cover the various types of painting prevailing in all the lands of Western Europe over a period of about three centuries. Even in France, where the epithet *roman* (whose English form is "Romanesque," sometimes "Romanic") originated, such comparatively recent writers as de Lasteyrie and Lauer extended it to the Merovingian and Carolingian periods and used it to designate all early medieval art. Nowadays, however, it is commonly agreed that the beginning of Romanesque art in France should be dated to the period following the year 1000 and the accession of the Capetian dynasty. The appearance of a corresponding type of art in England, associated with the Norman Conquest, may be assigned to approximately the same time. But the case was different in Germany where the 11th-century painters still kept to the practices of the previous epoch, that is to say to Ottonian art, which must certainly be distinguished from Romanesque. On the other hand, despite some infiltration of the Gothic, which was then predominant in France, the Romanesque style lingered on in German painting until well into the 13th century.

Moreover the life-span of Romanesque varied considerably in different parts of the same country, in France no less than in England; thus the Gothic style made its appearance north of the Loire in the middle of the 12th century, whereas in the south of France, as in Germany, the Romanesque style still prevailed in mural paintings as late as the 13th century. We find the same thing happening in Spain, where painters kept to the Romanesque type of mural decoration throughout the 12th and 13th centuries. In all these countries the dating of the rise of Romanesque is far from being definitely settled, and it is highly probable that a new chronology will need to be devised, varying according to the regions of transalpine Europe in which this new art form emerged. It is above all when we cross the Alps to Italy that the profound differences between Italian Romanesque and the corresponding art in France, England and Germany become apparent, and this despite the constant exchange of ideas between the countries concerned. Though contemporary with the Romanesque frescos of France and Catalonia, painting in Venice, southern Italy, Rome and Latium, Umbria, even in Piedmont and Lombardy, proceeded on very different lines. Also the evolution of art within Italy itself from the 11th to the 13th century not only followed a peculiar course, branching out in various directions in different places, but its ultimate fruition had little in common with the final phase of transalpine Romanesque. Whereas in the north of Europe Romanesque painting gradually gave place to Gothic and the art of the stained-glass workers, and was overshadowed by them, in Italy it followed a well-marked line of evolution, leading stage by stage to the achievement of those great artists of the close of the Duecento who ushered in the Renaissance: Duccio, Cimabue, Giotto and Cavallini. Obviously there can be no question of including these painters' works in a book dealing exclusively with Romanesque; their proper place is in a history of Italian art. We would, however, draw attention to the fact that such men as Cavallini and Cimabue derived the premises of their art from their immediate forerunners: for example the painters, usually anonymous, of the frescos at Ferentillo and Anagni and of the altarpieces and crucifixes of Tuscany.

Another important point arises in connection with this early Italian art. Paintings clearly foreshadowing Romanesque made their appearance in Rome as early as the close of the 10th and the beginning of the 11th century (in San Bastianello on the Palatine and, perhaps, in Sant'Urbano alla Caffarella), and notwithstanding their early date these should obviously be dealt with in the present work. Thus we shall discuss them and, in general, all the local manifestations in Italy and elsewhere which led up to Romanesque, since they help to an understanding of its nature.

It should be borne in mind, then, that, chronologically speaking, Romanesque painting assumed different forms in different places and that in Italy it followed a line of evolution independent of that in other countries.

In a general way, however, Romanesque painting flourished throughout Western Europe at the same time as Romanesque architecture, and perhaps even more abundantly than Romanesque sculpture. The destruction of so many mural paintings and the practical difficulty of personally examining the innumerable manuscripts disseminated in libraries in all parts of the world have tended to give an undue precedence to the study of sculpture in books dealing with Romanesque art. Yet it is the painting that should be studied most carefully, since it had continued without a break; even in the period of the barbarian invasions the painters always had models available and masters qualified to transmit their message to each successive generation. Moreover the technique of painting in books and on walls did not present so many difficulties as the rediscovery (for it was nothing short of this) of the techniques of monumental sculpture.

Thus there is no reason to be surprised by the great number of paintings figuring in manuscripts of the 11th, 12th and 13th centuries—whatever their country of origin—that have come down to us, or by the fact that Romanesque frescos have likewise been discovered in all parts of Europe, even in the humblest village churches and in remote valleys of the Tyrol and the Pyrenees. No earlier type of painting had ever been practised so extensively in Western Europe. Like the practice of building in stone, first reserved for religious edifices, then successively extended to those for private and official use, painting made rapid strides owing to the general increase of wealth and improved economic conditions. By the same token it became more "democratic," now that an ever increasing number of people could afford to buy works of art and were capable of appreciating them. For the progress of education played a part in the new demand for pictures, especially for illustrated manuscripts. Not only were there more readers and more books available but steps were also taken to create a new iconography intended to appeal to the more cultured reader.

As in the previous period, the great majority of paintings are anonymous and in many cases we are still in ignorance of the names of those commissioning them. However, in the case of illuminated manuscripts, the colophon often mentions the name of the person ordering the book. Most of the persons named were eminent prelates, in particular abbots of the great monasteries, but there are also some laymen and ladies of high rank. So far as can be judged, the artists employed were chiefly monks or laymen in the employ of monasteries. This certainly holds good for the illustrations of manuscripts that contain indications of their monastic provenance or can safely be ascribed to the scriptorium of a specific abbey. As regards the fresco painters, however, we know nothing about their social status or origins. Were they the same men as those who illuminated manuscripts? This is not impossible, but in view of the remoteness of many of the frescoed churches from the abbeys which possessed scriptoria we should have to assume that the monastic painters were free to travel far afield. And it may be questioned whether monks would be allowed to absent themselves for the length of time required for the execution of these commissions.

Like the professional stone-carvers who made statues and reliefs illustrating religious themes, the fresco painters may very well have been laymen who traveled from church to church in pursuance of their calling. In fact, since painted decorations could be carried out more quickly than the elaborate sculptures of a Romanesque church, it seems likely that the painters had to be constantly on the move if they were to earn a steady livelihood. There are very few instances of frescos inscribed with the names of their makers, for which reason those found in the region of Latium are of special interest. One of these 11th-century inscriptions records the fact that two brothers, John and Stephen, and a nephew, Nicholas, jointly decorated the walls of the abbey church of Sant'Elia near Nepi. Composed of three members of the same family (the first instance of a clan of artists), this team of workers had no connection with a monastery; moreover, in the inscription the three artists are described as "Romans"—which implies that they had to travel thirty miles to the scene of their labors. A large icon on wood (*The Last Judgment*, Pinacoteca Vaticana) seems to have been painted at Rome by the same group. A 13th-century fresco in the Sacro Speco at Subiaco displays the portrait and bears the signature of a painter who describes himself as a monk: *frater Romanus*. There was a large Benedictine monastery at Subiaco near the "sacred cave" (Sacro Speco) where St Benedict lived as a hermit, and among the monks of this monastery, which had its own scriptorium, there may have been some specialists in mural decoration. It is not known if this artist monk worked outside Subiaco; the theory that he took part in painting the Anagni frescos is no longer tenable. However, these two instances go to show that in the region of Latium monks as well as laymen practised monumental painting.

Unfortunately cases of this kind are rarely met with, and there is little to show which were the chief centers of pictorial art so far as mural painting is concerned. The only exceptions are such great Italian cities as Rome, Palermo and Venice, where it is known that ateliers of fresco painters and mosaic workers flourished in the 11th, 12th and 13th centuries. It is interesting to note that we have here the revival of a state of affairs that had obtained in an earlier age, when the artists' ateliers were located in large cities, where princes and high officials patronized the arts with a view to enhancing their prestige. During the Romanesque period the popes reverted to these practices, while at Venice and Palermo the Doges and Norman rulers, in imitation of the Byzantine emperors, carried on the same tradition.

It would seem that this custom was not revived till somewhat later in countries north of the Alps. Though schools of illuminators already existed in Paris and London, they were not necessarily under royal or princely patronage, while as regards monumental painting there is no positive evidence of the existence of ateliers of fresco painters in Paris, Toulouse, Cologne or any other large cities. Whether staffed by laymen or monks, they seem to have been located (like the workshops of the specialists in stained glass, mosaic pavements and figurative embroidery) in abbeys or in the neighborhood of scriptoria producing illuminated manuscripts.

These latter, as before and during the Carolingian renaissance and in Ottonian Germany, were usually housed in monasteries. But in the Romanesque period there was a remarkable increase in the number of monasteries employing staffs of illuminators, and while some of the older extra-monastic scriptoria maintained their output, others abandoned this form of activity. Since an account of the illuminators' workshops is given later in this volume, they do not call for detailed mention here.

We cannot but be surprised by the number of these workshops, each specializing in a distinctive branch of art. At first sight this might seem to be a consequence of the feudal system which was now coming into its own. But the proliferation of monastic workshops had already begun under the Carolingian, and had continued in Germany under the Ottonian emperors. The most that can be said is that it gained strength in the Romanesque period, when not only were there more workshops functioning simultaneously, but the output increased enormously. Despite the family likeness discernible in all Romanesque illuminations, each workshop had its own style and a specific repertory of images and motifs in which it particularly excelled. And since, as time went on, the supply of available models was constantly augmented, there was a parallel increase in the number of possible combinations of motifs inherited from the past or borrowed from other workshops.

This is not to say that there was a proportionate rise in the originality of the work produced; indeed the contrary would seem to be the case. While the Romanesque miniature is remarkable for its high average level of excellence, there are fewer really outstanding works than in the early Middle Ages—indeed one might almost speak of mass production. Interesting though these paintings are, they suggest that illumination was now by way of losing the privileged position it had enjoyed under the Carolingian and

Ottonian emperors. This was probably a consequence of the rapidly increasing demand for all forms of art in the 11th and especially the 12th century. The fact that this change is more apparent in the miniatures than in the frescos is due to the greater number of the former that have survived. For quite probably a similar need for intensive production led to the making of more frescos of a relatively inferior order, in which expert craftsmanship tended to replace the creative urge of the true artist. This, anyhow, is the impression we get from regions where a fairly large number of frescos have survived, notably in small country churches; in, for example, the Vendôme district of west-central France and the mountain valleys of Catalonia.

Not only were more paintings produced in the Romanesque than in the preceding period, but the artists' programs covered a wider field. Thus not only were the Old and New Testament narratives fully illustrated but at the same time (and this was distinctive of the age) a tendency developed to create cycles of elaborately planned pictures, appealing more to the intellect than to the eye and complementing the learned treatises of the theologians. Dogmas, mysticism and above all moral homilies were given iconographic expression inspired by the themes and methodology of contemporary tracts and sermons. There was also an increase of paintings illustrating the lives of the saints, which provided painters with opportunities for enlivening their works with local and, so to speak, topical themes such as forms of worship peculiar to specific dioceses, portraits of bishops and donors. Fostered by the popes during the investiture struggle between the papacy and the emperors and after the triumph of the former, this politico-religious art flourished, especially in Rome, during the 12th and 13th centuries.

Though many of the key works have disappeared, it is nevertheless possible to reconstitute some interesting aspects of this new form of art and get an idea of the conditions under which it developed, promoted by the medieval popes and guided mainly by considerations of political expediency. True, the workshops attached to the establishments of kings and princes ranked among the most important "schools" of art of the early Middle Ages. But it is only in Rome that evidence is forthcoming as to how the artists' workshops functioned, and the survival of this evidence is due to the fact that in Rome the secular element was tied up with the religious, and for that reason stood a better chance of escaping destruction. Certain works sponsored by the popes stand on the borderline between secular and religious art. Secular subjects had already been given a place among the illustrations of Carolingian books, but a much wider use was made of them in the Romanesque period. Illustrated calendars, bestiaries and geographies were produced in greater numbers; pictures intended to serve as records of legal decisions, with portraits of the parties concerned, had a considerable vogue; history books were embellished with depictions of the incidents described. Finally, the practice now developed of illustrating romances, *fabliaux* and verse chronicles.

It seems likely that these non-religious themes, whose cycles were being constantly enlarged, were also utilized by the painters called in to decorate the walls and ceilings of palaces and the homes of the nobility. But so few fragments of these decorations have survived that there is now no means of tracing the repertories of themes employed except by way of occasional reflections of them in other art forms: manuscript illumination, embroidery (and imitations of it in certain frescos), mosaic pavements, goldsmiths' work and wood-carving; also by way of the borrowings from palace art that sometimes figure in church painting. And scanty though this evidence may be, there is enough to prove that the repertory of non-religious themes employed by the Romanesque mural painters must have been considerable.

Yet, however extensive may have been the destruction of works of this kind which, not being objects of pious veneration, were far more vulnerable than religious works of art, there remains no doubt that throughout the Romanesque period the various art techniques, especially mural painting, were for the most part put to the service of the Faith. The repertory of subjects employed in churches remained very much the same as in the Early Christian era and, as in the past, a theophany was represented in the choir while narrative cycles figured on the walls of the nave. The few additions that had been made in Carolingian times were retained and there were some new contributions by the Romanesque painters themselves. However, these innovations seem to have been neither frequent nor far-reaching. On the contrary, in some transalpine churches (for example Saint-Savin near Poitiers) full-length historical cycles were replaced by sets of isolated pictures or by abridged cycles confined to a single part of the church, the other parts being left unpainted.

Only in the mosaic pavements do we find an enlargement of the repertory of Romanesque church decoration as compared with that of Early Christian and Carolingian basilicas. The motifs employed (classical in inspiration though usually adapted to the Christian view of life) were often of a scientific or literary nature—zodiacs, calendars, paradise gardens, animals; reminiscences of *fabliaux*, *chansons de geste* and historical events—but Old Testament scenes and characters also figure in them. The same subjects were used in embroidered fabrics and these were often reproduced in mural decorations. It was chiefly secular motifs of this type that Romanesque illuminators incorporated in their historiated initial letters. Though not the inventors of this form of illumination, they did more than any others to promote the use of big initials adorned with scenes and figures. Torn between a desire on the one hand to decorate the book and to entertain the reader with colorful pictures and, on the other, to stress the religious message of the text, the Romanesque illuminator drew freely on the aulic and scientific cycles of the age and adjusted his illustrations as best he could to the moralizing themes relished by his contemporaries. Strange beasts and acrobats were particularly in favor, since their bodies could be twisted to fit into the outlines of the "inhabited" initial letters that bulk so large in the illuminated manuscripts. In the mural decorations of churches, however, the non-religious elements were not allowed to encroach unduly on the religious, and Romanesque artists exercised much discretion in such cases. As it so happens, we are sometimes puzzled by partial reproductions of pictorial cycles which, in this fragmentary form, seem almost meaningless. Perhaps the explanation is that a mere "allusion" to a familiar theme, historical or fabulous, was enough, and the contemporary beholder could conjure up in his mind's eye what had been omitted.

On the whole the repertory of themes is considerably larger in Romanesque than in Carolingian and Ottonian painting, but, apart from those categories of images more noteworthy for their intellectual than for their artistic appeal which were a creation of the age, this greater wealth of thematic material is due to a revival of Early Christian motifs and, to a less extent, to borrowings from contemporary Byzantine art. Practised in Carolingian times and carried a stage further, in Germany, under the Ottonian emperors, this recourse to Early Christian and Byzantine sources, so rich in iconographic material, both Christian and secular, became still more frequent during the Romanesque epoch in all parts of Western Europe.

Esthetically too, Romanesque painting shows many affinities with the art of previous centuries in the lands around the Mediterranean basin and the countries of the West. As the immediate heir of the Carolingian and Ottonian styles of painting, it linked up by way of them with the Christian painting of an earlier age. A close study of the extant works, miniatures or murals, clearly reveals both these links with the distant past and the lasting effects of Carolingian art on Romanesque. Cases in point will be discussed later in this volume. Meanwhile, however, we would emphasize the part played by the Carolingian school of Reims and the Franco-Saxon school in shaping Romanesque esthetic in England and the north of France, where for several centuries miniature and fresco painters practised an expressive art which, for all its originality, owed some of its distinctive characteristics to the above-named schools. In other words, as regards their forms and general conceptions the Romanesque painters took the art of their immediate precursors as their point of departure.

But they also looked back for their models to the painting of an earlier age. Though this is most apparent in Rome, we find the same thing happening everywhere, for example in the frescos of Northern Italy and the region of Poitiers; also in English, French and Spanish miniatures of the period. The models which modern researchers have succeeded in discovering in various regions did not merely belong to a much earlier age, but were also of very different kinds, for example miniatures dating back to the first centuries of Christendom, frescos or mosaics figuring in very ancient churches. Moreover, not all Romanesque painters were equally receptive and the lessons they learnt from the monuments of antiquity were given various interpretations. In some cases the borrowings were limited to distinctive types of ornament; in others to the overall decorative arrangement employed in painting a book or a church. But sometimes, too, these artists went so far as to reproduce figures, scenes and even whole cycles of an earlier age. Thus in studying Romanesque paintings we must always allow for the latent influence, not only of the art immediately preceding them, but also of older forms of European painting, beginning with that of classical antiquity. The more closely we examine Romanesque art, the more numerous are the elements found to derive from these earlier sources and taken over by it at different stages of its evolution. For instance, that favorite motif of Romanesque painters, a garland tied with a ribbon, was obviously copied from 5th-century mosaics, while the palmette-candelabra in San Clemente at Rome and other churches of the same group go back to the "grotesques" of the Augustan age. The "historical" pictures containing representations of fortified towns seem to derive from paintings of the 3rd and 4th centuries, whereas the prototypes of the aureoled "Virgin in Majesty" figuring in decorations at Tahull and Aquileia cannot have been anterior to the 6th century.

Other versions of the same tradition of antique painting came to the notice of Romanesque artists through the intermediary of Byzantine works, some more or less contemporary, others much older. As early as the 7th century, Greek manuscripts with illustrations had been brought to England, where they were studied by indigenous artists and imitated in various periods, including the Romanesque. Italy was exceptionally favored in this respect; for many centuries mosaics and frescos made by Greeks and Syrians had been on view, and from the 7th century onward their art had kept much closer to the traditions of antiquity than had that of contemporary, even Roman, fresco painters. This was also the case in the late 11th and in the 12th and 13th centuries, not only in central Italy but in several countries of the West, where the Byzantine contribution can be assessed by the greater or less degree to which artists conformed to antique methods of modeling and sought to render plastic values. Finally, surprising though this may seem, the few cases of Moslem influence show that sometimes through this channel also, if indirectly, Romanesque painting drew inspiration from ancient Greco-Latin sources, as is particularly noticeable in imitations of Islamic historiated textiles.

Moreover, when we examine the style—i.e. the art proper as apart from themes and motifs—of Romanesque painters, we find, here too, a legacy of ancient Rome, though the presence of the classical tradition may not be so clearly visible. For instead of imitating the outward aspects of persons and objects (a form of art in which the painters of classical antiquity particularly excelled), the Romanesque painter aims at conveying their invisible essences in terms of a subjective, poetic interpretation of the optical phenomenon. Thus his creations are largely products of his imagination, and his representations are apt to deviate from the normal vision. Indeed he does not seem to take account of concrete visual experience in his work, except with a view to stressing some significant detail such as the curve of a wave, the shape of a leaf, the ornament on a costume, and using these as symbols: of the sea, of a tree, or of a personality, as the case may be. The artist makes no secret of the fact that what he represents is a creation of the mind and the imagination and this is especially true of his portrayals of human beings, the proportions of their bodies, their outlines, their movements and, naturally, their features. As in much modern painting, it is taken for granted that the painter has a right to ignore the objective data supplied by nature and, when it serves his turn, to give an object a contour differing from its "real" contour, to alter its shape and size (in relation to other objects), and to paint it whatever color he thinks fit. Nothing better reveals the basic conceptions of the new art than an analytic study of the historiated initials and other decorative paintings in which Romanesque painters felt free to give untrammelled expression to the tendencies described above.

It is clear that during this period the public of the age was quite ready to accept a principle that even today too many of our contemporaries fail to comprehend: the principle that the creative inspiration of a painter who has any claim to greatness entitles him to manipulate as he chooses the forms and motifs which are his natural means of expression, as words are the poet's and the orator's. Yet in the case of the latter we have no hesitation about according them the right of forging a language of their own and adding new shades of meaning to words of common use. The Romanesque painters went furthest in this direction in their handling of space, sometimes ruling it out completely, sometimes treating it as the fancy took them and giving it unequal extension in different parts of the same picture. And there are other striking deviations from visual actuality. Compressed into an extremely narrow plane parallel to the surface of the vellum or wall on which they are depicted, figures and objects in Romanesque paintings tend to appear flattened out and, so far as their "depth" is concerned, much like the figures on bas-reliefs. Likewise, the painter deprives them of the weight and sometimes even of the density basic to all that is opaque and, as a natural consequence, of the power of casting shadows.

Thus the beholder is constantly reminded of the artist's intention of setting before him not an exact transcription of reality, but his own interpretation of it or that of the artist whose work he has taken as his model. Obviously we should not be justified in claiming that such stylizations were always intended to body forth some esoteric message or poetic vision; those of human and animal forms in historiated initials were in many cases of a purely decorative nature. Probably many painters were drawn to these eccentricities of style instinctively, especially when they and their entourage had little acquaintance with the techniques of an art based on nature imitation, such as the Greco-Roman painting of the imperial epoch. In Western Europe during the 11th and 12th centuries, owing to the lack of direct contacts with the art of antiquity and of schools where its traditions had been maintained, the prestige of classical art could neither check nor control the vagaries of painters who were always tending to revert to the naive idioms of child art, of backward races and archaic epochs. There is unquestionably a strain of primitivism in Romanesque painting, and indeed it is to this that it owes much of its driving force, its expressive values and strikingly decorative effects. Nevertheless we should be wrong in assuming that this notion of "rusticity" is applicable to Romanesque art as a whole. Time and again a careful scrutiny of Romanesque works leads to a very different conclusion. It becomes clear that many of these pictures are designed with geometrical exactitude and proportions carefully calculated. Though the compositional schemes may not be immediately apparent in many cases, their presence is indisputable, and it presupposes the existence of a studio tradition stemming from antiquity that had been handed down from generation to generation.

A point in favor of this view is that the forms and motifs modified by Romanesque stylization can usually be traced to Greco-Roman sources. So there is no justification for describing Romanesque as in any sense a "folk" art, even though its style may have certain traits in common with the art of primitive peoples.

Indeed we would go further and point out that those selfsame tendencies of the Romanesque style in painting which seem to conflict with the Greco-Roman esthetic of antiquity had already made their appearance, during the preceding period, in much Mediterranean art and in works deriving from the Greco-Roman tradition. We have spoken of these early intimations of the Romanesque style in our *Early Medieval Painting*, notably with regard to fresco painting in Rome from the 6th to the 9th century. But there had been other precedents, chiefly in Byzantine and Coptic mural painting and, before them, in the 2nd- and 3rd-century murals of Dura-Europos in northern Mesopotamia. I do not think that we can continue to hold the view, current at the beginning of the present century, that all the paintings of the last phase of antiquity and the early Middle Ages which show tendencies towards an abstract style, flat color and, in general, towards forms not directly imitative of reality, are oriental in origin or anyhow subject to oriental influences. Any such view is negatived by the fact that in Rome during the 6th and 7th centuries it was precisely this style that differentiated the works of local, indigenous artists from the paintings imported from the Greek East. What we have here is, rather, one of the tendencies implicit in the complex of styles embodied in the art tradition of the imperial Roman age as practised in all the lands around the Mediterranean. Even in that epoch we find some works in which natural appearances were stylized in much the same way as many centuries later they were stylized by the Romanesque painters and which testify to the antiquity of the sources drawn on by the latter (see our *Early Medieval Painting*, Introduction and Part One).

Romanesque stylization is thus in the direct line from earlier art forms and this indeed holds good for all the characteristic traits of Romanesque painting. Its antecedents are not to be looked for in the remote (and very different) classical and Hellenistic phases of Greek art but in the painting of the late imperial epoch still in its full flowering when Christianity came on the scene, and it was this art that the early Christians enlisted in their service. But, even in the period before Constantine and Theodosius, there had existed, alongside works conforming to the Roman norm, others showing a tendency towards the stylization we are now discussing. Thus already, under the Empire, there were intimations of that plurality of styles, described in our previous volume, which led to the simultaneous emergence of works of art ranging from wholly realistic depictions in the classical manner to graphic stylizations of a more or less audacious order.

That Romanesque painters, when taking over the tradition transmitted century by century from the remote past, should adopt the ideas and practices of their immediate predecessors was to be expected. That this was what actually happened is proved by such works as have come down to us in a fairly complete state, such as the frescos of Latium, the Winchester and Limoges miniatures.

Attention has already been drawn to one of the most distinctive trends of these Romanesque stylizations based on the models of the preceding period. I have in mind the type forms which, after being formulated in certain Carolingian ateliers, chiefly those at Reims, were adopted during the Romanesque epoch in all the countries of northwestern Europe: in northern France, England, Flanders and western Germany. The fact that the Carolingian art tradition was perpetuated by the Romanesque painters was not fully recognized until quite recently, but it was a fact of capital importance for the evolution of Romanesque art. When we study the miniatures and frescos closely we cannot fail to see how considerable a part was played by this stylization, Carolingian in origin despite the new interpretations given it by the Romanesque painters.

Another type of medieval stylization which had a profound effect on Romanesque esthetic derived from Byzantine art forms of the Middle Ages. All the lands of Western Europe were acquainted with the discoveries and inventions of the contemporary Byzantine artists and turned them to account; indeed in some of these countries, those around the Mediterranean basin and in the Germanic empire, the forms assumed by Romanesque art reveal a more or less pronounced adoption of Byzantine idioms. Throughout the southern half of Europe Byzantine tradition had an influence on Romanesque art no less marked than that of Carolingian tradition (as sponsored by Reims) on the art of north-western Europe. It must be pointed out, in this context, that we are referring to the influence of medieval Greek works, not to that of East Christian prototypes of the first centuries of our era, which had by now lost their efficacity. The westward drive of Byzantinism made itself felt from the 10th century on, that is to say with the new flowering of Byzantine art under the Macedonian emperors. Nevertheless during the 10th century and well into the 11th these works were appreciated only by a cultured élite, chiefly at the court of the German emperors and in monastic ateliers working for the court. The prestige of the Byzantine monarchy largely contributed to the favor shown Byzantine art in these somewhat restricted milieux; it was only at the end of the 11th century that it achieved wider popularity, principally in Italy. Towards 1070, on the initiative of an abbot of the Monte Cassino monastery, artists and works of art were directly imported from Constantinople to that great center of monastic life in Western Europe. The popes too, at the time when the papacy was celebrating its triumphs over the secular authority of the Empire, turned to Byzantium for models of religious and political art. Rome was then the seat of a brilliant "Romanic" school with ramifications in all directions even in lands remote from Italy, which did much to popularize forms of Byzantine provenance (along with other influences) in various parts of the continent.

This trend gathered strength and became generalized towards the middle of the 12th century. Palermo and Sicily, Venice and the other great Italian commercial cities and, most of all, the Crusaders and other westerners who had settled in Greek territories, took a share in disseminating Byzantine works of art throughout the western world. These were enthusiastically welcomed and imitated by painters and sculptors in many parts of Europe, but it was particularly in the Rhineland and the Meuse valley—both exceptionally prolific during this period—and in the Germanic empire that Byzantine idioms had the most notable effect. The vogue for Byzantine art spread to England and, naturally, to all the lands of the western Mediterranean zone: Lombardy, Piedmont, the South of France and Spain. After the middle of the 12th century there were few schools of Romanesque painting and sculpture that owed nothing to Byzantine stylization. But it was in Italy that the wave of Byzantinism reached its culminating point, and it was under the aegis of the *maniera greca* that the painters and sculptors of Florence, Siena and even Rome produced what are rightly regarded as the first works of modern art.

Part One

MURAL PAINTING

TEXT BY ANDRÉ GRABAR

★

ITALY - SPAIN - FRANCE
ENGLAND - GERMANY AND AUSTRIA
SWEDEN AND DENMARK

THE TRIUMPH OF THE ARCHANGEL MICHAEL OVER THE DRAGON OF EVIL, FRAGMENT.
FIRST HALF OF THE TWELFTH CENTURY. FRESCO IN THE NAVE, SAN PIETRO AL MONTE, CIVATE.

MURAL PAINTING

Italy

IN Italy, as elsewhere, only a small fraction of the mural paintings of the Romanesque period have survived. And since the destruction or preservation of these works was essentially a matter of chance, the question arises as to how far those few that have come down to us can give a reliable idea of the general nature of Romanesque painting and its evolution in the 11th, 12th and 13th centuries. Thus in presenting a selection of the extant works, we are fully conscious of the insufficiency of our sources of information, an insufficiency all the more regrettable since, as a result of geographical and political conditions peculiar to Italy, the art of painting was practised in different manners, according to the province or region, and the paucity of works in any given province cannot be compensated for by those located in another province. For these reasons generalizations on Romanesque monumental painting in Italy are hypothetical at best and the safest course is to limit ourselves chiefly to such information as can be gleaned from a firsthand study of the surviving works.

The art of mural decoration was practised in all parts of Italy during the Romanesque period but by no means all the works produced come under the category of Romanesque art. I have in mind the Byzantine frescos and mosaics which, having been discussed and illustrated in an earlier volume of this series, *Byzantine Painting*, do not figure in the present work. Still it is important to bear in mind the fact that the 12th and 13th centuries witnessed the production on Italian soil of the superb mosaics at Palermo, Cefalù, Monreale, Torcello and Trieste, and in St Mark's at Venice; also at Ravenna where, after a long eclipse, there was a magnificent revival of this typically Byzantine form of art. Thus there were three flourishing centers of Byzantine mosaic workers in Italy—Sicily, Venetia and Ravenna—and it was in friendly rivalry with these Greek technicians that the indigenous Italian fresco painters practised their art in various towns and provinces of the peninsula. No such conditions prevailed in any other European country and their consequences were all the more apparent in Italy since Byzantine monumental decoration enjoyed such high esteem throughout the period in that country. This explains why Italian mural paintings bearing no traces of Byzantine influence are few and far between. In a general way every Italian artist of the period had to work out, so to speak, his own solution of Byzantinism, and until well into the 13th century it was in the stand he took vis-à-vis Byzantine tradition and the means by which he overcame its influence that he made good his personality.

THE MIRACLE OF THE SUBMARINE TOMB OF ST CLEMENT. LATE ELEVENTH CENTURY.
FRESCO IN THE NARTHEX, LOWER CHURCH OF SAN CLEMENTE, ROME.

But besides Byzantine elements, racial traditions and local usages going back to Early Christian times played a considerable part in Romanesque mural painting in Italy. Though the same thing happened in other countries, Italy was better placed to preserve these ancient indigenous traditions, for the good reason that in its earliest stages the art of Christian mural painting had had an exceptional flowering in Italy—anyhow in Rome and probably in Lombardy as well—and continued without a break in the succeeding centuries. The widespread use of monumental painting for purposes of church decoration (as in Byzantine countries) bulked large in the legacy bequeathed by medieval Italy to the Renaissance.

The revival of this art in transalpine Europe under the Carolingians and Ottonians was of comparatively small importance, all the more so since pre-Romanesque mural painting in the North (of which much less is known) often shows a reliance on models imported from Italy. Thus we should not expect to find many signs of northern influence in Italian Romanesque frescos. Even in the north of Italy the few surviving frescos vouch for the continuance of local indigenous traditions between the 8th and 12th centuries. In this context, however, a distinction must be drawn between mural paintings and miniatures. Although Carolingian and Ottonian illuminations had found their way to Italy and had exercised an influence on the miniatures produced in that country, mural painting seems to have been relatively unaffected. For instance, the large apsidal fresco at Aquileia, which contains a portrait of the Emperor Conrad II, has more in common with Roman 11th-century frescos than with the Ottonian frescos at Oberzell or Fulda. Another significant fact is that whereas Italian Romanesque frescos owe little or nothing to such contemporary French (or English) mural paintings as derived from the Carolingian tradition, they came much closer to those which were independent of it or owed least to it.

Under these conditions—the almost invariable presence, often to a marked extent, of a Byzantine strain and of reminiscences of Early Christian art; and, *per contra*, a total or almost total absence of elements deriving from the North—Italian Romanesque wall paintings show considerable differences from the works regarded as typically Romanesque in countries north of the Alps. Still there can be no question of refusing to the former the name of "Romanesque"; such are their numbers and so widespread was their efflorescence—from Spain to Germany—that mural paintings of the type obtaining in Italy represent approximately half of the extant works of the Romanesque period. This Mediterranean (i.e. Roman and Byzantine) form of Romanesque is no less significant than the northern type stemming directly from Carolingian sources. It is well to stress this fact since, as a result partly of the "romantic" outlook of an earlier generation and partly of the high artistic value and technical accomplishment of the Nordic artists, there is still a tendency to depreciate the achievements of the Southern schools as compared with the contemporary art of the Northerners. And the mural paintings, in particular, give us an opportunity of gauging the importance of the part played by Mediterranean art during the period.

To whose initiative were due the Romanesque paintings dealt with in this chapter? In a few cases, an inscription, a document or a portrait informs us that a work was commissioned by an eminent prelate: a pope, a bishop or an abbot. But it must not be forgotten that the great flowering of Byzantine monumental painting in Italy was promoted largely by the kings of Sicily and the Doges of Venice. For to both alike it seemed that, in conformity with the ideas of the age and the practices of the Byzantine emperors they aspired to imitate, it was incumbent on them to build luxurious palaces and churches, symbols of their power and piety.

After Canossa (1077) and the Concordat of Worms (1122) the prestige of the papacy was at its height and, following the example of the monarchs, the popes had frequent recourse to art, especially to mural painting, and with a similar intent. The art they favored conformed to the practices of monarchical art, not only as regards its propagandist bias and the use of symbolic motifs but also as regards the high quality of execution insisted upon and a more or less pronounced eclecticism as to the techniques employed. This is evident in the mural decorations commissioned by the popes, who however allowed some latitude to local painters. But in the case of manuscripts for liturgical use the exact nature of the illustrations was prescribed by the high ecclesiastical authority and the so-called "Atlas" Bibles which the popes disseminated around Rome may be regarded as the first productions of a "controlled" religious art in the West. (The idea of this type of art may have derived from the practice of the Eastern Church.) In the workshops established by the popes Roman art reached a remarkably high level, worthy of the Europe-wide dominion of the papacy of the epoch. Whereas the scriptoria of the miniature painters were housed in the great monasteries, Rome was, it seems, the headquarters of the fresco painters' ateliers. Though there are grounds for thinking that the frescos in Sant'Angelo in Formis near Capua were reproductions of monumental paintings at Monte Cassino, it was certainly not from there that the art of the 12th- and 13th-century frescos in Rome derived. That art was shaped in Rome itself. And it was also in Rome that, towards the end of the 13th century, Pietro Cavallini, while taking over the art of his anonymous local predecessors, developed a new version of it, pointing the way to the Renaissance.

Thus there were centers of Romanesque mural painting in Italy which kept to the traditions of aulic art, and this in my opinion was one of the "specialities" of Italian painting at the time. But it did not exclude the practice of other types of art in outlying districts, and the increasing wealth and political importance of the towns of Tuscany and, later, Lombardy led to an influx of artists into those parts of Italy. From the beginning of the Romanesque era Pavia, Milan and Verona were the headquarters of active schools of painting and in the 12th and 13th centuries the cities of Tuscany did much to shape the course of Italian art. Groups of painters and, before long, individual artists who signed their works established themselves in the towns, and in Lucca, Pisa, Florence and Siena a local art tradition arose, handed down from father to son. And in the second half of the 13th century, it was in the ambience of these local schools that there emerged the first world-famous Italian painters: Berlinghieri, Cimabue, Duccio and Giotto.

In Rome itself two small, humble, but altogether charming churches bear traces of mural paintings prefiguring the Romanesque frescos of a slightly later period. These are San Bastianello on the Palatine (ca. 1000) and Sant'Urbano alla Caffarella, near the Appian Way (1011). These paintings are also related to the famous frescos in the lower

Illustrations pages 26 and 29 church of San Clemente, which were made to the order of a Roman butcher's daughter (she figures in them with her family) who was fortunate in the artist she called on to do the work. If a woman of the lower commercial class, who was unlikely to have appreciated their merits, could commission paintings of such elegance, it was doubtless because she wished to follow in the footsteps of her "betters"—which goes to show that the Roman painters' workshops patronized by the popes had already to their credit large-scale works of at least equal merit. A detail, presumably inserted with an eye to the taste of the class to which the butcher's daughter belonged, clashes with the rest of the ensemble. It is a sort of tailpiece to a scene illustrating the story of St Alexis, and in it we see workmen struggling to lift a heavy pillar. To make the incident even more realistic, inscriptions are added recording the oaths and coarse remarks the workmen are exchanging as they go about their strenuous task.

Despite the willful vulgarity of this little scene and its inscriptions, the paintings in San Clemente are a masterpiece of the art of the fresco as practised in the city of the popes. There is a fine range of warm colors, reds, ochres and white predominating;

THE LEGEND OF ST ALEXIS. LATE ELEVENTH CENTURY.
FRESCO IN THE NAVE, LOWER CHURCH OF SAN CLEMENTE, ROME.

no attempt is made to render depth or perspective; tall, narrow buildings are echeloned in flat coulisses, sometimes viewed from outside, sometimes (in the interior scenes) with the front walls cut away so as to show what is taking place within. Motionless or in slow motion, unnaturally tall, with drooping shoulders, figures are draped in rich, bright-hued garments and surrounded by precious objects of all the kinds that could fittingly be introduced into a religious scene.

Some thirty miles northeast of Rome, at Castel Sant'Elia near Nepi, is a pilgrimage church containing the largest extant group of murals in the Latium region. In our Introduction we gave the names of the three artists, laymen and members of one family, who signed the frescos, describing themselves as "Romans." Less colorful and original than those of San Clemente, these paintings are similar in kind. Their iconography conforms to the standard type of Roman apsidal decoration: Christ standing amidst saints and, above, the Twelve Lambs and the Virgin with two archangels. A procession Illustration page 31 of virgin saints carrying crowns completes the decoration of the apse and, similarly, a Roman theme is illustrated in the transept (cf. chapel of San Zenone, in Santa Prassede, and San Bastianello). The twenty-four Elders and the prophets figure around the choir in accordance with a tradition going back to San Paolo fuori le Mura. To these files of figures are added a number of Apocalyptic scenes set out in three tiers, which together with another row of prophets complete the decoration of the transept. Here, too, on the south side of the east wall, is a panel depicting three episodes of an hagiographical legend, in which are naive but detailed representations of two churches, with a campanile and the bell-ringer.

It is clear that the artists working at Castel Sant'Elia made ample and, on the whole, successful use of the iconographical material and the techniques of rendering drapery and scenic accessories employed in Roman workshops such as that responsible for the San Clemente decorations. They are seen at their best in the delightful figures of angels, female saints and the Virgin in the apse, while no less effective, in the representations of the Elders of the Apocalypse, are the renderings of drapery delicately modeled on the surface. There are even some happy touches of inventiveness, for example in the treatment of the cloth on which are placed some vases, offerings to the Lamb. But the most successful elements of the Castel Sant'Elia frescos are the purely static figures, and in this respect they fall in line with all the Romanesque frescos of Latium, beginning with those of San Clemente. Was it because contemporary Byzantine mosaics provided excellent models for this type of figural art? In any case the fact remains that at Castel Sant'Elia the dramatic scenes are markedly inferior to the static. Gaunt and curiously wooden, the figures seem to find difficulty in communicating with each other; movements involve a painful effort, gestures are vague or hesitant. The imaginative sweep and feeling for the grandiose called for in illustrations of the Book of Revelation were sadly lacking here. Also on the technical side we find shortcomings, as when instead of integrating the motif of multicolored mountains into a coherent whole, the artists merely place the mountains side by side. Yet the naive candor of this art, from which all meretricious over-emphasis is excluded, adds a refreshing accent of sincerity.

PROCESSION OF VIRGIN SAINTS. LATE ELEVENTH CENTURY.
FRESCO IN THE APSE, BASILICA OF CASTEL SANT'ELIA (NEAR NEPI).

These frescos have a trait in common with all other Romanesque paintings both in the capital and in the region of Latium; in contrast with the appealing simplicity of the scenes depicted is the gorgeousness of the ornamental frames. Here the painters not only displayed quite remarkable powers of invention and imagination, but also reverted to traditional motifs that had figured in the "grotesques" of antique art. Thus at Castel Sant'Elia, besides the motif of a vase containing fruit alternating with parrots, we find, just under the cornice, a finely decorative row of peacocks on a white ground.

For the dating of the San Clemente and Castel Sant'Elia frescos no documentary evidence is available. Until quite recently the paintings in San Clemente were thought to have been made shortly before the sack of Rome by Robert Guiscard (1084). Now, however, both groups are commonly assigned to the last years of the 11th century, though some authorities would date the Castel Sant'Elia frescos to the beginning of the 12th. A closer comparative study of the frescos of this school than has hitherto been feasible will be needed if any reliable decision on the point is to be arrived at.

A careful analytic study should also be made of the apsidal mosaics in two Roman churches, San Clemente and Santa Maria in Trastevere, since they can throw much light on the chronology of 11th- and 12th-century Roman decoration in general. Made in 1128,

31

the San Clemente mosaics are noteworthy for their unusual wealth of decorative effects. Harking back to an Early Christian motif, the artists filled the conch with an allover design of acanthus leaves interspersed with animals and birds. Equally of Early Christian origin is the Nilotic landscape underneath this vision of the Other World, as also are the twelve doves (replacing the apostles) which the mosaicist had the idea of placing upon the cross and not (as usual) beside it. But along with these recalls of Early Christian motifs there are borrowings from contemporary Byzantine art, among them possibly the gold ground of the upper part of the apse and certainly that behind the small figures at the bottom of the mosaic. Twelve years later this same Byzantine influence, together with Early Christian motifs, played a considerable part in the apsidal mosaics at Santa Maria in Trastevere.

Made in the period when the medieval papacy was at the height of its power, these two mosaics are among the rare examples of a form of art designed to celebrate the spiritual and temporal authority of the popes and the triumph of the Head of the Church over the emperors; of the *sacerdotium* over the *regnum*.

It was shortly after this that the popes gave orders for remaking of the mosaics (unfortunately none have survived) in several great basilicas: St Peter's and San Paolo fuori le Mura (Innocent III: 1198-1216), Santa Maria Maggiore and St John Lateran (Nicholas III: 1277-1280). That the main purpose of the popes in commissioning such decorations was to extol their political successes is proved by descriptions of, and sketches for, the frescos (no longer extant) in the triclinium of their Lateran Palace, the chapel of St Nicholas and the two adjoining rooms. These depicted, as well as a portrait sequence of canonized and reigning popes grouped round a Madonna, Queen of Heaven, several popes of the period of the struggle over investiture, who were represented seated on thrones with their feet resting on the necks or backs of antipopes humbly prostrate before them; also the submission of Emperor Lothair, together with the entire text of the Concordat of Worms.

It seems that another fresco cycle, whose theme was likewise of a mixed religious and political nature, figured on the walls of Santa Maria in Cosmedin. Commissioned by the French pope Calixtus II (1119-1124), it contained not only a great number of Old and New Testament scenes but also a sequence of pictures related, so far as can be judged, to the legendary "Life of Charlemagne" wrongly ascribed to Archbishop Turpin of Reims (died ca. 800). From such faint traces of these paintings as have survived it would seem that they were intended to remind contemporaries of the balance of power between the Church and State—with precedence to the former, as in the time of Charlemagne—that had been achieved by the Concordat of Worms.

From a general survey of such 11th- and 12th-century frescos and mosaics as can still be seen, we get an impression of very high esthetic and technical qualities; of undoubted originality happily combined with fidelity to the traditions of an earlier art that had its own religious and political program, a repertory mainly consisting of elements belonging to the Early Christian period but including others deriving both from pre-Christian and from contemporary Byzantine art. Undoubtedly this Roman painting of the time when papal power was at its height merits more attention than is usually given it, since painters in many parts of Europe seem to have taken it for their model. One of the best examples is the Cluniac art obtaining at Berzé-la-Ville in Burgundy, and traces of its influence can also be found in the apsidal frescos in the cathedral of Aquileia and in the Nonnberg convent at Salzburg. Under the patronage of the popes this type of art continued to flourish in Rome and Latium in the 13th century and we shall encounter it again, under its later aspects, when we come to deal with the frescos at Anagni and Marcellina.

But before we turn from Central Italy, mention must be made of the paintings at Monte Cassino and the part played by that great center of monastic life in shaping Italian art at the end of the 11th and during the 12th century. It is well known that in 1070 Desiderius, abbot of Monte Cassino, summoned a group of artists and goldsmiths from Constantinople, but in the present state of our knowledge it is difficult to say what effect, if any, they had on the evolution of Italian mural painting. Did he call in Greek assistance because no competent artists were available at Monte Cassino or elsewhere in Italy? Similar instances might be cited in support of an affirmative answer to the question. But the records do not refer to any *painters* as being either among the craftsmen summoned from Constantinople or among the local monks sent by Desiderius to Byzantium to learn, or to perfect their knowledge of, some branch of art. What Desiderius wanted of the Byzantines were bronze doors, church furniture and those mosaic pavements which later gave rise to the Cosmatesque style of church decoration. The only fact suggesting that Desiderius took any interest in painting is the emergence of a school of illuminators at Monte Cassino during his abbacy.

However, in another monastery not far from Monte Cassino, Sant'Angelo in Formis near Capua, an entire mural decoration has survived, the oldest portions of which may well go back to the time of Desiderius. More Byzantine in style than any similar Italian work of the period—with the exception of the mosaics at Palermo, Cefalù and Venice— the Sant'Angelo frescos have always been thought to derive from those which formerly existed in the abbey church of Monte Cassino, no trace of which now remains. Defensible on historical, though not on archeological grounds, this theory can be neither proved nor disproved. And, after all, the Byzantine elements in the Sant'Angelo frescos might equally well derive from the neighboring province of Basilicata, where the Greek monks used models that were wholly Byzantine, or else from Sicily—in the latter case during the second half of the 12th century, after the making of the Palermo and Cefalù mosaics. But it is unlikely that we shall ever ascertain the immediate sources of the Sant'Angelo frescos. One thing, however, is clear: that they cannot all have been executed at the same time or by painters of the same school. While the archangel above the entrance and the two angels holding a medallion in the narthex are thoroughly Byzantine, the systematic linearism and the suavity of the angels' heads suggest that Italian painters had a hand in them. Almost equally Byzantine is the fresco in the apse, whose decorations are in any case the oldest of those in Sant'Angelo. Yet in addition to a bust of the Virgin and Child, in the righthand apse, obviously copied from a Greek Mother of God

Illustrations pages 34-35, 37-39

ABBOT DESIDERIUS, DONOR OF THE CHURCH. LAST THIRD OF THE ELEVENTH CENTURY.
FRESCO IN THE CENTRAL APSE, SANT'ANGELO IN FORMIS (NEAR CAPUA).

ANGELS. LAST THIRD OF THE ELEVENTH CENTURY.
FRESCO IN THE RIGHTHAND APSE, SANT'ANGELO IN FORMIS (NEAR CAPUA).

in the role of "Odigitria"—a parallel for which exists in the Cappella Palatina at Palermo
—we find in the main apse a group of three tall figures of archangels in the pure Roman
tradition, like those in San Bastianello and Castel Sant'Elia. Likewise, the placing of
the abbot donor in the apse follows a Roman custom; the Byzantine practice was to Illustration page 34
relegate portraits of donors to the narthex.

It is generally agreed that another group of artists made the frescos in the nave, Illustrations pages 37-39
where alongside numerous Byzantine mannerisms we find manifestations of a typically
Italic art that deviates persistently from any possible Byzantine models. The Byzantinisms might all be traced back to Greek 11th-century paintings, but unfortunately
there is no means of knowing whether the Sant'Angelo painters had opportunities of
seeing Greek originals and making re-interpretations of them in accordance with Italian

conceptions; or if the models they employed had already undergone this modification, that is to say were "westernized" versions of Byzantine prototypes. We are inclined to favor the second alternative for several reasons; firstly because even the frescos in the chevet, though coming closer than the others to the Byzantine norm, are obviously local versions of Byzantine originals, and secondly because the influence of Roman practice can be seen, if not in the actual choice of subjects illustrated in the nave, in the place given the scene of the Crucifixion and its presentation on a scale twice as large as that of the other scenes. And it is clear that this device of interrupting the rhythmic flow of the ensemble so as to give special prominence to the Crucifixion is not an improvisation on the painter's part but presupposes familiarity with a schema peculiar to the school of Rome (first employed in St Peter's). The other deviations from Byzantine usage (also in the nave) are innovations due to the tendency, so frequently found in Italy during the 12th and 13th centuries, to modify Byzantine prototypes in terms of direct observation

Illustrations pages 38-39

of reality. Thus, though the composition of the huge Last Judgment in the Byzantine manner covering the entire west wall of the nave contains many elements of the customary Greek iconography, the artist has not slavishly copied an Eastern model but includes both realistic details and reminiscences of the "Last Judgments" of western art from the year 1000 onwards, such as those at Müstair and Oberzell. Then again, in the biblical scenes in the side-aisles and the scenes in the narthex of the lives of the hermits St Anthony and St Paul, we find hardly any traces of Byzantinism, except in the technique. In short, these pictures, spaced out, it seems, over a considerable period ending with the 13th century, are certainly creations of an autonomous local art.

One of the most striking features of the Sant'Angelo decorations is that they include so many varieties of mural paintings, covering well over a century, placed side by side. Most revealing are the decorations of the nave leading to the apse, in which we see the successive changes, increasingly numerous as time went on, brought to the models which were their point of departure. These Italian painters displayed much skill in heightening the effect of Byzantine prototypes by means of accents, sometimes of a purely formal order since they modified only the drawing or the colors, with a view to stressing the rhythmic symmetry of the Eastern models. Elsewhere, however, attempts were made to catch the exact expression of a face, to add a telling gesture or to stress the emotive content of a dramatic scene. Throughout the 12th and 13th centuries we find original touches of this kind, unco-ordinated no doubt but purposeful and persistent. Thus each successive Italian artist added something of his own to his Byzantine models and, in so doing, opened up the path that was to lead to modern painting. Nevertheless, though we are justified in regarding the case of Sant'Angelo in Formis as typical of a tendency that was gaining ground in some parts of Italy (chiefly perhaps, after the middle of the 12th century), these decorations are, to the best of my knowledge, almost unique of their kind. The explanation of this surprising fact is probably that so many frescos of the period in the province of Campania have perished. Some admirable paintings in the apse of Santa Maria della Libera at Foro Claudio provide an idea of what they must have been like. However, in view of the limited information so far available on the subject, there are no good grounds either for seeing any positive reflections of the art of Monte Cassino in the Sant'Angelo frescos, or for assuming that their style had any repercussions outside the bounds of Campania. As a matter of fact the mural paintings in Rome and Latium are markedly different, and we have reason to believe that the Sant'Angelo frescos are of a type peculiar to Campania, which, though borrowing freely from the art of other parts of Italy, had relatively little influence outside its own sphere of activity.

From the Early Christian period onwards, under the Lombard kings and thereafter under the Carolingians, a great number of mosaics and frescos were produced in North Italy, nor was there any decline in the output during the Romanesque period. These

THE ENTOMBMENT. LAST THIRD OF THE ELEVENTH CENTURY.
FRESCO ON THE LEFT WALL OF THE NAVE, SANT'ANGELO IN FORMIS (NEAR CAPUA).

THE ELECT, FRAGMENT OF THE LAST JUDGMENT. TWELFTH CENTURY (?).
FRESCO ON THE WEST WALL OF THE NAVE, SANT'ANGELO IN FORMIS (NEAR CAPUA).

ANGELS IN ADORATION, FRAGMENT OF THE LAST JUDGMENT. TWELFTH CENTURY (?).
FRESCO ON THE WEST WALL OF THE NAVE, SANT'ANGELO IN FORMIS (NEAR CAPUA).

11th- and 12th-century works derived from different traditions and moreover were subjected to external influences, also of varying provenance—which adds to the difficulty of classifying such paintings as have survived; all the more so since they do not illustrate successive stages of a uniform evolutionary process. In the following pages we shall confine ourselves to pointing out what seem to us the basic characteristics of a limited number of mural decorations, selected as being both representative of the Romanesque painting of northern Italy and suitable for reproduction in color.

First come, chronologically speaking, the famous frescos in San Vincenzo at Galliano, Illustrations pages 40-41 near Cantù (south of Como). An inscription records the date of the consecration of the church (1007) and the name of its founder, Ariberto di Intimiano, a cleric who eleven years later was promoted to the archbishopric of Milan. His portrait (now removed and preserved in the Ambrosiana at Milan) figured in the apsidal decorations, which can thus be dated with some certainty to shortly before 1007. As regards the dating of the frescos in the nave, there are differences of opinion, some authorities believing

THE ARCHANGEL MICHAEL. CA. 1007. FRAGMENT OF THE FRESCO IN THE APSE,
SAN VINCENZO, GALLIANO.

they were made later, and others—more correctly, to my mind—holding that all the decorations at Galliano were made at the same time. But, needless to say, it does not follow that they are all the work of the same artist.

For the Galliano frescos differ from the majority of medieval church decorations in one important respect: that we can distinguish with some certainty the parts executed by the master painter (the chief figures in the apsidal vault and, notably, the heads of the donor and archangels) from the rest of the paintings. It is clear that he left the latter to his assistants who, though keeping to the same style and technique, took less pains and failed to measure up to him. The fresco in the apse is one of the key works of Romanesque art. On each side of a huge standing effigy of Christ surrounded by a luminous mandorla in the Roman manner, the prophets Jeremiah and Ezekiel are humbly adoring Illustration page 41

THE PROPHET JEREMIAH. CA. 1007. FRAGMENT OF THE FRESCO IN THE APSE, SAN VINCENZO, GALLIANO.

the celestial apparition. This inclusion of Old Testament characters in a theophany—an un-Roman practice—was presumably inspired by oriental, perhaps Palestinian models. Influences of the Christian East are often to be found, as here, in Lombard art and it is impossible to say whether the master artist employed at Galliano copied a Greek prototype directly or at second hand. The theme of this fresco may have been taken over by Italian artists from the Palestinian repertory long before, in the Early Christian era. In the Ascension of Elijah which figures in one of the spandrels over the apsidal arch we have another Old Testament motif (as in the row of small figures of prophets which runs all around the church beneath the cornice). Here we know for certain that the theme had come into use in Lombardy in Early Christian times, since it often figured on sarcophagi. Moreover we find Elijah (accompanied by Moses) given exactly the same place in a 9th-century mosaic in Rome (Santa Maria in Domnica). Nor was it from an eastern prototype that the Galliano painter took over the motif of Illustration page 40 the two archangels on either side of Christ, each of them holding a scroll, in the scene of the theophany. One is inscribed *petici[o]* and the other *postulatio*—which means that (following the conception of the Western Church) Christ is regarded as the Supreme Judge of the tribunal before which mankind will be arraigned on the Last Day. At His feet is another inscription proclaiming Him *dominus virtutum* and leader of the hosts of the Blessed. Moreover, in order to make it clear that the vision of Christ in Glory is to be located in highest heaven, above the firmament, the triumphal arch in front of the apse is decorated with a frieze of marine creatures evoking the celestial sea which, according to ancient cosmographers, separated the visible firmament from the heavens. The fact that vases figure in this frieze has no special significance; as in other compositions of the same class, this motif was inspired by paintings of classical antiquity. In the lower register of the apse, beneath the theophany, are several scenes illustrating the life of the patron saint of the church, St Vincent.

The saints and prophets figuring in such great numbers at Galliano may stand for the *agmina* (hosts) of Christ referred to in the inscription at the feet of the "Lord of Virtues." As regards the saints, we have here a departure from the norm of Romanesque church decoration, the customary Gospel cycle being replaced by two hagiographical cycles. Placed beneath a sequence of Old Testament themes (as at Müstair), these scenes of the lives of saints occupy the remaining surface of the lateral walls of the nave. On one side we have the life story of St Christopher dominated by an immense "portrait" of the saint, while the other wall chronicles the life of St Margaret. The choice of saints portrayed is significant and its purport emphasized by the dimensions given the figure of St Christopher. Both saints had a special appeal for the populace at large since they gave timely help in hours of peril, St Margaret's special function being to succor women in childbirth, and St Christopher's to preserve the Christian from a *malemort* (violent death) on the day he had been privileged to gaze upon his image. I doubt if it would be possible to find an earlier instance in Western Europe of a church which not only devoted so large a part of its murals to the lives of saints but also catered so manifestly to the popular cult of saints and their images.

When we examine the technique of the best of the Galliano frescos (those in the apse) we cannot fail to be struck by this unknown artist's fidelity to natural forms and his expert use of the antique methods of representation. We see this in his way of bringing out the modeling of heads in sculpturesque relief by means of dabs of green and red and, in a more general way, in his emphasis on the tactile values of bodies and drapery and his essentially painterly, not linear, rendering of the third dimension. His indebtedness to Carolingian esthetic is evidenced by certain mannerisms, such as a tendency to exaggerate movements (in the figures of prophets and the executioners of St Vincent) and relief (in the prophets' garments); also by his use of such typically Carolingian architectural elements as the curiously shaped stone pedestals on which St Vincent's torturers are standing, while the saint himself seems to be levitated in mid-air. But when we turn to the other frescos in this church—the small effigies of prophets, the figures in the hagiographical scenes and the portraits of bishops in the spandrels—we find frequent divergencies from the master's style. Whereas in the bishops' portraits both style and execution closely resemble the master's, elsewhere we find a growing tendency to schematize his procedures and to stress graphic at the expense of plastic values.

Thus the Galliano frescos admirably illustrate the transitional period of medieval art. When we turn from the architectural settings of the scenes of St Vincent's life to those of the hagiographical pictures in the nave we can trace the change-over from an art that still is basically Carolingian to one that is typically Romanesque. Indeed, probably no other edifice provides so lucid an epitome of the stylistic evolution that took place during the transition from the Carolingian to the Romanesque epoch. These frescos also prove that we should be wrong in regarding this evolution as slow and gradual; on the contrary, they illustrate two constant, co-existent tendencies of the same Mediterranean tradition, which had been operative persistently or alternately from the end of antiquity on. Another lesson to be gleaned from the Galliano frescos is that Romanesque esthetic and techniques can, on occasion, be regarded as products of a less sophisticated interpretation, at the hands of craftsmen, of certain forms that, handled by a master artist, kept closer to the earlier tradition.

But have we here no more than a continuance of the pictorial tradition of the 9th and 10th centuries in the West? The deeply grooved garments of the prophets in the apse Illustration page 41 recall the attempts that were being made by contemporary Greek mosaicists at St Luke's in Phocis and at Chios to recapture the plasticity of antique art. These are not the only traces of Byzantine influence to be seen at Galliano; we find them also in the extraordinary, bearded head of St Christopher, in the prominence given to theophanies including prophets, as also in the fact that the two saints celebrated in the nave were (as their very names imply) of Greek extraction.

Of the church decorations in Lombardy and Piedmont which, though posterior to the Galliano frescos, number among the most archaic, the surviving fragments in San Michele at Oleggio (near Novara), at Prugiasco (Ticino) and in the collegiate church of Sant'Orso at Aosta are of special interest; also the large, admirable ensemble in San Pietro at Civate (near Como).

THE TEMPEST ON THE SEA OF GENNESARETH, FRAGMENT. EARLY TWELFTH CENTURY.
FRESCO ON THE RIGHT WALL OF THE NAVE, SANT'ORSO, AOSTA.

The Aosta painters employed a formal language midway between the rusticity of Illustrations pages 44-45 the Carolingian art of Müstair and the more fully developed, better organized Romanesque style exemplified in the 12th-century frescos at Bohí in Catalonia and at Vic in Illustrations pages 92-93 France. What we have at Aosta is probably an early 12th-century solution of the problem confronting the painters of the period: that of the attitude to adopt towards the art tradition of antiquity. The fresco painters retained some elements of that tradition, those that had been taken over by Carolingian and also, to some extent, by Ottonian painting, but they replaced the sketchlike technique of antique forms (still evident at Müstair) by precise outlines and schematic draftsmanship, and organized images in purely surface patterns—without depth—in terms of that compulsive, all-pervading rhythm which is characteristic of Romanesque. All that remains of the Aosta paintings is a row of scenes

THE MARTYRDOM OF ST JAMES THE GREATER, FRAGMENT. EARLY TWELFTH CENTURY.
FRESCO ON THE RIGHT WALL OF THE NAVE, SANT'ORSO, AOSTA.

located on the clerestory walls above the present Gothic vaults. Devoted to the Apostles, Illustration page 44 they represent—most notably—St Andrew in a boat on the Sea of Gennesareth and the Illustration page 45 Martyrdom of St James the Greater; such is the rugged force we sense in their expressive features, so original and compelling is the artistry, that both figures leave an indelible impression on the memory.

Illustrations pages 24, 47-48 In San Pietro at Civate, perched on a hill-top some twelve miles east of Como, there are some archaistic paintings executed in an unusually interesting style; notably the fresco sequence extending from the narthex to the apse and forming a coherent picture cycle. Stylistically akin, some other paintings on biblical themes have recently been uncovered just below the roof of San Calocero, the parish church of Civate, but in their present condition they add relatively little to our knowledge of the art of Civate. The leading theme of the San Pietro frescos is the heavenly paradise. It figures directly Illustration page 48 on one of the principal panels where Christ the King and Savior is shown seated on a globe with the Lamb at his feet in a closed garden. In another vault we see the Four Rivers, and in the nave are grouped, in threes, the denizens of Paradise, saints and angels. The sequence ends with a vision of angels sounding the Last Trump, and balancing this, in the nave, is another dramatic scene inspired by the Book of Revelation: Illustrations pages 24 and 47 the triumph of the archangel Michael over the Dragon of Evil.

Once again there are considerable differences of opinion as regards the dating of these frescos, some authorities assigning them to the late 12th century, others to a much earlier date, about the year 1100. As so often happens in such cases, the problem is further complicated by borrowings from Byzantine art, which here are not only extensive but also differ from those we find in other frescos in this part of Italy. Thus the unusual presentation of angels and saints by threes is typically Byzantine and derives from Greek iconic calendars of the period. No less Byzantine than the iconography are the heads of the figures, their hooked noses and big eyes with eyebrows meeting above the nose; also the drawing, the arrangements of the folds of garments and their modeling. But, despite some traces of archaism, as in the heavily marked profiles of faces, these borrowings from Byzantine art cannot be dated before the beginning of the 12th century; the suppleness of movements and folds of garments, their striking plasticity and the elongated proportions of the figures tell against their attribution to an earlier period. The Galliano decorations certainly antedated them (though the two works are not in the same line of descent) and so did those at Aosta. As will be seen later, the style of the Civate paintings has much in common with that of the Catalan frescos at Pedret, which cannot be dated before the mid-12th century. And, finally, the "New Jerusalem" theme links up the art of Civate with that of several Romanesque church decorations in Germany and with Saint-Chef in France.

On the other hand, those frescos where Byzantine influence seems to have been *direct*—e.g. in the crypts of San Giovanni Domnarum and Sant'Eusebio at Pavia and on the west wall of San Michele at Oleggio—appear to have been made later, though the difference in time cannot have been great; the affinities between the Civate frescos and the earlier ones in Pavia are unmistakable when we compare the head of Christ

Aquileia were commissioned by the Patriarch Poppo (1019-1042), who did much to promote an artistic renaissance in that city. Enthroned, the Virgin and Child are being venerated by the martyrs of Aquileia, amongst whom we see the Patriarch himself, the Emperor Conrad II (1024-1039), the Empress Gisela and Prince Henry. Some strangely elongated saints figure in the lowest register and the sumptuous effect of the ensemble is enhanced by decorations inspired by antique prototypes (rows of heads enclosed in medallions). This composition has less in common with the Galliano frescos, to which it has been assimilated, than with early apsidal decorations of the Roman school, though it is impossible to reach any positive conclusion since all extant examples of such paintings (except those in San Bastianello) are later in date than those at Aquileia. Stylistically they come closest to the decorations of Sant'Urbano alla Caffarella (1011). The Aquileia frescos give us an excellent idea of the Italic prototypes followed in apsidal pictures north of the Alps, chiefly in Germany, but also in southeast France.

The majestic style of the paintings in the apse of Aquileia Cathedral is also found in the frescos on the walls and vaults of the crypt, though they postdate the former Illustrations pages 50-51 by nearly two centuries and differ from them in several respects. Famed for the beauty of their Crucifixion and Descent from the Cross, these decorations are by and large Byzantine in conception, though in many places the local painters have given rein to their personal inspiration. I have less in mind the emotive effect of the scenes of the Passion (the Byzantines had achieved similar effects in 1164 at Nerezi, in Jugoslavia) than the exceptional vigor of the draftsmanship and modeling, in which we sense the presence of an original artistic personality; and no less distinctive are the antique ornaments and simulated embroidery on the lower part of the walls. Here is an art Illustration page 51 that is Italian and Romanesque through and through. Reminiscences of this style are often found north of the Alps, in works produced within the Empire.

The Aquileia frescos were probably made after 1200 and thus belong to the period (late 12th and early 13th century) in which the activities of the ablest Italian painters had come to be localized in Central Italy and no longer in the North.

A number of decorative ensembles of a new kind were produced in Rome, in Latium and in Umbria round about 1200. Often of considerable size, they included lengthy cycles of narrative scenes and, as in Early Christian decorations, complementary episodes of Old and New Testament history facing each other on the lateral walls of the nave. The theophany in the apse was also of Early Christian origin but had continued to figure in church decorations during the intervening period. We have here, in fact, a revival of Early Christian programs, but these now were supplemented by scenes taken from Byzantine iconography, and it was also from this source, perhaps, that the representation of a Last Judgment on the wall above the entrance derived. But still more noteworthy are the borrowings from Byzantine technique, such as the methods employed for modeling bodies and draperies, for figure drawing and for the general layout of anecdotal scenes. It is interesting to note that the Byzantine models used by artists working in and around Rome in the late 12th and early 13th century must have been quite recent works, belonging to the last phase of the evolution of Byzantine art during the second half of

PROPHET (?). EARLY THIRTEENTH CENTURY. FRESCO IN THE CRYPT,
CATHEDRAL OF AQUILEIA.

the 12th century. Of all Italian schools of the period it is the Roman which, even before the Fourth Crusade (1204), shows most affinities with the more advanced Byzantine painting of the day and best reveals the manner in which its lessons were assimilated by contemporary Italians, before being used as a point of departure for the new art that achieved its full flowering in Cavallini's frescos. As pointed out above, the decorations which have been brought to light in the basilicas of Rome and its environs were executed under the auspices of the popes and celebrate the triumph of the spiritual power over the temporal, represented by the emperor. They are pendants, so to speak, of the famous "Atlas" Bibles commissioned in large numbers by the Holy See (cf. p. 28).

Illustrations pages 52-54

Each of the works of the Roman School that have come down to us has features peculiar to itself. Such portions of the mural decorations in the abbey church of San Pietro at Ferentillo (north of Rome, in the direction of Assisi) as have survived may be dated to the last quarter of the 12th century. The style and execution of the Creation cycle, which was included in the sequences of biblical subjects represented on the side walls, if somewhat rustic, are by no means lacking in vigor. The meander pattern adorned with fish that forms the frieze is wholly Romanesque, as is, generally speaking, the iconography of the various scenes. Nevertheless the picturesqueness of certain realistic

PAINTED DECORATION SIMULATING EMBROIDERY. EARLY THIRTEENTH CENTURY.
FRESCO IN THE CRYPT, CATHEDRAL OF AQUILEIA.

THE CREATION OF EVE. LAST QUARTER OF THE TWELFTH CENTURY. FRESCO IN THE NAVE, SAN PIETRO A VALLE, FERENTILLO (NEAR TERNI).

Illustration page 53

details (e.g. Adam naming the animals) and the concern for tactile effects prefigures what was to be one of the basic tendencies of Central Italian painting subsequently to 1200. In Rome itself the frescos in San Giovanni a Porta Latina—though predated by some fragments at Santa Croce in Gerusalemme (1144)—are among the earliest of the group, going back to the papacy of Celestine III (1191-1198). Alongside the depiction of the Creation with which the biblical cycle opens, we find a Last Judgment and scenes from the Apocalypse. Notable in the portrayal of the twenty-four Elders adoring the Lamb is the agitated quality of the line, while the artist's preoccupation with decorative effects makes itself felt even in the drawing of features and the coloristic treatment of heads. The Santa Croce fragments present analogies with such works as the decorations at Montmorillon near Poitiers, where we also find the Elders of the Apocalypse and the same emotive style ("Romanesque Baroque"), due to the infiltration of Gothic forms into works that were still essentially Romanesque in conception.

But while in the frescos of San Giovanni a Porta Latina, as in those of Santa Croce, we find traces of the Gothic spirit, there is nothing of it in other frescos made by the Roman School, and in these we find Byzantine influences pointing the way directly to the Early Renaissance. To begin with, we have the decorations in San Silvestro at Tivoli, south of Rome, where the apsidal frescos, while keeping to the traditions of the Early Christian basilica as regards their subjects, are interpreted in the "new style" of 1200 or thereabouts. The decorations recently uncovered in Santa Maria in Monte Dominico, in the neighboring town of Marcellina, offer close analogies to those of San Silvestro. The unknown painter responsible for the former was a talented and original artist; not only did he add themes, borrowed from the Byzantine repertory, to the familiar cycle of Old and New Testament imagery, but also, once he had mastered Byzantine techniques and draftsmanship, made skillful use of them with a view to giving more plasticity to bodies, more relief to draperies, more dignity to faces and gestures. In certain

ADAM NAMING THE ANIMALS. LAST QUARTER OF THE TWELFTH CENTURY. FRESCO IN THE NAVE, SAN PIETRO A VALLE, FERENTILLO (NEAR TERNI).

respects this was no more than a development of tendencies already latent in the decorations at Ferentillo and in San Giovanni a Porta Latina, but their assimilation of the most recent Byzantine discoveries enabled the Roman painters to make more rapid headway.

The culmination of these tendencies can be seen in certain mural paintings of the last three decades of the 13th century: in Santa Maria at Vescovio, in the Sabina district (ca. 1270), and at Grottaferrata (1272); then in the upper church of San Francesco at Assisi (Genesis cycle), said to be an early work of Giotto (1270-1280); and, lastly, in Pietro Cavallini's famous frescos in Santa Cecilia in Trastevere, Rome (ca. 1300). There is no need to linger over these late works in the present volume, since they are no longer Romanesque. But the earlier phases of this evolution call for mention here since, for

THE CREATION OF EVE, DETAIL: THE CREATOR. LAST QUARTER OF THE TWELFTH CENTURY.
FRESCO IN THE NAVE, SAN PIETRO A VALLE, FERENTILLO (NEAR TERNI).

one thing, they have been relatively seldom studied, and moreover much new light has been thrown on them by recent research work. Thus we have now a better understanding of the evolution of Roman and Romanesque art in Central Italy in the pre-Renaissance period and of the nature of the Byzantine art, then entering on one of its most fertile phases, from which the masters of the Roman and Umbrian Schools drew inspiration.

In every age of intense art activity, such as the Italian Duecento, we find a great variety of ventures and achievements, which do not necessarily run parallel or synchronize. Thus Roman painting, even at the time when it was heading in the direction of the consummate art of Cavallini, developed simultaneously another tendency whose presence is perceptible from the 11th century on. More conservative than the former, this art trend did not open up such wide perspectives on the future; nevertheless it led to the creation of several works of exceptional interest and accomplishment. Among these are the frescos in St Sylvester's chapel in the church of the Santi Quattro Coronati in Rome (ca. 1246) and those in the crypt of the cathedral of Anagni, south of Rome (ca. 1255.)

At the Santi Quattro Coronati a Roman Duecento painter was called on to make a decorative sequence inspired by the Donation of Constantine—a theme that had been in high favor with the popes during the quarrel over investitures in the previous century; and these paintings were intended to convey in pictorial form the doctrine, promulgated by the Holy See, of the supremacy of the spiritual authority over the temporal power of the emperor. In the two closing scenes the purport of the sequence is clearly indicated. First we see the emperor genuflecting as he makes over to the enthroned pope the tiara, Illustration page 56 parasol and a white, saddled horse; next, invested with these insignia of supreme temporal power, the pontiff makes his state entry into Rome, with the emperor playing the part of "squire," leading the pope's horse. This 13th-century symbolical cycle has many points in common with the fresco sequence in the chapel of St Nicholas in the Lateran made a century before, and relating as it does to a much earlier age, the theme is handled in a suitably medieval style. But here the artist, turning to account the technical procedures of the Byzantines, renders the plastic values of bodies and objects with extreme, not to say excessive, precision. In short, while employing the same methods and models as those of his contemporaries, this painter's addiction to minutely observed detail leads him to treat the mural as a miniature monumentalized into larger scale.

Far more elaborate and extensive, the decorations in the great crypt of Anagni were Illustrations pages 57-61 the work of several painters collaborating in the realization of the same iconographic program and, for the most part, contemporaneously. This cycle formed a sort of pictorial commentary on the liturgy employed at the consecration of the church and was presum- Illustration page 57 ably associated with the ceremonial inauguration of the crypt, following the placing in it, by the bishop of Anagni, of certain highly venerated relics. There is an ordered sequence of panels covering the vaults and walls, beginning with depictions of "scientific" subjects: the Universe, man the microcosm and the attributes of his moral and spiritual welfare. All these themes figured in the service appointed for the consecration of newly founded churches, in which, after an evocation of the creation of the world and the four elements composing it, reference is made to the place of Man in the scheme of things. Just as the purity of the sacred edifice is ensured by exorcisms, so the worshipper is called on to safeguard the health of his body, vehicle of the immortal soul. The painter has illustrated this part of the liturgy by representing two famous physicians of antiquity, Galen and Hippocrates, and an evocation of the four ages and four "temperaments" of man. Though, on the intellectual side, this is the most original portion of the decorations, it is not the most esthetically satisfying (or the best preserved). There is more beauty in the religious imagery deriving from the liturgy relating to the consecration of the church; on the one hand the Offerings of Abraham and Melchizedek, the Ascension of Elijah and various episodes pertaining to the Ark of the Covenant, and, on the other —near the apse and altars—theophanies described in the Apocalypse and portraits and scenes of the lives of local saints whose relics were enshrined in the crypt at the time of its dedication in 1255.

Illustration page 61

Illustration page 60

CONSTANTINE THE GREAT DELIVERING THE TIARA TO POPE SYLVESTER. CA. 1246.
FRESCO IN THE CHAPEL OF ST SYLVESTER, CHURCH OF THE SANTI QUATTRO CORONATI, ROME.

THE CONSECRATION OF THE CHURCH. CA. 1255.
FRESCO IN THE CRYPT, CATHEDRAL OF ANAGNI.

Fundamental to these paintings is the type of art we find in Roman frescos of the end of the 11th and the beginning of the 12th centuries. Thus the apsidal frescos of the twenty-four Elders and, in particular, the ornamentation, with its imitations of antique "grotesques," has obvious affinities (though here the effect is much more sumptuous) with the decorations at Castel Sant'Elia and San Clemente. Thanks to a wider acquaintance with Early Christian prototypes of late antiquity, the artists working at Anagni created decorations of an excellence unequaled until the 15th and 16th centuries. It was also to these ancient models that they owed the method of adorning the interior of a cupola with a band of consecutive scenes grouped around a central ornament such as a disk or floral device. These cupolas predate the similar arrangement of the mosaics in

Illustration page 59

the north narthex of St Mark's in Venice (of the same period) and also those in the narthex of Kahrieh Djami at Constantinople (made shortly after 1300). Since layouts of this kind are peculiar to monumental painting, there can be no question of their deriving from illustrations in manuscripts.

One of the salient characteristics of Roman mural art from the 9th century on is its skillful use of the decorative motifs styled "grotesques," in which organic forms are interwoven with flowers and foliage, and this reflects the taste, fostered by the popes and their entourage, for works of classical antiquity (including sculpture and the sumptuary arts). We find the same thing happening in Sicily, during the long reign of Frederick II (1208-1250), and this was in fact a courtly art, much appreciated by the kings and nobility of the day.

The aulic arts of Europe and the Late Middle Ages tended towards eclecticism, Byzantine forms of expression being no less freely used than those of classical antiquity, and Roman art was no exception to the rule. Thus the Anagni painters, as in duty bound, paid tribute to Byzantinism both in their iconography and in their style, but, on the other hand, they drew on actual visual experience for their renderings of individual figures and groups of figures, costumes, gestures, garments and simply but strongly characterized facial expressions. We find the same compact groupings as those (described at a previous page) in San Clemente and the Santi Quattro Coronati in Rome, but frequently enlivened by some picturesque and telling detail. Though, differing in spirit from those other paintings of the time which point the way to Cavallini and Giotto, the Anagni frescos may not represent the peak point of 13th-century art, they rank none the less among the most brilliant achievements of the school to which they belong.

The quest of realistic and emotive effects and colorful presentation which we find in the scenes of the lives of saints at Anagni was continued by many of the painters of the altarpieces, triptychs and wooden crucifixes that were produced in large numbers from the mid-12th century onward in the neighborhood of Rome (for example the famous triptych in the cathedral of Tivoli), and above all in Tuscany. This type of medieval painting is to be found only in countries where Byzantine influences were strong: in Italy and Spain, and to a lesser degree in Germany. The production of portable paintings of this kind was stimulated by the importation of icons from Greece and the Balkans and by the imitations of them made in Venice and elsewhere. Byzantine art played a vital part in shaping the course of Romanesque painting in Italy, and it was by way of their several and personal responses to the works they imitated that the forward-looking Italian painters made good their personalities.

We see this process at work in the large effigies of Christ and the Virgin, often forming a triptych, which were produced at this period in Central Italy. For a long while the leading figures were treated in the Byzantine style, that of the icons figuring on iconostases. But, even so, the Italian painters showed a tendency to "loosen up" such figures, whose hieratic, otherworldly nature was deliberately stressed by the Byzantines, and to give the Madonna a more human appeal. Similarly they sought to make the narrative scenes on the wings of the triptych more dramatic, more colorful and closer

THE ELDERS OF THE APOCALYPSE, FRAGMENT. CA. 1255.
FRESCO IN THE APSE OF THE CRYPT, CATHEDRAL OF ANAGNI.

THE OFFERINGS OF ABRAHAM AND MELCHIZEDEK. CA. 1255.
FRESCO IN THE CRYPT, CATHEDRAL OF ANAGNI.

to ordinary life (we saw the same tendency at work at Anagni in the hagiographic scenes). While the triptychs of Latium have an interest of their own, the most striking illustrations of this trend of Italian art are to be seen in Tuscany: those painted wooden crucifixes Illustration page 64 which were a purely Italian speciality and whose earliest known example dates from the end of the 12th century (Museo Nazionale, Pisa, No. 15). Since no Romanesque frescos have survived in Tuscany, the painted crucifixes constitute the finest specimens of this style to be found within that province. These works were essentially monumental in nature; fixed to the beam marking the separation of choir from nave, the cross and the figure of Christ Crucified painted on it towered above the congregation in the church.

THE TWO GREAT PHYSICIANS OF ANTIQUITY: GALEN AND HIPPOCRATES. CA. 1255.
FRESCO IN THE CRYPT, CATHEDRAL OF ANAGNI.

ST FRANCIS AND FOUR SCENES OF HIS LIFE. MID-THIRTEENTH CENTURY. (45×60¾")
ALTAR PAINTING, TREASURE OF SAN FRANCESCO, ASSISI.

Rigid at first, with staring eyes, these depictions kept pace with the evolution of Byzantine effigies of Christ, whose figure gradually came to bear the signs of death, with closed eyes, drooping head, the body limply sagging and forming a graceful arabesque on the lines of antique prototypes. While some of the heads of Christ figuring on these crucifixes are charged with an intense expressive power and quite remarkable beauty, we are bound to admit that they show little real advance on contemporary Byzantine interpretations of the same theme.

Byzantine makers of reliquaries preserving relics of the True Cross had begun to group more or less haphazard around the crucifix (which contained a fragment of the wood of the Cross) scenes of the Passion of Christ and figures of saints. Italian painters adopted the formula and enlarged its scope in their painted crucifixes. Often they represented the entire cycle of the Passion up to the Pentecost (as was done on Greek portable icons) and, despite the fact that these paintings were far too small to make their full effect at such a distance from the congregation, included a host of figures and scenes of minute dimensions in the picture sequence. Some of them are little masterpieces

ST FRANCIS AND FOUR SCENES OF HIS LIFE, FRAGMENT: THE HEALING OF THE WOMAN POSSESSED BY A DEVIL. MID-THIRTEENTH CENTURY. ALTAR PAINTING, TREASURE OF SAN FRANCESCO, ASSISI.

COPPO DI MARCOVALDO (ACTIVE IN 1265). CRUCIFIX. (112×94")
PAINTING ON WOOD, PINACOTECA COMUNALE, SAN GIMIGNANO.

in their own right, so graceful is the rendering of figures, so finely balanced are the compositional rhythms and so charming the color accords telling out on a gold ground. Other painters, as in the altarpieces, enlivened the stereotyped scenes by introducing here and there an expressive detail, a figure done from the life, a speaking glance or gesture, or an object of everyday use. Towards the middle of the 13th century some of these artists are known to us by name, and not only do we have signed works by them but also some record of their careers. Among them were two painters whose work has a dramatically emotive appeal, Bonaventura Berlinghieri and Coppo di Marcovaldo; but greatest of all was Cimabue, who adapted the traditional painted crucifixes to a monumental art of compelling power. Like his Roman contemporary Cavallini, Cimabue, while taking over the inventions and discoveries of several preceding generations of painters schooled in the Romanesque tradition, transmuted these into an art of a beauty hitherto unknown, heralding the Renaissance.

ST PETER, DETAIL. TWELFTH CENTURY. FRESCO FROM SAN PEDRO DEL BURGAL (LÉRIDA). MUSEUM OF CATALAN ART, BARCELONA.

Spain

No other mural decorations of the Romanesque period have been so minutely studied as those of Catalonia and, given their high quality, they richly merited the loving care with which they have been transferred, piece by piece, from the walls on which they figured to the art museums of Barcelona, Vich and Solsona, where they are no longer exposed to the gradual deterioration that has played havoc with so many frescos of the period. No less praise is due to the energy and taste of the Catalan archeologists who have done so much to direct attention to Spanish Romanesque painting. They have not only brought to light and published a number of highly original works, but particularly applied themselves to uncovering facts concerning the great artists who created them, and their disciples. Thus whereas the mural paintings in other countries are usually studied without reference to biographical research, those in Spain are now envisaged from what might be described as a humanist angle. Our readers will, however, notice that in the following account of such Spanish frescos as have escaped destruction we prefer to keep to the methods employed in dealing with Romanesque pictorial art in general; that is to say, differing from our Spanish colleagues, we shall study them chiefly in the light of well documented facts of art history, without any special insistence on the—often largely hypothetical—personalities of individual artists.

In all the provinces of Spain which were under Christian rule during the Romanesque period certain mural paintings have survived, but (as elsewhere in Europe) they are few and far between. There is, however, an exception to this general rule; in Catalonia we find a "family" of Romanesque frescos more numerous than in any other part of the continent, and proliferating across the frontier into the Roussillon district of France. Thus the many Romanesque decorations which have survived in churches sheltered in remote valleys of the Pyrenees provide much information, rarely to be had elsewhere, about the activities of local schools of fresco painters in the 12th and 13th centuries.

In a previous volume in this series we described several frescos in Spanish churches dating to the close of the first millennium of our era. Do the Romanesque murals in Spain, as is the case with those in other countries, stem from an earlier tradition? Generally speaking, I believe that this is so, but I would point out that the type of painting carried over into the Romanesque epoch differed from that of the frescos at Oviedo (Asturias) and Tarrasa (Barcelona) illustrated in our *Early Medieval Painting*. For the intervening period had witnessed the rise of the Christian art commonly known as "Mozarabic" (i.e. the style employed by Christian artists in Spain when the country was under Moslem domination) and it was presumably this art which, when the Romanesque painters came on the scene, stood for the local tradition. Unfortunately Mozarabic art is known to us almost exclusively by way of architecture and manuscript illuminations, since no Mozarabic wall paintings have survived. All the same the Mozarabic miniatures—and the original Moorish paintings they imitated—enable us to trace motifs that must have figured in the vanished art of the Mozarabic frescoists, and the great majority of Spanish Romanesque frescos testify to the continuance of that tradition.

The strain of Moorish art in Spanish Romanesque becomes particularly noticeable when we compare the mural paintings of the peninsula with contemporary frescos in France and Italy. And since what we have here is an essentially regional tradition, it may well have arisen at different periods, sometimes relatively late, and under various forms; all the more so since certain traces of the influence of Moslem painting (often confused with Mozarabic painting) suggest stylistic changes due to contacts with more recent forms of Moslem art that had developed in neighboring Arab states.

No one region of the peninsula was specifically or exclusively exposed to Mozarabic influences, and during the 12th century Christian art was equally affected in all parts of Spain by Arab or Arabizing tendencies. The themes of the works of art produced in this period show how Mozarabic (Christian) elements in Spanish painting gradually gave ground to Arab (i.e. "pagan") influences.

But there were also contributions from foreign countries, from Italy for the most part but also France. Indeed there is much to support the view that the Romanesque fresco was "imported" into Spain—into Catalonia first and thence into Castile—in the course of the crusade launched by Pope Calixtus II, and owed much to the art of northern Italy. There can be no denying this Italian influence, though further research work will be needed before its scope can be satisfactorily determined. At the time when a French abbot at Saint-Benoît-sur-Loire called in a Lombard painter, it is more than likely that other Lombards made their way to Spain, newly liberated from the Moslem yoke. But, as in France, none of the original works produced by these North Italian artists has survived. In the case of all the Spanish frescos known to us—including those in which Italian influence is most evident—everything points to the fact that the actual painting was done by Spanish artists. And though their interpretations of Italian models differed considerably from each other, all alike were foreign both to the Italian temperament and to Italian style.

In the case of San Isidoro at León, I question if we should speak, as some have done, of French inspiration. True, an examination of the sculpture lends color to this view, but the frescos show no affinities whatever with any French mural painting known to me. On the other hand there can be no doubt, in my opinion, of the penetration of the Spanish fresco into French territory; first into the Roussillon, that region of France just across the Pyrenees where Catalan painters had established a firm foothold. But there are also reasons for believing that Iberian influences streamed northwards into Auvergne, where they came into contact with art currents deriving from the Germanic Empire, but chiefly from Lombardy and, as a result, with the North Italian art forms which were making headway simultaneously in Spain.

That so few of the mural decorations in Spanish churches can be dated satisfactorily is due to the lack of inscriptions or documents relating to them. The first well authenticated date is 1123, in which year the church of San Clemente at Tahull was consecrated, and there are good grounds for believing that the San Clemente frescos, which rank among the masterworks of Romanesque mural painting, may be dated to that year. The frescos in another church at Tahull, Santa Maria, are usually assigned to the same date. This dating may well be correct, though stylistic differences seem to tell against it; in the Santa Maria decorations we can trace the work of three separate hands and in no case does the style tally exactly with that of San Clemente. In Santa Maria at Tarrasa near Barcelona, on the other hand, a clue to the dating is supplied by the apsidal fresco representing the death of St Thomas Becket, which took place in 1170. However rapid may have been the spread of the cult of the murdered archbishop (canonized in 1172), it seems highly unlikely that the scene would have been depicted in a Spanish church earlier than about 1180. But though this *terminus a quo* is helpful so far as it goes, the style of the Tarrasa fresco is so exceptional that its dating does not give much aid as regards that of many other frescos.

To the same period belong the frescos in the Panteón de los Reyes, in the narthex of San Isidoro at León; commissioned by Ferdinand II, king of León, they must have been made some time between 1157 and 1188. But here again the artist's remarkable originality makes it impossible to use them as a chronological *point de repère*.

This much, however, is clear: that the style of the great majority of the Romanesque mural paintings in Catalonia proves that they should be ascribed to a period earlier than that of the paintings in Santa Maria of Tarrasa; that is to say, prior to ca. 1180. But I am less disposed to follow those who hold that all were subsequent to those in San Clemente at Tahull and therefore should be dated after 1123. The very perfection of the San Clemente paintings (which contain many reminiscences of Mozarabic art) presupposes great activity on the part of local painters over a period preceding this outstanding success. To this period, previous to 1123, might also be ascribed the paintings in Santa Maria at Tahull, San Juan at Bohí and San Quirce at Pedret. For when we seek to establish a chronology (hypothetical, no doubt, at best) of the evolution of Spanish art during this period, it would seem that the above-mentioned frescos, and some others, should be dated before those of San Clemente; in the case of the frescos in Santa Maria at Tahull and San Juan at Bohí, because they contain so many recalls of Mozarabic art, and in the case of San Quirce at Pedret, because the style retains so many formal elements deriving from antiquity—whereas that of San Clemente, despite the early date, is wholly Romanesque. However, it would be unsafe to draw any definite conclusions from purely stylistic considerations of this order. Since Mozarabic and Moorish influences did not die out at the beginning of the 12th century, the linearism of the San Clemente frescos may be regarded as a continuation of the Mozarabic style, whereas the illusionist modeling of antiquity returned to favor after the mid-12th century as a result of the increasing influence of Byzantine art in the peninsula. Like those at Burgal, the Pedret frescos may perhaps link up with this revival of antique art by way of Byzantium; in which case the Burgal decorations may have been made later than those at Tahull and fall into a period when more recent borrowings were being made from the fresco art of northern Italy.

At the turn of the century and thereafter Spanish artists continued to have recourse to Byzantine models. The justly famous frescos in the Sala Capitular of the monastery of Sigena, which mark the peak point of Byzantinism in Spain, should probably be dated to the first years of the 13th century. Should we assume (as has been suggested) that

ZACHARIAS AND THE SCRIBE. CA. 1123. FRESCO FROM THE NORTH WALL OF SANTA MARIA DE TAHULL. MUSEUM OF CATALAN ART, BARCELONA.

the tendencies they illustrate were transmitted to Spain by way of England or (as seems to me more likely) that they derived from the painted ceilings then in vogue in Sicilian churches? The probability that their place of origin was Palermo is strengthened by the fact that we find at Sigena, along with Byzantine idioms, new borrowings from Moslem art, such as are also noticeable—and even more pronounced—in the decorations of another chapter-house, that of San Pedro at Arlanza. As might be expected, Moslem elements bulk larger in those parts of Spain where the Christian painters could study at first hand the "pagan" art of the Arabs. Thus the somewhat later decorations (still extant) in a large hall of the castle of Alcañiz were directly inspired by Moorish frescos similar to those in the Alhambra at Granada.

There are other grounds for holding that the beginnings of large-scale mural painting in Spain should be dated well before 1123, the year of the consecration of the Tahull church. Thus round about 1130 the entire façade of the abbey of Ripoll, in Catalonia, was faced with a sculptured replica of a previously existing interior decoration. Presumably the model of this sculptured façade (believed to be unique of its kind) resembled the two sets of Spanish frescos in which Mozarabic influence is most apparent, those of San Juan, Bohí, and Santa Maria, Tahull, where we find the same layout: a row of narrative scenes above, tall figures under arches in the middle register, and depictions of bizarre creatures on the plinth. The large scene, in the Bohí frescos, of Nebuchadnezzar and his mountebanks is supplemented at Ripoll with a frieze depicting David's musicians. This inclusion within the normal biblical cycle of motifs not *per se* religious and more in keeping with the courtly life of the day affiliates the Ripoll decoration to another cycle of 12th-century frescos, also marked by Mozarabic influence: those of San Baudelio at Berlanga, in Castile. This has perhaps some bearing also on the large place assigned to Old Testament scenes in the decorations at Ripoll, as in Santa Maria of Tahull and Bohí.

Whereas the arrangement of the scenes on the four lower registers of the Ripoll façade keeps to the decorative layout of a nave, the highest register corresponds to the decoration of the interior of the apse and contains a Christ in Majesty framed in a mandorla, Evangelist symbols and Apostles engaged in a "sacra conversazione." As a general rule, apsidal paintings are in a better state of preservation than those in other parts of Romanesque churches and it is in them that we can trace most clearly variations of style, since the basic iconographic elements remain much the same from one church to another. In the apse fresco of San Quirce at Pedret, however, we find a departure (which had no sequel) from the general rule; the painter has represented not only the theme of the Wise and Foolish Virgins but other eschatological motifs such as the Four Horsemen of the Apocalypse. No less rare outside Catalonia is the use of the theme of the Adoration of the Magi—e.g. in Santa Maria of Tahull and Santa Maria of Esterri de Aneu —for the decoration of apses. But, generally speaking, the painters of Spanish churches did not feel called on to enlarge their range of subjects. When we have cited the Last Judgment at Santa Maria of Tahull, a few abridged cycles of the Childhood and Passion of Christ, and a limited number of lives of the patron saints of churches and chapels, we have exhausted, to all intents and purposes, the repertory of themes they drew on.

The thematic programs of Spanish 12th-century frescos were much the same as those of Romanesque mural paintings in other countries. But there were also elements deriving from Mozarabic tradition such as the motif of Nebuchadnezzar's mountebanks, mentioned above. In the Bohí fresco the scene is embellished with a wealth of entertaining details, also found in a very fine miniature in the Ripoll Bible. To a similar source may well be due the dramatic scenes of the torments of the Damned that figure on a wall in Santa Maria of Tahull; they have much in common with the agitated groups of human and animal figures on the borders of the famous ivory crucifix made for King Ferdinand I and his wife Sancha in 1063 and now in the Archeological Museum of Madrid. At first sight the prevalence of Old Testament scenes in these early Spanish decorations may seem rather surprising; the explanation is probably that such "salvation" themes (e.g. David and Goliath) were much employed in early Christian imagery; nor should we forget that Old Testament subjects were even more widely used in the Romanesque churches of northern Italy (at Galliano, for instance). In some cases these correspondences with north Italian art are so to speak involuntary, but, in others, direct borrowings of themes and motifs are apparent. Examples are the two archangels standing beside the throne of the Supreme Judge, who play the part of advocates, each holding a roll inscribed with a *petitio* or *postulatio* (at Galliano in Italy, in Santa Maria of Tahull and Esterri de Cardós in Spain); or, again, the representation of St Andrew carrying a cross with a long shaft: an iconographic device stemming from Constantinople, acclimatized first in Lombardy (e.g. at Civate), and thereafter in Spain (e.g. in the church of San Pedro at Seo de Urgel). These affinities extend to the style as well; in fact the art of the Pedret wall paintings is much like that at Civate.

The ensemble of Spanish Romanesque frescos, a considerable number of which have survived in good condition, lends itself to presentation in various ways. The color plates in this volume have been chosen largely with a view to illustrating the exact position of Spanish frescos in the wider context of European Romanesque painting in general.

Illustration page 70

A fresco in Santa Maria of Tahull illustrates the pictorial methods of a Catalonian painter still addicted to the techniques and, above all, the style of Mozarabic art. In it we see a well-marked linearism, a total absence of plasticity and—most notably—a type of face that, by way of Mozarabic painting, links up with Moslem art. Thus heads are long and triangular, with large eyes placed close beside the nose, which is demarcated

Illustration page 209

by two parallel lines, and tiny mouths (cf. the Prophet Nahum in the Biblia Hispalense and the Christ in the apse of Esterri de Cardós). But the heavily marked contour lines characteristic of the Mozarabic miniature are tending to lose something of their rigor in the fresco. Other pictures in the church of Santa Maria of Tahull, for example the scenes of David's combat with Goliath and of the torments of the Damned in Hell, likewise recall the Mozarabic antecedents of this type of art.

Very similar in inspiration, the frescos in San Clemente of Tahull were the work of an exceptionally gifted painter who kept to the same Mozarabic formula in his rendering of the face of Christ in the apsidal decoration. But he infused new life into it by the use of a highly personal rhythm—hence the remarkably expressive power of all this artist's paintings. The pure, bright colors, the dynamic line, the unusual conformation of the faces stamp themselves on the memory like the words of an inspired preacher. The face of Christ and that, exceptionally narrow, of the Virgin (she is holding a peculiarly shaped vase from which rays of light stream forth: perhaps the eucharistic chalice) are charged with an intense, mysterious spirituality, intimations of Faith at its sublimest.

ST PETER'S BOAT. TWELFTH CENTURY. FRESCO FROM THE CENTRAL APSE OF SAN PEDRO DE SORPE (LÉRIDA). MUSEUM OF CATALAN ART, BARCELONA.

THE VIRGIN AND ST JOHN. TWELFTH CENTURY. FRESCO FROM THE APSE OF SAN PEDRO DE LA SEO DE URGEL.
MUSEUM OF CATALAN ART, BARCELONA.

GROUP OF APOSTLES. TWELFTH CENTURY. RIGHTHAND PANEL OF THE ALTAR FRONTAL FROM LA SEO DE URGEL.
MUSEUM OF CATALAN ART, BARCELONA.

THE CREATION OF EVE AND THE TEMPTATION. FIRST HALF OF THE TWELFTH CENTURY.
FRESCO FROM THE ERMITA DE LA VERA CRUZ, MADERUELO (SEGOVIA). PRADO, MADRID.

Illustration page 73 We find the same Faith reflected at San Pedro of Sorpe, but in more human guise, in the facial expressions and even in the gestures of the two apostles in their boat which, small though it is, flies at the masthead a standard "with a proud device," like the *vexillum* borne at Roman triumphs. But here the Faith triumphant celebrated by the artist is the simple faith of the first believers.

Illustration page 74 In one of the frescos, stemming from a different atelier, in San Pedro at Seo de Urgel, we have the work of a 12th-century Catalan artist who diverged still further from Mozarabic techniques, notably in the handling of drapery and figures. It has more in common with Romanesque paintings in other countries, France and England in particular. All the same, when we look closely into it, we can detect reminiscences of Mozarabic art in the drawing of faces. Hence the special interest of this picture since it throws light on the gradual transformation that came over antique art in the process of becoming "Romanesque." Though what happened in Spain was paralleled in other countries during the early Middle Ages, there was an innate vigor, a compelling power, in Spanish art which may well have had repercussions beyond the Pyrenees. This opinion has often been expressed as regards the sculpture of the period; it holds good for wall painting Illustration page 209 also. When we compare a head of Christ from San Clemente of Tahull with another from the church at Revello in Piedmont, there can be no mistaking the parallelism of the stylistic developments that were then taking place in Spain and in the north of Italy.

Given the close resemblance between them, there can be no question that one must stem directly from the other and, since the Spanish fresco clearly belongs to the period of Mozarabic influence, it seems certain that it antedated, and served as model for, the Italian work. Perhaps we have here a back-flash, so to speak; that is to say, an instance of the penetration of Spanish Romanesque into a region from which Spanish artists meanwhile were borrowing iconographic themes as well as numerous "Byzantinisms."

In the decorations of San Pedro of Burgal we find a tendency at work that characterizes much Spanish fresco painting of the second half of the 12th century: a gradual toning down of the extreme geometric linearism of Mozarabic art in favor of Byzantine plasticity. Thus while the faces in San Pedro have the same general structure as those in Tahull, the clear-cut contour lines demarcating noses, cheeks and eyes are here replaced by passages in half-tints; also we find a new concern with modeling and painterly effects. Similar developments can be observed in the treatment of drapery.

Outside Catalonia, as already stated, too few wall paintings have survived for us to be able clearly to trace a similar evolution. Nevertheless such frescos as remain suggest that here, too, mural art passed through two phases: being archaic to begin with and relatively uncouth, and then acquiring a more fluent style—though it does not necessarily follow that the change was due to Byzantine influences.

There are such striking resemblances between the Catalan frescos at Tahull and the Castilian frescos at Maderuelo and Berlanga that some authorities have assumed —wrongly, in my opinion—that both groups of paintings should be attributed to the

WARRIOR WITH SPEAR AND SHIELD. FIRST HALF OF THE TWELFTH CENTURY. FRESCO FROM SAN BAUDELIO DE BERLANGA (SORIA). PRIVATE COLLECTION.

ELEPHANT AND CASTLE. FIRST HALF OF THE TWELFTH CENTURY.
FRESCO FROM SAN BAUDELIO DE BERLANGA (SORIA). PRIVATE COLLECTION.

same artists, these being presumably Catalans or Italians who, after being employed in Catalonia, were summoned to the kingdom of Castile. There is no question, however, that, so far as the paintings dealing with religious subjects are concerned, marked affinities exist, and that both groups can probably be dated to the first half of the 12th century. Moreover in the second group, as at Tahull, there are many indubitable borrowings from Mozarabic models, these being particularly noticeable in the double scene from Maderuelo, with Adam and Eve. The treatment of the nude figure, the Illustration page 76 movements and attitudes, and the drawing of trees, all alike are reminiscent of Mozarabic 11th-century art. Despite an all too evident clumsiness in the execution, this representation of the Garden of Eden, with its sinister-looking trees, like skeins of writhing serpents, and its gaunt, no less forbidding denizens, has an eerily evocative power. Indeed in this so typically Spanish work, God alone seems human!

This indebtedness to Mozarabic art is even more pronounced in the Berlanga frescos. Illustrations pages 77-79 Also the architecture of the small church of San Baudelio which housed these paintings (most of which have been detached and are now in the United States) is Mozarabic. In the frescos Moorish influences are exceptionally noticeable, since they include a large number of non-religious motifs and it was in their renderings of these that medieval artists made most lavish use of oriental models. The style employed in the scenes of the Passion of Christ is certainly effective and the frequent borrowings from Arab painting

HUNTING SCENE, WITH THREE HOUNDS DRIVING TWO RABBITS INTO A NET. FIRST HALF OF THE TWELFTH CENTURY. FRESCO FROM SAN BAUDELIO DE BERLANGA (SORIA). PRIVATE COLLECTION.

THE ANNUNCIATION TO THE SHEPHERDS. CA. 1157-1188.
FRESCO ON THE VAULT OF THE PANTEÓN DE LOS REYES, SAN ISIDORO, LEÓN.

(particularly evident when we bear in mind the art of the earliest Islamic miniatures) heighten their expressive power. All the same the most interesting, and also the most original, elements of the Berlanga frescos are those whose themes are frankly "pagan," such as the warrior, the elephant and the hunting scene. Originally covering the Illustrations pages 77-79 lowest register of the walls, these paintings were intended to simulate textiles hung over a balcony and it is interesting to note that they exactly reproduce motifs found in the most ancient art of Islam. Always shown in side-view and quite flat, the figures of men and animals are edged with colored lines, which sometimes reappear on an animal's hide, so as to indicate, for example, the separation of the limbs from the rest of the body. This was a device much employed by 10th- and 11th-century Mozarabic artists and the painter of the Berlanga frescos, working in the first half of the 12th century, merely imitated them. Here, as at Sigena, we can see how greatly the decorative art figuring in the residences of the Moorish aristocracy contributed to the spread of oriental influences in Spain. Thus in the Alhambra there are painted hunting, fighting and banqueting scenes which offer analogies to the Berlanga frescos.

When we turn to the remarkably beautiful frescos in the Panteón de los Reyes at Illustrations pages 80-83 San Isidoro of León, we find relatively few of these oriental mannerisms. As already

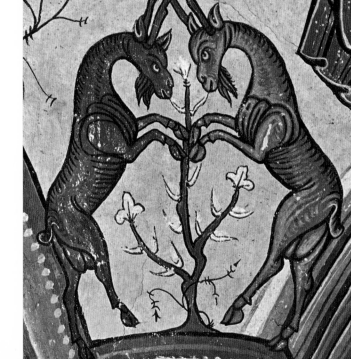

mentioned, they date to the reign of King Ferdinand II (1157-1188) and some believe them to have been made by French artists. Figuring on six vaults of the narthex, these panels deal with subjects more or less independent of each other—the Childhood and Passion of Christ, and a theophany deriving from the Apocalypse—and are ill adjusted to the shape of the vaults; obviously the painter was unaccustomed to working on concave surfaces. This was only to be expected in Romanesque Spain, where all the extant paintings (with the exception of those in apsidal conches) have straight walls as supports. The León painter, it seems, had to make shift with models intended to serve for flat surfaces. The white grounds and a frequent use of arches as frames for scenes and figures remind us of the layout of mosaic pavements, such as that, now in the Museo Civico at Pavia, which originally figured in the 12th-century cathedral of that city, Santa Maria del Popolo. But most noteworthy

THE ANNUNCIATION TO THE SHEPHERDS, DETAIL: CONFRONTED GOATS. CA. 1157-1188. FRESCO ON THE VAULT OF THE PANTEÓN DE LOS REYES, SAN ISIDORO, LEÓN.

THE ANNUNCIATION TO THE SHEPHERDS, DETAIL: THE ANGEL. CA. 1157-1188.
FRESCO ON THE VAULT OF THE PANTEÓN DE LOS REYES, SAN ISIDORO, LEÓN.

THE ANNUNCIATION TO THE SHEPHERDS, DETAIL: A SHEPHERD. CA. 1157-1188.
FRESCO ON THE VAULT OF THE PANTEÓN DE LOS REYES, SAN ISIDORO, LEÓN.

at León is the new fluency of the drawing; the figures, their hands and feet, gestures and garments, have little of the stiffness found in so much earlier Spanish art, and the modeling of bodies, also, displays much greater suppleness. In fact the artists responsible for these frescos seem to have drawn on new sources of inspiration, among these being, quite likely, contemporary French miniatures. All the same we need only study the faces of the figures to be convinced that the painters concerned were Spaniards since, notwithstanding the stylistic changes apparent in the San Isidoro frescos, they fall in line with the general trend of Spanish art in the first half of the 12th century, these affinities with earlier Spanish painting being particularly noticeable in the drawing of animal and plant forms.

EPISODES FROM THE LEGEND OF THE ARCHANGELS. THIRTEENTH CENTURY. ALTAR FRONTAL FROM AN ATELIER AT VICH (?). MUSEUM OF CATALAN ART, BARCELONA.

As in Italy, a very large number of Romanesque paintings on wood have survived in Spain, chiefly in Catalonia. Some consist of panels resting on beams above the altar table and taking the place of baldachins; on them are represented Evangelist symbols, effigies of Christ in Majesty, and sometimes other figures. Other paintings on wood were used as altar frontals, replacing and sometimes imitating the structures in goldsmiths' work which had been produced in such large numbers during the early Middle Ages. The two characteristic examples of Romanesque altar frontals which we illustrate make Illustrations pages 75 and 84 it clear that, in a general way, they very much resemble contemporary mural decorations. In fact there is every reason to believe that the paintings figuring on walls and those on fronts and sides of altars were in almost all respects identical. At Civate in northern Italy there still exist, besides the frescos on the walls, a painting in the concave interior of an altar canopy and painted effigies of saints on the four sides of the altar. In both cases we have merely adaptations of the type of painting elsewhere employed for decorating walls to the holy table used for the celebration of the Eucharist, and at Civate it is obvious that the same artists made both sets of decorations. We first reproduce the side of a very handsome retable in which six Apostles are grouped pyramid-wise with Illustration page 75 their faces turned towards a Christ in Majesty (on the left). This comes from Seo de Urgel and its similarity to the frescos there is unmistakable. Moreover, the themes on the walls of the choir and on the front of the altar are the same; to begin with, a Christ in Majesty, alongside figures of Apostles and scenes of the life of St Peter, the church's patron saint. This identity of themes brings out the stylistic affinities of both sets of paintings—with this difference, however, that the altar paintings are distinguished by their hard, expressive line and often display, in a purer state, those specific traits of Spanish Romanesque painting which derived from Mozarabic art. The paintings on the retable of Sagars (with scenes of the life of St Andrew) and on that of Espinelvas (Gospel scenes), now in the museums of Solsona and Vich, are the best examples of this archaic —or archaizing—art, full of Mozarabic reminiscences, such as are sometimes also found on the ornamental frames enclosing pictures, for example at Espinelvas.

As is the case with frescos, there is no dearth of altar frontals in which Byzantine tendencies are evident to a greater or a less degree (e.g. the Valltarga frontal in Barcelona Museum), and also influences of French Gothic (e.g. the frontals from San Jaime of Frontanyá and San Cebrián of Cabanyes, now in the museums of Solsona and Vich respectively). Here we find (as in Italian altarpieces) an effigy of the church's patron saint replacing that of Christ or the Virgin in Majesty. As regards another altar frontal Illustration page 84 (Barcelona Museum), which illustrates four episodes from the legend of the archangels, we agree with José Gudiol that it may equally well hail from a workshop at Vich or one in the province of Navarre. Our choice of this work was determined by the graceful drawing of the figures, the elegant composition and finely balanced rhythmic movement of each scene. In this 13th-century painting we can see the "classical" elements of a typical Romanesque masterpiece at their best, and the two angels carrying a soul remind us of the similar, no less elegant group that figures on a wall at Brinay in France: two angels carrying the white linen for Christ's use on the occasion of His baptism.

SCENES FROM THE LIFE OF JOSEPH: JOSEPH SOLD BY HIS BROTHERS. CA. 1100. FRESCO ON THE VAULT OF THE NAVE, LOWER REGISTER, SOUTH SIDE. SAINT-SAVIN-SUR-GARTEMPE (VIENNE).

France

Of all the Romanesque frescos known to me, the most refined and elegant are those in the abbey church of Saint-Savin-sur-Gartempe, near Poitiers. But it is not for their elegance alone that these frescos have a special interest; they also form the most extensive group of Romanesque paintings in a large church that has escaped the well-meant but ill-advised attentions of 19th-century restorers. Originally the entire church (with the probable exception of the walls of the side-aisles) was adorned with frescos, beginning with the barrel-vaulted ceiling above the choir, the walls of the radiating chapels and the crypt beneath the choir, and extending to the western gallery above the porch and the porch itself. The paintings in the transept are almost entirely obliterated and in the choir only traces remain of the standing figures in the upper portion of the walls. Also the frescos in the chapels, depicting lives of saints, have faded rather badly. Happily, however, the works of some exceptionally gifted Romanesque artists have survived in excellent condition in four parts of the great church of Saint-Savin: in the porch, in the western gallery, in the ceiling of the nave and in the crypt.

The esthetic merits of these four groups of frescos vary considerably and it is obvious that the paintings in the crypt were the work of underlings. But there can be little doubt that the same atelier was employed throughout, since the technique, the choice of colors, the renderings of bodies, drapery, vegetation and buildings have all a family likeness. However, as was only to be expected, we find occasional differences of style, due partly to the location of the frescos and partly to the idiosyncrasies of the artists employed on them. Thus the proportions of the figures change according to their height above ground-level, the result being that those in the nave and on the walls of the gallery are somewhat taller and slimmer than those in the porch and the crypt. Actually this systematic adaptation of the dimensions of forms to the elevation of the support on which they figure confirms the view that the entire decoration was carried out by one and the same atelier. As regards the composition of the atelier in question, its origin and period of activity, the frescos themselves are our only source of information, since no documentary records are available, nor is their any portrait of the donor. On internal grounds we are inclined to date all four groups of frescos to about the year 1100.

It is impossible to say whether all the paintings in Saint-Savin conformed to a well-defined iconographical program, but those which have survived by no means rule this out. On the contrary, it is easy to imagine what the frescos that are missing (notably in the transept) may have represented and, by integrating them into what has survived of the ensemble, to arrive at a tolerably clear mental picture of the original layout. None of the paintings in the apse is extant, but in each of the chapels opening off the choir we find a hagiographical cycle appropriate to the saint to whom the chapel is dedicated (individual cycles deriving from martyria). In any case the architecture of the church did not lend itself to elaborately developed sequences, the only exception being the transept, which contained a full cycle of scenes of the Childhood of Christ (supplemented, perhaps, by miracles).

The portion of the nave west of the transept was reserved for laymen and it was there, on the barrel-vaulted ceiling, that scenes of Old Testament history were depicted together with images of prophets (these have lost much of their color). The gallery facing the choir comprised a private chapel, with a wide bay giving on the nave. In it were represented martyrs and sainted bishops of Poitiers, along with two hagiographic scenes, as in the radiating chapels. But the chief feature of these decorations was an extensive cycle of scenes from the Passion of Christ, which were presumably supplemented by a (no longer extant) group of scenes of Christ's Childhood, in the choir. The central scene of the former cycle is a large Descent from the Cross on the wall above the arch communicating with the nave. An Entombment and the Three Marys with the Angel of the Resurrection number among the most elegant and graceful Romanesque paintings still in existence (unfortunately their colors have badly faded). Lastly, conforming to a well-established practice, there figured in the porch a depiction of the Second

Illustrations pages 90-91

Coming of Christ and two rows of Apocalyptic scenes.

The Old Testament cycle in the nave contains several sequences of narrative paintings: the six days of Creation; the story of Adam and Eve and their children up to the curse of Cain and the translation of Enoch into heaven; the tale of Noah, the Tower of Babel, the life of Abraham and, lastly, two symmetrical cycles of the lives

Illustrations pages 86, 89

of Joseph and Moses. The final scene shows Moses receiving the Tables of the Law from God who is appearing in a blaze of light, to the sound of celestial trumpets. In short we are shown the early history of the world and mankind *ante legem*; up to the time, that is, when, on Mount Sinai, God made known his Law to man. It is impossible to say if the Saint-Savin frescos formerly included scenes of the later period of Bible history, the period styled by medieval theologians as *sub lege*. But the fact that the fresco cycle in the vault stops short at the scene on Sinai may well mean that the person or persons responsible for the layout of the decorations conformed to the practice of the theologians who divided the early history of the race into two periods: "before the law" and "under the law."

We have already suggested that the skillful arrangement of the subjects and separate cycles comprised in the Old Testament sequence proves that the artist in charge was a man of exceptional ability and gave much thought to the balanced co-ordination of form and content in the paintings on the vaulted ceiling. It is an interesting point that the symmetry between the Noah, Joseph and Moses cycles becomes apparent only when we take the apex of the vault as the axis of the decorative layout—that is to say, adopt a viewpoint differing from the so to speak normal one, in terms of which the pictures figuring on each side of the intrados of a vault are contemplated separately, as though they were prolongations of the decorations on the vertical walls upon which the vaulting rests. But it seems that only after he had made a certain portion of these pictures did our painter realize how greatly the decorative effect would be enhanced by presenting the biblical scenes in the manner of a continuous frieze extending from end to end of the vault, treated as a uniform concave support aligned to the axis of the nave. Thus after he had come to the third span, he ceased inserting simulated transverse arches like those which in the previous sections of the vault had divided the paintings into separate compartments, and took to painting the scenes in an unbroken sequence. However, in so doing he did not limit himself to using the uniform white surface of the vault as a background for his figures, or to the horizontal colored bands that emphasized the continuity of the friezes. He had the ingenious idea of placing behind the figures rectangular "screens" of varying colors and sizes, and thus inserted a certain number of accents and variations in a composition in length that otherwise might have appeared monotonous. These "screens" do not always fill the background of an entire scene; sometimes they serve to throw only a part of it, perhaps a single figure, into prominence. In this respect they differ, as regards their decorative function, from the trees intercalated between the scenes. Like the maker of the almost contemporary Bayeux tapestry, the Saint-Savin painter uses these trees to bridge the gaps between successive scenes and thus to give an air of continuity to a series of pictures which, in actual fact, are independent of each other.

SCENES FROM THE LIFE OF MOSES: THE CROSSING OF THE RED SEA. CA. 1100. FRESCO ON THE VAULT OF THE NAVE, LOWER REGISTER, NORTH SIDE. SAINT-SAVIN-SUR-GARTEMPE (VIENNE).

ANGELS IN ADORATION. CA. 1100. FRESCO IN THE PORCH.
SAINT-SAVIN-SUR-GARTEMPE (VIENNE).

At Saint-Savin, as in the Bayeux tapestry and also in the miniatures of the famous Joshua Roll, the artist has produced the effect of a continuous frieze by the device of inserting "neutral" motifs between successive episodes of the narrative.

It is more than probable that the idea of composing a frieze-like sequence was suggested to the painter not by any pre-existing model but by the shape of the ceiling he was working on. However, he may also have had in mind contemporary embroideries, like the Bayeux "tapestry," which took the form of long, narrow bands of linen and were intended to be hung on walls. This rapprochement seems to me all the more justifiable since in the Bayeux tapestry, which, as already indicated, was made at about the same time, we find two of the most distinctive features of the Saint-Savin frescos: not only composition in a frieze of scenes placed side by side, but also the combination of elements deriving from *fabliaux* with a leading theme of an historical order. In the Bayeux tapestry, these essentially extraneous elements (scenes from Aesop's fables and the like) were relegated to the decorative borders. But the man who painted the Saint-Savin nave had the ingenious idea of intercalating in his pictures the animals of the old fables—the Fox and the Crow, the Cat hung by Rats and so forth—as well as decorative trees between the scenes. This bold innovation does not seem to have won favor with contemporaries; in any case no other church decorations of the period display so copious an intermingling of religious imagery and the lore of the medieval *fabliers*.

The Saint-Savin frescos were the work of several hands. Their esthetic value varies considerably from scene to scene and the painter first employed was definitely inferior to his successors. Nevertheless in a general way all these artists, members of the same atelier, were experienced craftsmen with a fine feeling for pictorial values. They had, for one thing, a sense of the exigencies of monumental art that had been lacking in the majority of Christian painters of Western Europe since the making of the decorations of Santa Maria Maggiore (Rome) in the 5th century and those at Müstair (Switzerland) in the 9th. Bearing in mind the great height of the Saint-Savin vault, they spread out the figures, simplified the simulated architectural frames, emphasized outlines and oppositions of color and reduced the modeling of bodies and garments to a small number of uniform white "lights." This conventional modeling did little more than hint at tactile

APOCALYPTIC SCENE. CA. 1100. FRESCO IN THE PORCH.
SAINT-SAVIN-SUR-GARTEMPE (VIENNE).

values and, generally speaking, there is no suggestion of depth. The fascination of these paintings is largely due to a subtle interplay of patches of pure color; also to the expressive outlines and rapid movements of the figures. They have small heads, prominent, almond-shaped bellies, and spindle legs. All alike seem possessed with a curious agitation, gesticulating and swinging around rapidly, their legs crossed and the extremities of their garments billowing out around them as they turn. Faces are flat and elongated, with square chins and, when drawn in profile, display big, beak-like noses.

These painters evidently owed much to a type of Carolingian art that had obtained in miniatures from the 9th century on. The Saint-Savin frescoists probably became acquainted with it through the medium of somewhat later works; for it was only in the 10th and 11th centuries that this style came into vogue, playing a prominent part in the art of Ottonian Germany and Anglo-Saxon England, and also in the miniature painting of Northern France and Flanders. Many of the distinctive traits of Carolingian art in general were embodied in these later works; among them the dynamic rendering of figures, heads with broad chins, crossed legs, bell-shaped contours, rounded backs, which we find at Saint-Savin. Also in the intervening period between the 9th and 11th centuries there had developed a tendency towards a curiously metallic quality in Carolingian

THE ARRIVAL AND THE ADORATION OF THE MAGI. SECOND HALF OF THE TWELFTH CENTURY. FRESCO ON THE EAST WALL OF THE NAVE. SAINT-MARTIN, VIC (INDRE).

figure drawing. Not only were bodies flattened out, but their outlines and the edges of folds and highlights were given more geometric forms. The Saint-Savin painters took over the Carolingian heritage in this final phase of its evolution, which may suitably be described as Romanesque. Nevertheless here, as elsewhere in Romanesque France (at Brinay, Tavant and Vic, for example), we would lay stress on the presence of this Carolingian element, since it not only constitutes a family tie between the wall paintings in a whole series of French churches, but also differentiates them from another group of churches decorated by painters schooled outside the sphere of Carolingian influence. Although church decorations midway between these two extremes were being produced at the time, chiefly in Italy, such ateliers as were unaffected by the Carolingian tradition relied for the most part on Byzantine formulae. And though both traditions perpetuated many elements of Early Christian art, these elements differed considerably. Thus there is no reason to predicate any real affinity between the Saint-Savin frescos and contemporary Byzantine painting, whether in Constantinople, Cappadocia or elsewhere.

The frescos in the porch illustrate eschatological themes: the Second Coming of Christ accompanied by the apostles and adored by angels, twelve scenes from the Book Illustrations pages 90-91 of Revelation, and the signs of the zodiac. The tympanum contains a Christ in Majesty,

THE ENTRY OF CHRIST INTO JERUSALEM. SECOND HALF OF THE TWELFTH CENTURY. FRESCO ON THE SOUTH WALL OF THE CHOIR. SAINT-MARTIN, VIC (INDRE).

while the other subjects occupy the arch surrounding the tympanum, the two vaults in front of it, and the supporting arch which divides the two vaults. The style of the paintings in the porch closely resembles that of the other frescos and here again—if we are to judge by the iconography of the Second Coming and Apocalypse scenes—the artist relied strongly on models in the Carolingian tradition.

At Saint-Pierre-les-Eglises, a village not far from Saint-Savin, there can still be seen an apsidal decoration which seemingly antedates the frescos discussed above. Thus we might expect to find in it an early intimation of the Saint-Savin style. This, however, is not the case, and the decoration at Saint-Pierre-les-Eglises, very different in kind, may well be a rustic work comprising borrowings from older forms. (Frescos of a similar type, archaistic in appearance but not particularly old, were produced in Spain at Santa Maria of Tahull.) When we look for antecedents of the Saint-Savin frescos, we are better served if we turn to the big portraits of sainted bishops in Notre-Dame-la-Grande at Poitiers which clearly foreshadow those in the Saint-Savin gallery; or when we go down into the crypt of the same church, where a Christ in Majesty, the Lamb and Evangelist symbols figure on the vault, and, on the walls, a row of martyrs carrying crowns and books. Both the themes and the manner of their presentation, together with their ornamental motifs, form a link between Carolingian and Ottonian frescos on the one hand and those of Saint-Savin on the other. The Last Judgment on the vault above the choir of Notre-Dame-la-Grande clearly derives from a Carolingian model.

It would seem that cycles of scenes from the Book of Genesis resembling that on the ceiling of Saint-Savin, often figured in Romanesque churches. One has recently been discovered in the church of Château-Gontier (Mayenne), a dependency of the abbey of Saint-Aubin at Angers. Though more schematic, the style of these paintings has a marked resemblance to that of Saint-Savin, and the presence of a work of this type in the neighborhood of Angers tends to confirm our theory as to the Northern strain in the tradition followed by the Saint-Savin painters. A further proof of this is to be found Illustration page 112 in the South of England, at Hardham, where the scene of Adam and Eve (ca. 1125), though even more schematic than that of Château-Gontier, is remarkably similar in style to the Saint-Savin frescos. The Château-Gontier paintings may be assigned to the early 12th century, to which period also belongs, in all probability, a curious fresco in the crypt of Auxerre Cathedral, representing a large cross and Christ in front of it on horseback—a striking work, clearly of Northern inspiration.

Illustrations pages 92-93 In the village church of Vic (commune of Nohant-Vicq), in the Bourbonnais, the paintings in the choir have survived almost intact. As in other churches of this part of France, the choir is divided from the nave by a solid wall pierced by a communicating door. This wall, too, is adorned with frescos, obviously by the same artist who painted the other decorations and executed at the same time. The dating is uncertain, but everything points to their having been made in the 12th century, after the Saint-Savin frescos. For all its originality, this artist's style owes a good deal to the art of Saint-Savin (or to other similar works of the same period), but differs from it sufficiently to suggest a date somewhere in the second half of the 12th century. This is confirmed

by the Vic artist's predilection for plastic form (notably in the treatment of drapery) and also, in the choir, by the more sophisticated drawing of zoomorphic ornaments in imitation of historiated textiles. Moreover, compared with Saint-Savin and the paintings at Poitiers, these frescos are obviously of a much more "popular" order.

At first sight it may seem surprising to find scenes of St Peter's crucifixion and Herod sitting in judgment placed side by side under the Christ in Majesty in the choir. But the former scene figures in the same place at Tavant and the latter on the east wall of the Saint-Savin gallery. The choice of subjects illustrated shows that, despite their many and conspicuous differences, all these works produced in Central France belong to the same family. The paintings in the choir at Vic give a condensed version of the *ante legem* cycle which is reproduced in detail at Saint-Savin, with an emphasis on the Fall as an essential antecedent of the Passion of Christ. At Vic the latter theme, in virtue of its bearing on the Redemption, complements and answers to the Genesis theme and here, too, we find the two pictorial cycles figuring at Saint-Savin, scenes from Genesis and scenes of the Passion, one in the nave, the other in the gallery. To these are added, firstly, a large wall painting of an incident in the life of St Martin of Tours, patron saint of the Vic church, and, secondly, a didactic panel associated with the "Salvation" theme, illustrating the parable of the Rich Man and Lazarus (Luke XVI, 19-31). The same moralizing trend is manifested in the representation of a "Combat of Virtues and Vices." Finally, the wall between the nave and choir is frescoed with a well-ordered sequence of scenes on three registers. The central Christ in Majesty may have been inspired by one of those altar frontals still to be seen in all the countries around France, whose type form had been standardized in the Carolingian epoch. Attended by the apostles, Christ presides over the celestial court—as in the Saint-Savin porch. Lower down, as at Saint-Savin and Tavant, the Redemption theme is evoked by a Descent from the Cross (in all these decorations it replaces the Crucifixion, which is omitted). But, as against this isolated scene of the Passion, we find at Vic several episodes of the sequence of Christ's Childhood: the Annunciation, the Arrival and Adoration of the Magi (in two episodes), Candlemas and a scene of Joseph reproaching Illustration page 92 Mary. Hence it is difficult to believe that the "Childhood" cycle was omitted at Saint-Savin; it probably figured in the transept and has gone the way of so many frescos of the period. The repertory of themes drawn on by the Vic painter has much in common with the cycles, lengthy or curtailed, employed in other churches of Central France, and he arranges them, like those at Saint-Savin and Brinay, in scenes placed side by side, frieze-wise, without any separations. In my opinion, their thematic analogies justify our holding that all these paintings stem from a common art tradition.

Stylistically, however, they have far less in common with other frescos in this part of France—and this is why the elements affiliating the Vic frescos to the common tradition are apt to be overlooked. For the harshness of the linework, the rotund, owl-eyed faces and the excessive dynamism of the figure drawing (often pressed to the point of caricature) seem to be at a far cry from the decorations of Saint-Savin. Nevertheless among the Saint-Savin paintings, especially those in the porch, are some groups of

P. Ro. 49

THE MARRIAGE AT CANA. FIRST HALF OF THE TWELFTH CENTURY. FRESCO ON THE SOUTH WALL OF THE CHOIR, UPPER REGISTER. SAINT-AIGNAN, BRINAY (CHER).

crowned heads closely packed together that adumbrate the heads of the Magi on horse-back—including their curious facial expressions—in the Vic frescos. There is already a hint of exaggeration in the figures of the angels in the Saint-Savin porch and gallery, bending almost to the ground as they hasten forward, and the garments, unnaturally drawn in at the knees, give their forms an outline that, though quite unconvincing, has a rhythmic beauty of its own.

Illustration page 92
Illustration page 90

Several other paintings of the late 11th and early 12th century help to an under-standing of the Vic style, so baffling at first sight. Jean Porcher has pointed out the affinities between the art of Vic and a manuscript from Moissac (Paris, Bib. Nat., lat. 5058), another from Le Mans (City Library of Le Mans, MS 214), and a third from Saint-Omer (City Library of Saint-Omer, MS 698, see page 148). These hail from three widely different parts of France, a fact that is perhaps significant since the two wall paintings most similar to those at Vic are even more distant from each other: one being at Aosta in Piedmont, the other at Bohí in Catalonia. That paintings whose style offers closest analogies to those at Vic should be situated at such a distance from each other makes it unlikely that these works were in any sense interdependent. The most probable explanation is that all had a common ancestry, being offshoots of a type of art that had

Illustration page 149

Illustrations pages 44-45

THE BAPTISM OF CHRIST. FIRST HALF OF THE TWELFTH CENTURY. FRESCO ON THE SOUTH WALL OF THE CHOIR, UPPER REGISTER. SAINT-AIGNAN, BRINAY (CHER).

found its way into all the lands of Western Europe. Moreover it is clear that at Aosta and Bohí we have reflections of pre-Romanesque works and that the Saint-Omer miniatures derive from Ottonian painting. Though quite as elaborate as any fully developed Romanesque work of the same kind, the Vic frescos fall into the class of slightly more rustic work retaining a greater number of pre-Romanesque characteristics. The limited palette (red, ochres and a few blues) which we find at Vic and the dynamic exuberance of the figures are survivals from Carolingian times.

The church at Brinay, in the province of Berry, has a walled-off choir like that at Vic, communicating with the nave only through an arch in the cross-wall isolating the chevet from the rest of the building. Also as at Vic, the choir walls are frescoed, though here the "façade" of the choir, towards the nave, is left unpainted. The Brinay painters aligned their frescos on two registers running around three sides of the choir (north, east and south walls) and confined themselves to a single narrative theme: the Childhood of Christ. Though separated by painted pillars, the scenes form an unbroken sequence, beginning, as was the custom, with the Annunciation and ending with the three episodes marking the beginning of Christ's public life: the Baptism, Illustrations pages 96-97 Temptations and the Marriage at Cana.

DANCING FIGURE. TWELFTH CENTURY. FRESCO IN THE CRYPT.
SAINT-NICOLAS, TAVANT (INDRE-ET-LOIRE).

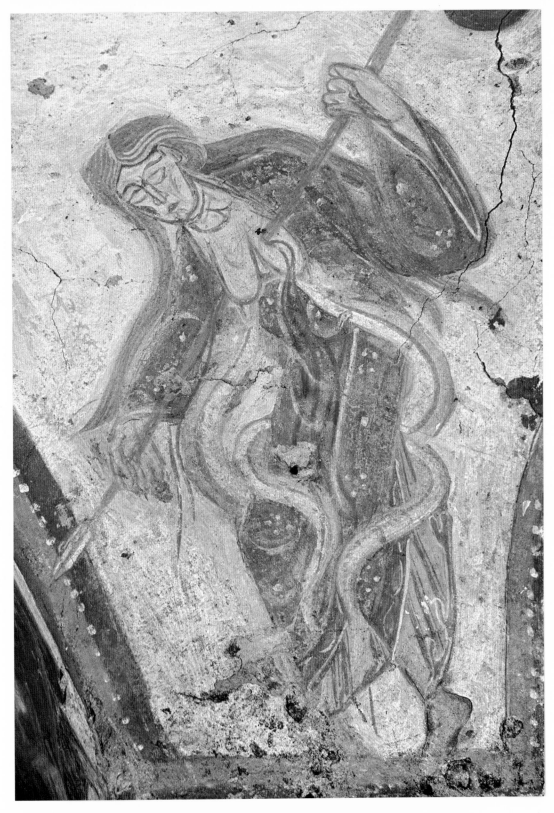

PERSONIFICATION OF LUST. TWELFTH CENTURY. FRESCO IN THE CRYPT.
SAINT-NICOLAS, TAVANT (INDRE-ET-LOIRE).

Illustration page 99

As a whole, the paintings in the Tavant crypt do not form a complete cycle, but give the impression of being a selection from a larger, more fully developed sequence, and the choice of themes appears to follow the iconographic program of those 12th-century bronze doors which give a sort of preview of the imagery within the church: Christ in Majesty, the Descent from the Cross and the Harrowing of Hell, martyrdoms of saints, the David and Samson legends, and the unbiblical motif of the archer (Sagittarius). The Passion cycle is replaced by the two scenes of Christ's Death and Resurrection (at Tavant the Childhood cycle is in the choir); the figures of Adam and Eve epitomize the story of the Fall, and those of David and Samson the cycle of Old Testament heroes.

Illustration page 101

The same holds good for the depictions of the Virtues and Vices and the Sagittarius figure—in fact the painter of the Tavant crypt limited himself to "samples" of the full-length cycles, and this applies equally to such antique motifs as Atlantes and birds.

The iconographic program of the Tavant painter is of no great interest, confined as it is to the vaults and arches of the central aisle (he left the walls and ceilings of the side-aisles of the crypt untouched). What holds us in his work is its remarkably high esthetic quality; indeed this unknown master was undoubtedly a man of genius. Like the Vic artist, he kept to the traditional Carolingian dynamism, but he alone among Romanesque fresco painters succeeded in giving his work that sketch-like spontaneity and lively movement in which the Carolingians had excelled and which, after the School of Reims, reached its apogee in English miniatures and drawings of the 10th and 11th centuries. Indeed, there can be little doubt that the nervous intensity and agitated movements of the Tavant figures derived from the brilliant achievements of contemporary English art, whether directly or at second hand by way of continental works inspired by English paintings; for example, the Evangelist portraits in a late 11th-century manuscript made at Corbie (City Library of Amiens, MS 24). In this manuscript we find many distinctive characteristics of the Tavant style: the twisting movement given bodies, dance-like attitudes, and the practice of rendering folds of garments in almond-shaped or close-set parallel curves. While in all other frescos of Central France we are unable to determine their immediate models (though their affiliation to the Carolingian tradition is manifest), the case is different with those at Tavant, and this rare exception to the general rule is of the utmost interest to students of the period. It is probable that more intensive studies of other frescos will lead to new discoveries of this kind, which will be especially welcome as regards the contributions of Ottonian art. For, *a priori*, it would seem likely that, in view of the great flowering of art in the Ottonian Empire, Germanic influences took effect in France during the 10th and 11th centuries. So far, however, no definite evidence of this has been forthcoming as regards wall painting—as was only to be expected, considering that in Germany itself so few Ottonian frescos have survived.

None the less, the present work, covering as it does the whole field of medieval painting in all the countries of the West, brings out more clearly than any previous compilation the kinship between 11th- and 12th-century frescos in Burgundy and Savoy, in Southern Germany, in Austria and in Northern Italy from Aquileia to Piedmont. Were these affinities due to the geographical factor—the proximity of these parts of

Europe—or to some historical cause and, if so, to what cause? Until such time as detailed and comprehensive studies have been made, region by region, of the most typical works produced in the above-named countries, no definitive reply can be given. But, without prejudice to the conclusions of future scholars, we would remind our readers that most of the regions in question were geographically in close contact with Italy across the Alps; and also that all were included in the "Holy Roman" (Germanic) Empire. Unfortunately, owing to the fact that no large-scale Ottonian painted decorations have survived and to the wanton destruction of the abbey church of Cluny early in the 19th century, we are deprived of many essential, perhaps decisive data that would have facilitated the analysis of the frescos we now shall deal with.

It is in Savoy, in the chapel of the Château des Allinges (above Thonon), that the earliest group of frescos stylistically akin to those of South Germany and Northern Italy can be seen. Judging by the style of the drawing of figures, hands, feet, faces and garments (cf. the archaic paintings at Civate), these frescos cannot be dated later than the 11th century. In two other, equally archaic frescos we find Majestas which, as regards their iconography, resemble those at Les Allinges, though it must be admitted that their artistic quality is relatively mediocre. One group is situated in the vault of Saint-Michel d'Aiguilhe at Le Puy, the other in the crypt of the church at Ternand, some twenty-five miles northwest of Lyons.

The frescos in Le Puy Cathedral seem to have been made a good deal later, for which reason we do not discuss them at this stage and begin by an account of two churches, in Burgundy and the ancient province of Viennois, which contain the most striking Romanesque paintings extant in that part of France: the chapel of Berzé-la-Ville near Mâcon and the church of Saint-Chef in the neighborhood of Grenoble.

Berzé-la-Ville was a priory affiliated to the abbey of Cluny, some seven miles distant; thus there is every reason for believing that the paintings in the chapel were inspired by the art of that famous monastery. This is borne out by their exceptionally high quality and there can be little doubt that they were the work of a skillful executant coming from Cluny itself. Unfortunately their dating is highly problematic. In the absence of any inscription bearing on this point (the portrait of an abbot is of no help, since we do not know his name), the Berzé frescos are usually assigned to the first decade of the 12th century (1103-1109), since it is on record that the famous abbot of Cluny, St Hugh, took a special interest in the Berzé priory, often visited it towards the end of his life, and bequeathed funds for structural improvements and defraying the cost of Masses on anniversaries of his death, which took place in 1109. But, interesting though they are, the records make no mention of the chapel or its decorations (the buildings restored by St Hugh were intended for lay use) and throw no light on the dating of the frescos. Thus whether St Hugh carried his interest in Berzé to the point of commissioning the decorations in the priory chapel remains an open question.

Illustrations pages 104-105, 109

Originally all the walls and vaults of the upper chapel at Berzé-la-Ville were frescoed (some vestiges of painting can also be seen on the lower floor). But of the nave decorations, which included figures of saints and Gospel scenes, only isolated fragments have survived.

THE MARTYRDOM OF ST BLAISE. MID-TWELFTH CENTURY (?). FRESCO IN THE APSE.
CHAPEL OF BERZÉ-LA-VILLE (SAÔNE-ET-LOIRE).

THE MARTYRDOM OF ST VINCENT. MID-TWELFTH CENTURY (?). FRESCO IN THE APSE.
CHAPEL OF BERZÉ-LA-VILLE (SAÔNE-ET-LOIRE).

Among the Gospel scenes we can identify an Entrance into Jerusalem; the others are indistinct. In keeping with an ancient practice which still obtained in the Carolingian and Romanesque periods (for example at Prüfening, see p. 119), the entrance to the choir was adorned with portraits of the founders, in this case two unnamed abbots each wearing a cowl and carrying a pastoral staff. The apsidal frescos are in relatively good condition and there is no mistaking their high esthetic quality. Not only have we here a work of exceptional technical accomplishment, but the artist has displayed much skill in grouping harmoniously together within a limited space an unusual number of religious motifs. Whereas in the large neighboring abbey church at Cluny the apsidal decorations, datable to before 1125, consisted merely of a Christ in Majesty and the four Evangelist symbols, the decorator of the Berzé apse adorned the vault with a scene unique of its kind in France: Christ enthroned in the midst of the twelve Apostles, blessing St Paul who

Illustration page 109

is represented on His right—and at the same time delivering an open scroll to St Peter who is holding up the manuscript with his right hand while in his left he clasps the keys. I regret my inability to decipher the words written on the scroll, which are generally assumed to relate to the "donation" of the monastery of Cluny to the Apostles Peter and Paul at the time of its foundation (in 910). All the same, if this was so, one would have expected a portrait of William I, the Pious, duke of Guienne (Aquitaine) to figure in the fresco, since it was he who made that famous "donation." But William is not represented, and it is difficult to see why, if the painter's aim was to suggest a link between the temporal prince, the donor, and the two "princes of the Apostles," the handing-over of the scroll should have been assigned to Christ Himself and why the whole company of Apostles was included in the scene.

Hence the probability that what is actually represented in the apsidal fresco at Berzé is neither the "donation" of William of Aquitaine nor (as has been suggested) the making-over of the New Covenant to St Peter, but that specifically Roman theme: Christ accompanied by the twelve Apostles, headed as was natural by Sts Peter and Paul, to whom He is delivering the New Covenant. And by reverting to this theme, so often used in Roman apses, the monks of Cluny signified their allegiance to the Holy See. Typically Roman, too, is the way the artist places at the feet of the giant figures of the Apostles the tiny kneeling figures of four saints: two deacons on the left, two bishops on the right. Moreover, the names of the sainted deacons are recorded, Lawrence and Vincent, and these two, always in association, were the objects of a special cult, Roman in origin, that had spread all over Europe; similarly the two sainted bishops figuring in the frescos were presumably Roman popes.

Some other paintings, too, beneath the Majesty, bring us back to Rome: in the

Illustration page 105
Illustration page 104

blind arcade on the right, the Martyrdom of St Vincent (probably not St Lawrence), and in the corresponding arcade on the left that of St Blaise. It is common knowledge that St Vincent was one of the saints most venerated in medieval Rome, but not so generally known that Blaise also was in high favor, and that from the beginning of the 10th century on the cult of this saint had been making rapid strides in Rome, where, between the 10th and 13th century, no less than ten churches were dedicated to this famous bishop, martyred under Diocletian at Sebaste or Caesarea. The sainted virgin martyrs depicted beneath the two scenes of martyrdom at Berzé bear Roman names and all of them figure in the Liturgical Calendar of Cluny, as also do the male saints, mentioned above, represented in the apse. It is an interesting point (I owe this piece of information to the erudition of Dom Dubois) that here the virgin martyrs are assimilated to the Wise Virgins of the parable, as is evidenced by the lamps they are holding up towards Christ. And since the analogy was of an exclusively moral order, their number could exceed the scriptural five. The Berzé painter knew of and conformed to the practice of representing the Virgins of the parable in apses, as exemplified at Gorze, near Metz, in the 9th century, and at Pedret in Catalonia, at Summaga near Venice and at Pürgg in Styria in the 12th and 13th centuries. (It was only later that they were "transferred" to the portals of churches and cathedrals.) The influence of these apsidal frescos makes itself felt in a curious iconographical blunder on the Berzé painter's part; the virgin martyr on the extreme right of the group assimilated to the Wise Virgins of the Gospel story carries, instead of a lamp, the cross with a long shaft which in traditional illustrations of the parable is an attribute, not of any of the virgins, but of Christ the Bridegroom. Is it due to mere chance that the virgin carrying the Bridegroom's cross is given the apt name of Consorcia?

Finally, on the lowest register of the wall of the apse, above the usual simulated textile decoration of the plinth, are the half-length figures of nine saints, the names of all but one of whom can still be deciphered. All writers on the subject have pointed out that these are eastern saints, and have associated this choice with the Byzantinizing tendencies of the Berzé artist. As a matter of fact, however, nearly all these saints (who figure in the "Book of Saints" of Cluny), whatever their nationality, either suffered martyrdom in Rome (e.g. the Persians Abdon and Sennen; also, according to Father Delahaye, Sts Dorotheus and Gorgonius) or were martyrs whose relics were preserved in Rome (e.g. St Sebastian), or else were particularly venerated in that city (four Roman churches were dedicated to the Syrian St Sergius in the period preceding Charlemagne). The only ones with no Roman associations were the two French saints, Denis (Dionysius) and Quentin (Quintianus). Thus, like the rest of the decoration, the "portrait" sequence in the apse derives from the Roman repertory, and it is in fact in the choice of their thematic material and by the use of specifically Roman motifs that the Berzé painters most clearly show both their allegiance to the art of Cluny and their conformity to the liturgical practices of the great abbey. This is borne out also by the exceptionally sumptuous decorations of the apse, especially typical of the Roman tradition being the floral garland encircling it.

Ever since their discovery in 1887, the Berzé frescos have attracted much attention and it has often been pointed out that this Cluniac painting differs considerably both in style and technique from its equivalents in Poitou and the Loire valley. Stress has also been laid on its "dependence on Byzantine tutelage." The Berzé artist's palette is far richer and more varied than that of the Saint-Savin and Tavant painters. Combining dark blue grounds with passages of red, ochre, grey-green, purplish-brown and white, he builds up color accords as striking as they are original. That he was a skilled and experienced technician is proved by the ingenious composition of the apse decorations, where, despite their rich diversity, figures and ornaments are integrated into an harmonious whole. The two scenes of martyrdom are particularly interesting since they demonstrate the painter's mastery of the problems of rendering and organizing space, and thus mark a decisive forward step in the evolution of the Romanesque style.

Illustration page 105

In the scene of the martyrdom of St Vincent, spatial recession is indicated by the frequent use of diagonals and the face of the judge is skillfully foreshortened. Noteworthy in all these frescos is the close attention given to the modeling of forms and garments, and here we have, moreover, criteria which help in a general way to the dating of Romanesque paintings. Spatial composition by means of diagonals and slanting figures makes its appearance in the famous fresco at Civate, in Northern Italy, datable to the

Illustration page 24

first half of the 12th century and representing the triumph of the Archangel Michael. But such systematic, elaborately developed modeling as we find in the Berzé scenes of martyrdom belongs to a somewhat later period and for this reason I have never been able to endorse the view that these frescos should be dated to the abbacy of St Hugh, i.e. to the first decade of the 12th century. The emphatic rendering of three-dimensional values and the fully plastic treatment of drapery suggest that this must be a mid-12th century work. Since no equivalents are to be found in France, mention may be made of the frescos in the Allerheiligenkapelle in the cloisters of Regensburg Cathedral and those in the neighboring monastery of Prüfening, both of which date to shortly after

Illustrations pages 122-123

1150; also of the fine paintings in the Nonnberg church at Salzburg (ca. 1154).

This comparison between Berzé-la-Ville and the Regensburg-Salzburg groups of frescos is all the more justifiable since Prüfening took part in the Cluniac reform movement and all the above-mentioned churches lay within the Holy Roman Empire. Both in their style and in their emphasis on plastic form, the German frescos offer close analogies to those at Berzé, and in both alike Byzantine influences are strongly marked. At Berzé we see them not only in the technique employed and the iconography of the portrayals of Christ, the Apostles and St Blaise, but also in the drawing and modeling of drapery and costumes. Indeed, the Berzé painter has copied Byzantine models with such fidelity (e.g. his renderings of folds, and bundles of folds, with patches of white to mark the highlights) that it facilitates the dating of these frescos, since the models he followed cannot belong to a period earlier than that of the Comnene dynasty, and it is difficult to believe that the influence of this style could have reached faraway France before the middle of the 12th century. In this context it should, however, be pointed out that the Berzé frescos also bear unmistakably the imprint of Roman art (see above) and that it is quite probable that the Byzantine elements we find in them derive equally from Rome, since, from the second half of the 11th century on, there flourished in that city, under the patronage of the popes, a form of art which comprised extensive borrowings from contemporary Byzantine painting. It is clear that this infiltration of eastern influences gathered strength with the years—a fact which tends to support our view that the hagiographical frescos in San Clemente at Rome antedate those at Berzé. And the

CHRIST IN MAJESTY WITH THE TWELVE APOSTLES, DETAIL: ST PETER. MID-TWELFTH CENTURY (?).
FRESCO IN THE APSE. CHAPEL OF BERZÉ-LA-VILLE (SAÔNE-ET-LOIRE).

San Clemente frescos were certainly made after 1084 and can hardly be posterior to the close of the 11th century. On the other hand, the new apsidal mosaics of San Clemente (1128) and Santa Maria in Trastevere (ca. 1140) display Byzantine mannerisms resembling those of Berzé, and the same style makes its appearance in Sicily after 1148. If we are to judge by the monumental art of Rome and Sicily—and also by the South German frescos (see p. 118)—the style of the Berzé paintings justifies us in dating them somewhere around the middle of the 12th century.

The wall paintings in the abbey church of Saint-Chef, in Dauphiné, reflect an art akin to that of Berzé and to the frescos of South Germany and North Italy. All alike saw the day in lands that then formed part of the Holy Roman (Germanic) Empire and the common political background goes far to explain the obvious resemblances in the techniques and programs of these decorations.

The frescos in the choir and transept of Saint-Chef have been repainted and in their present state are little more than shadows of their former selves. However in a chapel in the transept, on the upper storey, some of the original paintings have survived intact. The decorations of this chapel, which is dedicated to three archangels and St George, are located at the north end of the transept above a vault frescoed with the Rivers of Paradise. Doubtless all the frescos in the church were made at the same time, but only those in the chapel have escaped (if not entirely) the attentions of restorers.

As patron saints of the chapel, the three archangels figure on the wall of the apse, exactly as at Sant'Angelo in Formis, but here they are accompanied by St George, fourth patron of the little oratory. All the other frescos center on a single theme and are adapted with much skill to the layout of the walls, spanned by a single vault. They comprise a depiction of the Heavenly Jerusalem and its inhabitants: the angelic hosts, the Mystic Lamb, the Virgin and saints. All the holy figures are placed in superimposed tiers, the angels occupying the upper register, with the exception of those whose function it is to escort the souls of the Blessed, newly arrived in the celestial sphere, to the gates of the City of the Lamb. Since the scenes are not limited (as is often the case) to a single wall but cover all the walls alike, their effect is to convert the entire chapel into a small-scale replica, as it were, of the Celestial City. We find a similar imagery in those contemporary miniatures which depict the soul of a dead Christian being conveyed by angels through the courts of Heaven before being finally admitted into God's presence. At Saint-Chef, too, the painter conjures up before us that paradisal world which is the home of the Elect when their earthly pilgrimage is over.

This notion of decorating a chapel in such a way as to assimilate it to the City of God is paralleled in several other Romanesque ensembles; in South Germany, Austria and North Italy (e.g. the Allerheiligenkapelle of Regensburg Cathedral, Prüfening, Gurk, Civate). The theme was frequently employed for the adornment of edifices with vaulted ceilings in the southern provinces of the Empire, and in all cases Byzantine influences played a part in these visions of the Celestial Paradise. They are particularly noticeable at Saint-Chef, for example in the figure of the Virgin in her blue mantle and in her gesture as she raises both hands to her breast; also in the row of saints seated side by side on a long bench. No less typically Byzantine is the drawing of faces and garments and the modeling of drapery. The beginnings of this tendency can be traced, it seems, in the Nonnberg paintings at Salzburg (ca. 1154) and the two fresco sequences, mentioned above, at Regensburg (ca. 1150). We assign the Civate frescos to about the same time (see p. 46). The affinities between all these works justify us in assuming that the Saint-Chef paintings may likewise be dated to somewhere around 1150. However, the exact chronology is less important than the presence of a marked family likeness, as pointed out above, between these decorations, in all parts of the Empire and around the Alps.

In a less degree we find the same affinities in the frescos at Berzé-la-Ville which, like Cluny, lay near the frontiers of the Empire, and also, to a still less degree, in two groups of wall paintings in Auvergne. While both of these groups contain sporadic reminiscences of contemporary Byzantine art, these are interpreted in a manner less concordant with its spirit.

We will begin with the paintings in a church located in one of the grottoes at Jonas near Besse-en-Chandesse, just south of Clermont-Ferrand, capital of the ancient province of Auvergne. These rustic frescos have stylistic analogies with certain illustrations of the Exultet theme stemming from ateliers in Central Italy and such painted Catalan retables as those at Sagars and Espinelvas.

In the cathedral of Le Puy, also in Auvergne, the two arms of the transept were formerly painted with a large and elaborate fresco sequence. Unfortunately the paintings on the south side have been completely destroyed and all we have to go on are some rather poor sketches of them made in the middle of the 19th century, while those on the north side, after some rough handling at the hands of restorers, are now half-obliterated. Since, however, this is the only known example of a *cathedral* decorated wholly in the Romanesque style, the Le Puy frescos merit careful examination. The lost frescos in the south gallery originally consisted of a cycle, inspired by the liturgy, in which Old and New Testament scenes were arranged in pairs, with an eye to their concordance. On one of the walls of the north gallery, however, much of the painting has survived. It includes an exceptionally large scene representing the Archangel Michael (object of a special cult at Le Puy) accompanied, as at Regensburg and Essen, by prophets and martyrs. There can be little doubt that the Byzantinisms of the archangel and saints were at a far remove from their eastern prototypes and derived from Italy. The rudimentary style of these frescos seems all the more surprising when we consider that not only do they figure in a cathedral but must have been made in the second half of the 11th century (during the bishopric of Pierre II, ca. 1050-1073). Still here it is perhaps less accurate to talk of "rusticity" than of an independent style found not only in Exultet miniatures but also in those 12th-century Catalan altar frontals (at Sagars and Espinelvas) which we have already cited in connection with the decorations in the Grottes de Jonas—the style which, in Spain, developed out of contacts with Mozarabic art. It would seem indeed that these two groups of frescos in Auvergne were influenced by the art of the contemporary Spanish retable, though how this came about, and through what channels, is a problem that has not yet been fully solved.

ADAM AND EVE. FIRST THIRD OF THE TWELFTH CENTURY. FRESCO ON THE WEST WALL OF THE CHANCEL.
ST BOTOLPH'S, HARDHAM (SUSSEX).

England

There was a great flowering of the pictorial arts in England during the Romanesque epoch but, whereas many illuminated manuscripts have survived (these are discussed at a later page), the case is very different with English wall painting. And though the rare examples that have escaped destruction have been the object of intensive study by specialists, it must be admitted that there are not enough of them to warrant any broad generalizations as regards the activities and achievements of the English fresco painters during the period we are dealing with.

The chief scriptoria producing illuminated books were situated in the South of England and it is also in that part of the country that we find the few Romanesque frescos which have come down to us. Sometimes they are only quite small fragments, or else, as a result of modern restorations, mere shadows of their former selves. If these be excluded, what we have to go on, in our study of this branch of English painting, is limited to a few groups of 12th-century frescos in tolerably good condition. One is at Hardham, near Chichester (on the South Coast); another, recently discovered, similar in style, is at Coombes (also in Sussex), and a third, obviously the work of a quite different school, consists of fragments in two chapels of Canterbury Cathedral.

St Botolph's, the little church of Hardham, contains a single nave communicating through an arch with a rectangular chancel abutting on a flat apse. Of the big Majesta which originally figured at the center of the east wall of the chancel, only two figures of cherubim or seraphs flanking the central effigy of Christ have survived. The paintings in the chancel were laid out in two zones, the upper one containing two symmetrical groups of figures: first the Elders of the Apocalypse, then (on the west) the Apostles aligned under an arcade. Originally the Hardham decorations comprised a full-length eschatological sequence, in which the scenes described above, concerned with man's Salvation, counterbalanced two scenes on the same register on the west wall of the chancel (above the arch communicating with the nave): on the south side Adam and Eve beside the Tree of Knowledge; then, on the north side, Eve again and beside her not the familiar snake but a curious dragonlike quadruped. Presumably the artist's intention was to illustrate in the chancel the Fall of Man and his Redemption. The paintings in the lower zone are in very poor condition; so far as can be made out, they represented the Arrest of Christ and the Last Supper on the north wall and, on the south wall, the Entombment. Thus scenes from the Passion linked up the imagery in the chancel with the rite of the Eucharist solemnized within it.

Illustration page 112

All four sides of the nave were covered with paintings set out in two zones, as in the chancel, the lowest portion of the walls being filled with painted draperies. Here the iconographic scheme is easy to follow; above the arch, on the east wall of the nave, figures the Adoration of the Lamb, recalling the cycle in the chancel and overlooking scenes of the Labors of the Months—a Christian substitute for the pagan "Annus." Of these "Labors," which formerly surrounded the big arch leading to the chancel, only two, those on the south side, remain. Facing the Lamb and the sequence of Labors of the Months, reminders of the "Triumph of Time," the frescos on the west wall evoked a vision of the End of Time, answering to the corresponding motif in the chancel, where the figures of Christ, the Apostles and the Elders of the Apocalypse conjured up the Kingdom of Heaven and the bliss of the Elect. But at the west end of the nave the painter represented the nether world, peopled by sinners and demons. It is to be regretted that this fresco is in so poor a state, since it obviously offered a quite original interpretation of the Torments of the Damned. On either side of a window that has been enlarged we have glimpses of cowled demons with blue bodies and red tongues manipulating awesome cauldrons in a sort of Devil's Kitchen.

On the east and side walls is a long sequence of Infancy scenes, beginning with the Annunciation and ending with the youthful Christ preaching in the Temple and the Baptism—two scenes prefiguring the dual function of the Church, doctrinal and sacramental. Many of these frescos have faded almost to invisibility but enough remains to show that the theme of the three Kings of the East was treated at exceptional length. (We find a similar cycle at Lambach, in Austria, and also—an interesting point—in an English book, the Albani Psalter.) While the upper register is reserved exclusively to scenes of the Infancy of Christ, the lower register of the side walls contains a sequence of hagiographic paintings. On the north wall we can still make out a representation of the soul of Lazarus being borne heavenwards by two symmetrically posed angels and, on the opposite wall, a handsome knight, perhaps St George, riding a white charger and carrying a large banner with five streamers.

As Francis Wormald has observed, the style of these paintings (datable to the first third of the 12th century) contains unmistakable reminiscences of pre-Norman painting; it recalls even more closely the miniatures in an exceptionally fine Winchester manuscript belonging to the same period (Brit. Mus., Nero c. IV), in which we also find several of the iconographic motifs of the Hardham sequence. This fidelity to Anglo-Saxon pictorial traditions is evidenced in the artist's emphasis on design; everywhere in the Hardham frescos we find the same linear technique: strongly marked contours combined with schematic renderings of the anatomy of nude figures and of the garments worn by others. These are distinctive traits of Anglo-Saxon art, as are the elongated proportions of bodies, unnaturally small heads, narrow, drooping shoulders, slightly bent knees, long, heavily built limbs. Another interesting point about these frescos is that in their choice of subjects, their style and general layout, they have many affinities with the decorations of a number of 12th-century Danish country churches, for example those at Ørreslev (near Jellinge), Fjenneslev and Jørlunde. In both countries we get the impression of an art distinctively Anglo-Saxon in origin and conception. None the less at Hardham, as in other works of the same style, the basic characteristics of the artist's figure drawing can be traced back to type forms created by Carolingian draftsmen and the School of Reims. For the influence of Carolingian models was no less considerable and persistent in England than on the Continent; hence the fact that the style of English wall paintings like those at Hardham has so much in common with such French frescos of the same period as kept to the Carolingian tradition. We have in mind,

ST PAUL AND THE VIPER. LATE TWELFTH CENTURY. FRESCO, ST ANSELM'S CHAPEL,
CANTERBURY CATHEDRAL.

particularly, the Château-Gontier paintings and their representations of Adam and Eve. Since the frescos at Tavant and in the central apse at Montoire were made at a later date, they have no direct bearing on those at Hardham, but we shall not be surprised if frescos similar in style are, one day, discovered in England; for this highly dynamic interpretation of the style originated by the School of Reims was followed up with striking success by the Winchester school of illuminators.

But not all Romanesque frescos in England were of this kind; as in France, we find, along with mural decorations in the Carolingian tradition, others whose style is obviously influenced by contemporary Byzantine art. In France the Byzantinizing trend manifested itself chiefly in the southeastern provinces, i.e. those included in the Empire or adjoining it. Through the intermediary of the central power these provinces were in touch with Italian art, first to be penetrated by Byzantine influences. Also, the contemporary frescos of west and south Germany reflected, as a general rule, these specifically Byzantine trends of Romanesque.

As regards England, the surviving works do not enable us to localize this Byzantine style of painting in any particular part of the country, and we find both types of art, native and imported, existing side by side in the south. Thus Hardham is not far from Canterbury, where the best examples of Byzantinizing frescos are located. And though the Hardham style, as already mentioned, has affinities with certain Winchester illuminations, it is in another famous group of miniatures issuing from the same workshop (those, for instance, in the Winchester Bible) that the closest analogies to the Canterbury frescos can be found. The explanation of this seeming anomaly lies in a difference of date, since the Winchester miniatures of the second group were made in the second half of the 12th century and the Canterbury frescos may safely be dated to the same period; whereas the Hardham frescos and the Winchester miniatures resembling them were made nearer the beginning of the century, that is to say before English artists had come under Byzantine influence. A parallel stylistic evolution can be traced in the illuminated psalters produced in England during the 11th and 12th centuries; while reproducing the same pictures, these artists brought them into line with the taste of each successive period. The wall paintings in both chapels of Canterbury Cathedral are productions of the second half of the 12th century, but those in St Gabriel's Chapel, situated in the crypt, were executed first. As at Hardham the frescos in the apse have undergone considerable modifications, with regrettable results. There can still be seen on the soffit of an arch (which formerly, it seems, contained a window, now walled up) a series of small Apocalyptic pictures: at the top, seven stars in a medallion and beside these the scene of St John writing the Book of Revelation (the letters *Apocal...* can be made out on his scroll) and seven angels carrying candlesticks or in the orans attitude. The vault of the small chancel contains a Majesta and two scenes from the life of Zacharias, father of St John, in which the archangel Gabriel figures as God's messenger.

The paintings on the intrados of the two arches between the nave and chapel reveal some pentimenti, where the artist partially remade his motif of medallions on an ornamental ground. In the medallions are busts of women, personifications or female saints, carrying torches or in prayer. Of the decorations which originally covered the four groined vaults of the nave all that can still be seen are some medallions, containing half-length figures holding scrolls, telling out on a ground of rinceaux. Done in yellow on dark blue, these decorations greatly resemble the frescos in the Norman church of Petit-Quevilly, near Rouen—a fact which supports the view that the latter, unique of their kind in France, were of English origin.

The style of the paintings in St Gabriel's Chapel is strongly marked by Byzantine influence. This is evident in the drawing of heads and draperies, in the modeling of garments and in the color scheme. The decorative pattern of the vaults (medallions on ornamental grounds) goes back to the same source and might seem to imply firsthand acquaintance, on the English artist's part, with Byzantine monumental painting. It is, however, most unlikely that he had seen anything more than frescos of a Byzantinizing tendency—doubtless on a visit oversea. That he had kept abreast of developments across the Channel is suggested by the treatment of certain details such as the Apocalypse scene in the apse and the motif of busts within rectangular frames adorning the interior curves of arches; or, again, the long floating scrolls held by figures. There is nothing Byzantine in these practices, but we find many instances of them in the continental countries of the West after the mid-12th century.

Whereas the frescos in St Gabriel's Chapel cannot have been made long after 1150, those in St Anselm's Chapel (dedicated to Sts Paul and Peter)—which gives on the ambulatory of the choir of the Cathedral—were evidently made a generation later, somewhere around the close of the 12th century. Only one panel has survived, the famous scene of St Paul and the viper on the north wall of the apse. This fragment, which we reproduce, Illustration page 115 is in exceptionally fine condition. An examination of the drawing, modeling, colors and general technique reveals its affinities with the frescos in the crypt, discussed above. But this later artist shows an advance on his predecessor, both in his handling of forms and in the use of patches of color to suggest the plastic volume of garments, instead of the network of lines employed in St Gabriel's Chapel. The head is treated similarly, notable being the smoothness of the modeling and the suavity of expression, verging on mawkishness, that the artist has imparted to the saint's face. Both the color, intense but subtly modulated, and the style in general recall the Winchester and Canterbury miniatures of about 1200 (e.g. the Winchester Bible and the Psalter, MS 8846, in the Bibliothèque Nationale, Paris). But the St Paul picture has also many analogies with the frescos at Sigena, in Spain, in which some modern authorities claim to see traces of English influence. That a certain kinship exists between them is undeniable but, pending further comparative research, I prefer to reserve judgment in the matter. Unfortunately such research is handicapped by the lack of adequate data; since not only have some parts of the Sigena decorations been destroyed, but in the "St Paul" we have the one and only English example of *wall* painting in this style. Provisionally, I am inclined to think that the Sigena painter derived his style (with its pronounced Byzantinisms) from contacts, not with English, but with Italian painting, whose influence on the Spanish fresco was considerable and continuous throughout the Romanesque period.

Germany and Austria

As a result of the intense and constant art activity prevailing in that country throughout the 10th and 11th centuries, the division between pre-Romanesque and Romanesque frescos is less clearly marked in Germany than elsewhere. Thus this chapter of the present work might well have opened with a description of the mural decorations at Oberzell (Reichenau), Goldbach and Fulda. Actually, however, it seemed best to include them in our previous volume, *Early Medieval Painting*, since chronologically they are associated with the miniatures—definitely pre-Romanesque—of the 10th and the first half of the 11th century.

Many German churches were adorned with paintings during the Romanesque period, but most of these have disappeared, while others have been ruined almost completely —from the esthetic point of view—by restorations carried out in the 19th and at the beginning of the present century. This applies particularly to frescos in the region of the Lower Rhine; none of them, in our opinion, has today the authenticity which would justify its reproduction in color. What makes this all the more regrettable is that some of them must, in their original state, have been works of remarkable beauty: which is why they were the first of German medieval frescos to be the subject of an erudite and exhaustive study, that of Paul Clemen published in 1916. If we take them into consideration in the present volume, this is less for their artistic merits than for the light they throw, despite the alterations they have undergone, on the enlargement of the iconographic programs of Romanesque monumental painting in its later phase.

Among the unrestored fragments of decorations that illustrate the earliest period of Romanesque wall painting in Germany, mention may be made of those in the churches of Burgfelden near Balingen (Württemberg) and Krosingen, not far from Freiburg-im-Breisgau. The Burgfelden Last Judgment and the Scenes of the Life of John the Baptist at Krosingen clearly belong to a tradition inherited from the preceding period. This may also be true of the frescos in the west chancel (dedicated to St Denis) of the abbey church of St Emmeram, situated at the gates of Regensburg. This great monastery housed, from the 10th century on, an active and famous school of illuminators. The big rectangular apse is decorated with a sequence of scenes relating to the lives of St Peter and (probably) St Denis—i.e. Dionysius the Areopagite—and above this is a row of large standing figures of saints, while in the vaults in front of the apse is a depiction (apparently) of the Ark of the Covenant and a sequence of ornamental motifs alternating with figures of prophets. One of them, a grey-bearded prophet, gives a good idea of the technique and modeling —both strongly marked by Byzantine influence—practised by the painters of these frescos, datable to about 1052.

To the same atelier of painters, still domiciled at Regensburg but active a century later (ca. 1150), we owe—in addition to the Frauenchiemsee fragments—two interesting fresco cycles which have marked affinities both stylistic and thematic. This is natural enough since they are quite near each other, one of them figuring on the walls of the Allerheiligenkapelle (All Saints' Chapel) which gives on the cloister of Regensburg

THE ADORATION OF THE MAGI. LATE ELEVENTH CENTURY (?). FRESCO ON THE VAULT OF THE GALLERY.
ABBEY CHURCH, LAMBACH (NEAR LINZ).

Cathedral, and the other on the walls and vault of the choir of Prüfening Abbey, only a few miles from Regensburg. The former group of frescos has recently been cleaned of certain 19th-century retouchings; the second still awaits similar treatment, but happily some fragments in the nave and the decorations in the side chapels have been relatively little tampered with.

The Prüfening choir consists of an apse and a square bay, with a cupola above, whose imagery conjures up a vision of the City of God, dominated by the figure of Christ, attended by the apostles, in the upper zone of the apse. At the top of the cupola is a representation of the Ecclesia, and on the walls are three zones of saints arranged in the order of their hierarchy. The general effect resembles that of the frontispieces in

Romanesque copies of St Augustine's *De civitate Dei*. Next, we have at the bottom of the side walls the kneeling figures of the donors, a king and a bishop (usually identified with the Emperor Henry V and Otto, Bishop of Bamberg). Much of the painted surface is occupied by ornamental motifs and imitations of marble, with slightly exaggerated veinings. The north chapel is frescoed with scenes of the Life of St John the Baptist and another vision of the Celestial City (in the vault), while in the symmetrically shaped chapel on the south the same positions are occupied by scenes of the Life of St Benedict and the Dove of the Holy Spirit surrounded by the Apostles. Lastly, in front of the choir, above the pews reserved for the monks, there are four large panels, on two of which the figure of Christ attended by the three theological Virtues counterbalances one of the Madonna with two angels, while the paintings on the other two panels reflect the politico-religious doctrines of the day. Thus on one of these (the panel on the north) we see St Peter handing a sword to a king and another to a cleric—a reminder of the Roman doctrine that both the civil and the religious powers derived their authority from the pope. Since Prüfening was a Cluniac foundation, this composition may well conform to an iconographic program sponsored by Cluny, its ultimate source being presumably the Carolingian mosaic in the Lateran which depicts St Peter in the act of blessing simultaneously Leo III and Charlemagne.

The Allerheiligenkapelle in the cathedral cloister of Regensburg is a vaulted structure with three conches and a dome supported by a drum. All the paintings in this chapel relate, so far as can be seen, to the theme of the Heavenly Jerusalem or "City of God." It would be possible to speak more definitely had the many inscriptions which once accompanied the figures not been obliterated. (Professor H. Krempl, who recently cleaned these frescos, assures me that the "readings" of the inscriptions given by J.A. Enders in a work published at the beginning of the present century were based on insufficient data.) At the summit of the cupola is the figure of Christ surrounded by angels; lower down, between the windows, are eight depictions of a group consisting in each case of an aged man (Christ?) and the three theological Virtues whose names are inscribed beside them. To express the notion of the Church "sealed with the blood of martyrs," scenes of the violent deaths of several saints are represented on the inner surfaces of the arches framing the windows of the drum beneath the cupola. The angels on the pendentives hold out long inscribed scrolls towards the archangel Michael who, posted at the back of the apse, seems to preside over all the decorations in the arches (as at Le Puy and Essen)—a reminder of the original, funerary, intention of the chapel. For on each side of the archangel, who is standing on the solar disk, are twelve small scenes representing the Angel of the Lord marking representatives of the twelve tribes of Israel with the sign of the Elect; which shows that we have here the New (Christian) Jerusalem, city of the Blest, while the sign imposed is that of the Cross, token of Salvation. Finally, in the lateral apses, male and female saints, linked together by bands bearing inscriptions (now effaced), represent the Elect who have won admittance to the courts of Heaven. It is not unlikely that a minute study of these figures would lead to their identification, despite the poor condition of the painted surface; for thanks to recent cleanings we can now see them as they were previous to the 19-century retouchings. But even at that time many of their original elements must have already disappeared. On a few of the draperies the streaks of white used to indicate highlights and the modeling of figures can still be seen, but faces are oddly blank and inexpressive. Enough remains, however, to make it clear that the artist's source of inspiration was Byzantine, and this applies also to the iconography of the paintings in the cupola. Thus the representation of Christ attended by eight angels obviously stems from Byzantine domical decorations such as that in the Cappella Palatina at Palermo. There are also marked analogies both with certain French frescos —those at Saint-Chef in Dauphiné (the "Heavenly Jerusalem" cycle in the gallery chapel) and those of Le Puy (the composition, dominated by a big figure of the archangel Michael, also in the gallery chapel)—and with North Italian frescos such as those at Civate, where we find much the same thematic arrangement: angels and saints in threes. Like those of ca. 1150 at Regensburg and Prüfening, all these decorations show Byzantine influences.

We find them also in the Romanesque painting of northwest Germany, on the Lower Rhine: at Schwarzrheindorf near Bonn (1151-1173); in St Gereon's at Cologne (late 12th century); in the choir of Soest Cathedral (ca. 1160) and in Essen Cathedral; in St Martin's Church at Emmerich (ca. 1150) and at Knechtsteden (1162). For the reasons given above the present condition of these paintings prevents their being considered—so far as their esthetic is concerned—typical of North German Romanesque. But despite the retouchings they have undergone, there is no mistaking the Byzantinism not only of the iconography but also of their style, and this despite the modifications brought to it by the German painters; for example the peculiar modeling of faces and garments at Emmerich and Knechtsteden, and the jagged *(Zackenstil)* draperies in the St Gereon frescos. These paintings have, moreover, a distinctive feature—rarely found in the Romanesque frescos of other countries—which at once continued and carried a stage further a tendency already noted in the two Regensburg ensembles—in the Allerheiligen-kapelle and at Prüfening. I have in mind the practice of composing complex and coherent cycles, whose various elements, displayed on all available surfaces, including vaulted ceilings, were integrated *inter se* and with the leading theme of the ensemble both by an ingenious layout and also by the use of inscribed scrolls ("phylacteries") weaving among the figures and linking them together. There are grounds for believing that the Saint-Denis frescos in Abbot Suger's day had the same characteristics, which remind us of the sophisticated, ultra-intellectual imagery of the decorations found in much 12th-century Mosan goldsmiths' work (also of stained glass and miniatures revealing the same sources of inspiration). In fact the Rhineland frescos may be regarded as enlarged versions of these productions of contemporary monastic workshops.

What is today the frontier between Germany and Austria separates the two chief centers of medieval Germanic painting: Regensburg and Salzburg. In each there flour-ished a distinct though similar type of book illumination, but we cannot be sure if this was also the case with wall paintings since so few of them have survived. Such information as can be gleaned from the rare examples to be seen in Salzburg is limited to a relatively brief period, the mid-12th century, though it is a known fact that the painters' ateliers

ST BENEDICT. CA. 1154. FRESCO IN THE VESTIBULE, KLOSTER NONNBERG, SALZBURG.

in that city had been active since the Carolingian epoch. In the preceding volume of this series we discussed the only wall paintings of the early period that presumably derive from the Salzburg school, those at Naturno, in the Italian Tyrol.

The lack of any frescos that can be positively accredited to this school and are datable to before 1150 is due to the wholesale destruction of the medieval churches of Salzburg and the disappearance of its Romanesque cathedral. So completely was this form of art obliterated that the oldest group of Romanesque frescos in Austria, though less than

ST FLORIAN. CA. 1154. FRESCO IN THE VESTIBULE, KLOSTER NONNBERG, SALZBURG.

fifty miles from Salzburg, bears no trace of Salzburgian influence. I am referring to the decorations on the vaults of the gallery, fitted out as a chapel, west of the nave in the Illustration page 119 abbey church of Lambach; this is the only part of the church in which the frescos have not been totally remade. Building of the church began in about 1060 but the high (western) altar, dedicated to the Virgin, was not completed until 1089. It was at this date presumably that the surviving frescos were painted; around a central image of the Virgin and Child enthroned, in line with the main axis of the building, the artist grouped

PORTRAIT OF A DONOR. CA. 1200. FRESCO IN THE CHOIR.
CHAPEL OF ST JOHN, PÜRGG (STYRIA).

an extensive cycle illustrating the story of the Magi and stopping short with the scene of the three Wise Men of the East worshipping the Divine Child. It is impossible to determine the scope of the original cycle as only those parts of it which figured on the vaults remain intact. Chronologically, it begins with the scenes (in the southern barrel vault) of the Wise Men before Herod and the King's counsellors interpreting to him the portent of the star seen in the East. The rest of the cycle is located in a central cupola where three scenes, following without a break, are grouped around a star: first we see the Wise Men sleeping, then on their journey, guided by the angel, and finally presenting their gifts to the Child held by the Virgin enthroned. In this last scene there is a curious detail, not found elsewhere; a woman is standing beside the Virgin's throne, a follower apparently of the Three Wise Men. (According to Professor Swoboda, this woman's presence is accounted for by a legend relating to the Magi which is recorded in a manuscript preserved at Lambach.) The cycle ends with two scenes in the northern barrel vault: the Wise Men on horseback "departing into their own country" and the Presentation in the Temple.

This Infancy cycle centering on the story of the Magi and completed by the Presentation in the Temple has points of similarity with another cycle figuring in a chapel on the left of the crypt of the Petersberg (Ottonian) church at Fulda. The Fulda frescos —unfortunately in poor condition— may be dated, in my opinion, to the

11th century and seem to be imitations of the paintings in the Andreaskirche discussed in our *Early Medieval Painting* (p. 83). That the Lambach frescos were inspired by those at Fulda is all the more likely since the founder of Lambach was a former bishop of Würzburg, not far from Fulda. In any case the silhouettes and attitudes of the figures, their bent knees and rounded backs are reminiscent of Ottonian figural art, and the same is true of their faces, notably the large, square chins. There are other, equally pronounced archaisms, such as a curious stiffness in the figures' movements and the rudimentary modeling of the white garments with streaks of green and red. This type of modeling is also found in miniatures of the Ottonian period and the works of Greek 11th-century painters; also the deep blue grounds of the Lambach frescos may have a similar origin. Some of the figures recall those in the mosaics at St Luke's in Phocis, but the Byzantinisms at Lambach are mostly of an iconographical order (e.g. the Theotokos enthroned). However, Austrian artists had not as yet adopted the Byzantine technique of modeling faces and draperies. On the other hand these archaic Romanesque artists, while following in the footsteps of their Western predecessors, often show an unusual boldness in their handling of details. Thus we find touches of forthright realism, for example in the scene of a pedestrian and men on horseback passing below an arch, in which the horses are rendered in foreshortening, from different angles. No less striking is this artist's predilection for rich chromatic effects in defiance of natural appearances, as when the horses of the three Magi are not only white and brown but one is painted vivid blue!

The frescos in the ancient nunnery on the Nonnberg, at Salzburg, date from about 1154 and are thus contemporary with the Regensburg decorations. The same is true of the Romanesque miniatures produced by schools located near these two great art centers, but independent of them; in these miniatures we find many Byzantine touches, their immediate source being, presumably, the city of Aquileia at the head of the Adriatic, near Venice. For a while the seat of a patriarchate, Aquileia made its influence felt throughout northeastern Italy and even beyond the Tyrolese Alps, and as one of the outposts of Byzantinism in the Western world did much to propagate it throughout Austria, Bavaria and even Bohemia, in versions conforming to the art obtaining in Venetia during the 12th century.

The Nonnberg frescos constitute what is undoubtedly the keywork of this branch of Romanesque mural painting. A vestibule set apart for the devotions of nuns of high degree flanks the west wall of the church. Three of the walls contain niches probably used for seating purposes, and in these are painted half-length figures of saints, a little over life-size. St Benedict is represented in the central niche of the bottom wall and on either Illustrations pages 122-123 side of him are six sainted bishops and popes, each in his niche, holding an open book, while five deacons and martyrs occupy the niches in the northern wall (those of the south wall no longer exist). A large composition above the niches depicts the Virgin enthroned flanked by two symmetrical figures, probably angels. Though this decoration is far from being complete, enough remains of the big images of saints to prove that they were the work of a highly expert and painstaking artist; numerous marks of the points of a compass can still be seen along the outlines of the geometrical designs underneath the images of saints, and their mathematical correctness has been verified. No less remarkable is the purity of the colors employed, their balanced orchestration and the grace of the delicately molded faces. These heads have all the nobility of Byzantine effigies, and the martyrs wear silken garments patterned with "aces of spades" in the manner of Byzantine textiles. But it is above all the modeling, which with a few deft touches brings out the plastic values of a face, that proves these artists' careful and rewarding study of models in the best Greek or Byzantine tradition. We should be wrong, however, to describe the Nonnberg frescos as Byzantine, despite the frequent presence of Greek elements; these were certainly taken over at second hand by way of Rome or Aquileia, and much of their interest lies in their demonstration of what a talented Romanesque painter could make of Byzantine techniques when exploiting their esthetic content in terms of his personal inspiration. Also of much interest is the date of these paintings—the middle of the 12th century—since it serves as a *point de repère* for the chronology of other esthetic and technical innovations of the same kind in countries around the Alps.

Several churches in Carinthia and the Tyrol contain Romanesque frescos. Nauders is the only one in which these are 12th-century works; the decorations in the others (all in the south of Austria) were made subsequently to the year 1200. The latest of the group is probably datable to 1267, the year when the chapel in the gallery at Gurk was consecrated. Though these later works contain some Gothic forms, the Romanesque tradition held its ground, by and large, in Austria until the middle of the 13th century.

The fact that most of these paintings are to be found in smallish churches explains the absence of lengthy, fully developed iconographic programs. At Gurk, however, where there is a fairly large vault, and also at Matrei (where the frescos are a little earlier), we find large-scale representations of that ever-popular theme, the City of God. In the uppermost of two superimposed chancels at Matrei, four caryatid angels uphold a mandorla within which is an effigy of Christ; at their feet stretches the Celestial City, peopled with Apostles and Evangelist symbols. Also, just underneath the vaulting, is a row of portraits of saints enclosed in frames. The decorations in the lower chancel consist of a series of scenes from Genesis: the creation of Adam and Eve, the Garden of Eden and so forth. The much more elegant frescos at Gurk comprise depictions of the Heavenly Paradise on two adjoining vaults and, on the walls, some Gospel scenes and the famous picture of the Mother of God seated on the throne of Solomon with lions on each step of the dais below the throne—as on the façade of Strasbourg Cathedral. Stylistically these paintings show a great advance on their predecessors; here the vigorous renderings of broken folds and festooned clouds signalize the final phase of Romanesque, transitional to the Gothic.

Of the same high artistic quality as the Gurk paintings are the frescos, in a very fragmentary state, which have been discovered above the Gothic vaults of the church of Bressanone (Brixen). These include some admirable personifications of Virtues and Vices linking up with a large composition depicting the Heavenly Jerusalem, datable to about 1220, which contains some picturesque, strongly expressive figures of prophets.

But most remarkable of all the decorations in the country churches of the Austrian Alps are, in our opinion, the frescos (ca. 1200) at Pürgg, in Styria. Thanks to a recent cleaning which has rid them of accretions due to 19th-century restorers, we now can see them in their original state. In the chancel of the little church we have the "classical" scene of the Lamb with the usual figures of worshippers and saints in niches. The Offerings of Cain and Abel figure on the arch in front of the chancel; also the two donors, a cleric and a layman: two solidly constructed portraits, a trifle ponderous but Illustration page 124 instinct with life. Heads and hands are rendered with a meticulous precision rarely found outside the miniature, while the modeling of faces combines remarkable boldness with a fine sense of nuances. In brief, we have here a painter of quite unusual sensibility. The frescos in the nave have similar qualities; true, the bodies are bulky, with over-large feet, but faces have a singular beauty and are fully plastic; draperies are sculpturesque, broadly treated; movements slow, a shade ungainly; and emphasis is laid on telling details. There are unmistakable links of various kinds between the Pürgg decorations and such earlier frescos as those at Nonnberg and also with contemporary paintings in the baptistery of Portogruaro near Venice. Iconographically they had precedents in Austria, as is evidenced by the 12th-century frescos at Friesach in Carinthia (e.g. the scene of the Miracle of the Loaves and Fishes). The limitation of the Gospel cycle at Pürgg to three scenes having little real connection with each other (the Nativity, the Miracle of the Loaves and Fishes, the Parable of the Wise and Foolish Virgins) is quite exceptional, and more remarkable still is the presence of a theme culled from the non-religious cycle sometimes found in Romanesque and Gothic decorations: the Battle of the Mice and Rats. In the Pürgg frescos we have an excellent illustration of the great variety of art currents that intermingled in the mural painting of the Austrian Alps throughout the Romanesque period. The influence of the art stream running from south to north—from Aquileia and Venice towards Salzburg—was usually, it seems, predominant, though undergoing changes on its northward way. But once art centers arose under the lead of local Austrian painters in such towns as Salzburg, they tended to strike out in new directions, while assimilating both the influences of mixed Italian and Byzantine provenance that were gaining ground towards the close of our period and also some of the idiosyncrasies of German 13th-century painting.

Sweden and Denmark

Following in the wake of the Christian missions, Romanesque wall painting reached Denmark and Sweden in the 12th century by way of Germany. It is chiefly in the province of modern Sweden known as Skåne (Scania) which lies nearest Denmark and then formed part of the Danish kingdom, and in the island of Gotland, that vestiges of Romanesque frescos can still be seen. Smaller, but not without an interest of their own, are those in the province of Östergötland (Kaga, Fornåsa). Unfortunately most of these paintings have undergone restorations, sometimes of a drastic order, and provide but a garbled version of the mural art of Scandinavia during the Romanesque period. True, an old photograph gives a fair idea of what the Christ in Majesty in the apse of the church at Övraby must have looked like, but even here we cannot help suspecting that the fresco had already been tampered with—if relatively discreetly—when the photograph was made. In Skåne we find a series of frescos centering on those at Finja which are in better condition than others in this part of Sweden.

The Gotland frescos have been less affected by retouchings but, so far as the 12th century is concerned, all without exception have a markedly Byzantine aspect. They are not so much Romanesque frescos tinctured with Byzantine influences as productions of an art that, while including some vaguely Romanesque elements, was closely affiliated to the Byzantine tradition. In fact the Byzantinism of these Gotland paintings (especially those at Garda) is more pronounced than that of the frescos made in Rome—even in Venice and Aquileia—in and shortly before the 13th century. The fragments of mural decorations that can still be seen in two Gotland churches (it is known that frescos survive in other churches on the island, buried beneath a coat of limewash) have obvious affinities with contemporary frescos at Novgorod, the great trade center of northwest Russia, which had active commercial relations with Gotland during this period. These frescos are of a high order, both technically and esthetically, and a closer study of them might make it possible to trace the sources of the influx of Byzantine influences into the north of Europe which, though contemporaneous with the similar Byzantinizing trend of Romanesque art in other parts of Europe, through the medium of Italy, was independent of it. This more immediate contact with Byzantine art is also evidenced by the Romanesque sculpture of Scandinavia, notably that of the baptismal fonts.

Traces of Romanesque frescos have been discovered in more than eighty Danish country churches. But once again we have to deplore the damage done by tasteless restorations made in the 19th and early 20th century, with the net result that it is hard to form an opinion of the esthetic of the art known to have flourished in Denmark (chiefly in the island of Zealand, but in Jutland also) during the 12th and 13th centuries.

Only copies are extant of the frescos in the Royal Church at Jellinge, in Jutland, but we find a similar type of art in the paintings (ca. 1125) in two smaller churches, at Tamdrup and Ørreslev. On the intrados of the triumphal arch is a scene of the Offerings of Cain and Abel, under a medallion of Christ; here the execution is exceptionally

HORSEMEN. CA. 1150-1175. FRESCO, CHURCH OF SKIBET (JUTLAND), DENMARK.

vigorous, with an emphasis on line and geometric patterning. Bodies are elongated, with the lower portions of the figures fanning out bell-wise. Modeling of faces is replaced by abstract white lines, and colors are subdued. We are reminded of the frescos at Hardham, in the south of England. All the paintings on the island of Zealand—with the exception of some fragments, thought to be earlier in date, at Sostrup—figure in small churches built in the second half of the 12th century. Those in Fjenneslev and Jørlunde, though restored, give a good idea of the artists' handling of cycles of the Childhood and Passion of Christ. Here again we have representations of the Lamb and the Offerings of Cain and Abel, their function being to direct the thoughts of worshippers to the Redemption, the Eucharist and the Last Judgment.

To the group of paintings made in the province of Jutland in the mid-12th century belongs the fresco reproduced on this page. It figures in Skibet church, where a great many Gospel scenes (of the Childhood and Passion of Christ) can still be made out on the ancient walls, though these are hidden in part by Gothic vaults made at a later date. Most of the figures represented in this extensive Gospel cycle have been modified by restorations. On one section of the wall, however, recently uncovered, we can see several Romanesque frescos (a little faded) in their initial state. The figures in two Gospel scenes are large and greatly elongated; but by far the most interesting of these decora-

Illustration page 129

tions is the frieze running below an arcade in which we see a cavalcade of riders, rendered with consummate elegance. Ranking undoubtedly among the masterpieces of Roman-esque mural painting, this decoration illustrates to happiest effect its final phase, when Romanesque esthetic was in the course of merging into Gothic. The long line of mounted men has no clearly defined subject and falls into the class of the strips of paintings showing riders on the march or engaged in combat—a semi-pagan motif—examples of which are found in other Danish churches, at Højen and Aal, as well as in France (Poncé), in England (Claverley) and in Northern Italy (Novara and Broletto, and also in a mosaic pavement at Bobbio). Sometimes these friezes depict crusaders on the long trek to the Holy Land; sometimes scenes of the war between the Greeks and Maccabees. Such pictures not only had a popular appeal but lent themselves to moralistic interpretations. The Skibet fresco, which belongs to this category, is perhaps intended, like other paintings of the kind, to simulate a strip of embroidery. But among all the extant friezes representing cavalcades, that at Skibet should certainly be given pride of place so far as delicate design and execution are concerned. Particularly attractive is the outline drawing of the men and horses, whose graceful arabesques foreshadow the elegant intricacies of Gothic draftsmanship.

Byzantine influence, which began to make itself felt in Denmark only at the end of the 12th century, took effect not only on the iconography of the Gospel scenes but also on the style and technique of Danish painters. Through what channels this influence found its way to Denmark has yet to be determined, but it seems likely that its proximate sources were the Rhineland and Westphalia. All the same the possibility of its being derivative from the Byzantinizing art of Winchester and Canterbury cannot be ruled out—e.g. in Ferring; this view is supported by the fact that imitations of English forms have been traced in Jutland, in other branches of contemporary art.

Part Two

BOOK ILLUMINATION

TEXT BY CARL NORDENFALK

★

DURATION AND DIFFUSION OF ROMANESQUE BOOK ILLUMINATION
PRINCIPAL TYPES OF MANUSCRIPTS
ROMANESQUE INITIAL LETTERS
PICTORIAL STYLES IN THE ROMANESQUE MINIATURE

THE SAINT-SEVER APOCALYPSE. THE STARS FALLING FROM HEAVEN. SAINT-SEVER (GASCONY), MID-ELEVENTH CENTURY. (14⅜ × 11″) MS LAT. 8878, FOLIO 116, BIBLIOTHÈQUE NATIONALE, PARIS.

ROMANESQUE BOOK ILLUMINATION

IN the previous volume of this series, *Early Medieval Painting*, it was shown that the evolution of the pre-Romanesque illuminated manuscript fell naturally into a series of easily differentiated periods. Late Antique, Insular, Merovingian, Carolingian, Mozarabic, Anglo-Saxon and Ottonian illumination—each had characteristics peculiar to itself, and each covered a well-defined period of time whose beginning and end were marked by conspicuous changes of style. Indeed we might almost adopt the terminology of the pre-historian and speak of different "cultures."

When we turn to Romanesque illumination, the situation is rather different. We are not simply confronted with yet another period, clearly demarcated and easily definable. Romanesque illumination, like Romanesque art in general, is not on the same footing as the independent styles of the Early Middle Ages. We find something new and different taking place, sharply distinguishing this art from all that had preceded it. Historical events were bringing about a change in the cultural situation, whose developments from now on become more widespread and intricate, less easy to grasp in their entirety. Hitherto we were dealing, so to speak, with a series of experimental prologues; now the curtain rises on the play itself. In other words, it is almost as if medievaldom, after casting round for its natural mode of expression during the early centuries, finally came into its own in the Romanesque period.

When, however, we consider the role of book illumination in the history of medieval art as a whole, it must be acknowledged that in moving on from the early medieval schools we leave the Golden Age behind. The miniature bulked large in the art history of the first millennium of our era. It was an age in which the minor arts (among which book illumination is certainly to be reckoned) played a more important part than in any other period, and it is not unreasonable to suppose that this was a result of the esthetic outlook of the Northern peoples, for whom art was practically synonymous with ornament. The focal point of early medieval decorative art became the altar, and in the illumination of books the most lavish and costly ornamentation was reserved for such liturgical volumes as were intended either to figure on the altar itself or to be used nearby during the celebration of the Mass. The Romanesque period, too, produced a wealth of liturgical books and *objets d'art* for ecclesiastical use, but these ceased to predominate as in the earlier age. Interest was now diverted to another problem: the embellishment not only of the altar, but of the entire church, its portals, capitals, walls and façades.

The revival of monumental sculpture is the outstanding phenomenon of Romanesque art and overshadows all its other achievements. Mural painting, too, benefited from the general trend towards monumentality during the 12th century and had a brilliant efflorescence, as André Grabar has shown in the first part of this volume.

Yet if we are asked what class of extant works of art illustrates to best effect the stylistic trends of Romanesque painting, it is not so easy to give a conclusive answer. It is true that if we balance, so to speak, the number of church decorations against that of illuminated manuscripts—or even that of the scriptoria—we find that wall paintings are still in the minority. There are whole regions, moreover, as regards which, when we seek to form an idea of the evolution of Romanesque painting, we have to rely solely on the evidence of the illuminated books. On the other hand, it must be remembered that the painting of large wall surfaces was always a major undertaking and called for a greater command of painterly resources. Whenever it is possible to confront and compare contemporary frescos and miniatures—for example in Rome, Salzburg, Burgundy and Canterbury—there can be no question that the quality of the wall painting is, to say the least, on a par with that of book illumination. And when we come upon miniatures of a particularly monumental quality, it is not unreasonable to ask ourselves whether these are not the work of a mural painter who only incidentally—perhaps in the interval between two major undertakings—gave a "guest performance" in a scriptorium where normally only minor craftsmen handled brush and color.

Apart from specific instances, it is difficult to say categorically what form of art held the lead during the Romanesque period. However, all things considered, we get the impression that from now on book illumination had become a derivative art whose style, in the last analysis, depended on achievements in other fields; this is also the chief reason why in this volume more space has been devoted to frescos than to miniatures. On the other hand, it should never be forgotten that book illumination always remained a specialized branch of art. Owing to the close relationship, the give-and-take, between text and picture, calligraphy and ornamentation, the miniature painter was called on to solve problems which, in other fields of art, arose either not at all or only to a very limited extent. To such problems we shall devote particular attention in the course of our survey of Romanesque book illumination.

Duration and Diffusion of Romanesque Book Illumination

Romanesque illumination is an integral part of Romanesque art in general, and no sooner do we try to fix its chronological limits than we realize how hard it is to tell precisely when it began and when it ended. In the preceding volume of this series we treated the Ottonian, Anglo-Saxon and Mozarabic miniatures of the 10th and 11th centuries as works of the Early Middle Ages; but envisaged from another angle, they might quite as well be described as Early Romanesque, which is the description commonly applied to the miniatures produced during that period in France and Italy. In any case, the latter do not form so distinctive a group, stylistically, as the former, linked up as they are with subsequent developments. Ultimately, everything depends on the exact meaning to be assigned to the term "Romanesque": a complicated question, which can be adequately dealt with only in the course of our study of the works themselves.

Similarly, it is no easy matter determining the exact time when Romanesque illumination gave place to Gothic. We encounter much the same difficulty in connection with the handwriting of the manuscripts, but here definite criteria have been formulated which can be taken into account in deciding whether any given script should be described as "Gothic." As for the paintings in manuscripts, however, it is less easy to lay down any cut-and-dried rules. Most authorities now concur in designating the Psalter of Queen Ingeborg of France, produced at the beginning of the 13th century (and now at Chantilly), as our first specimen of Gothic handwriting. That may well be so. But in Germany and Italy the Romanesque style lasted considerably longer, and in fact gave rise in the 13th century to interesting transitional forms in which Romanesque and Gothic characteristics are so harmoniously blended that it is almost impossible to say whether the resultant style should be described as Romanesque or as Gothic. The delimitation of the main periods of art history from the Romanesque epoch onward has given rise to endless controversies among scholars, and we can deem ourselves fortunate that by general consent the entire 12th century, anyhow, is always classified as "Romanesque." So far as miniature painting is concerned, the Romanesque style reached its culminating point in the middle and third quarter of that century.

The basic difference between the Romanesque and the Early Medieval period is also brought out by a study of the various schools in terms of their geographical diffusion. For the successive pre-Romanesque styles were not only strictly delimited in time, but also in space; each had its own habitat, Late Antique illumination being localized chiefly around the Mediterranean basin, Merovingian and Carolingian illumination mainly in France, Ottonian illumination in Germany, Mozarabic illumination in Northern Spain, and so forth. Indeed Anglo-Saxon illuminated manuscripts of the 10th and 11th centuries came to be named after a single place: Winchester.

By the 12th century such precisely localized styles had ceased to exist. Romanesque book illumination is the first that does not call up thoughts of any particular country; on the contrary, we find its style evenly diffused throughout the length and breadth of Europe. Not only did those countries which hitherto had remained outside the pale of Christian culture, such as Scandinavia and the East European borderlands, now begin to contribute to the common art heritage of the Latin West, but even the age-old cultural centers south and west of the Alps were stimulated to a participation far greater than in the previous centuries. Southern France and Italy, which had played a relatively undistinguished part in the history of early medieval book illumination, now come to the fore with a corpus of works remarkable both for quality and quantity.

The extent of the change is strikingly brought home to us when we direct our attention to Rome. So far as can be judged from extant manuscripts, there was never any real "school" of Roman book illumination in the period between the pontificates of Gregory I and Gregory VII (roughly from 600 to 1050). Thus it was a significant phase in the evolution of the miniature when, during the second half of the 11th century, the Papal States began to make their voice firmly heard in the concert of Europe. The Illustration page 137 so-called *bibbie atlantiche*—the large "Atlas" Bibles, usually in two or more volumes, being produced from now on in Rome and Umbria in ever increasing numbers—may not provide the choicest examples of Romanesque illumination. All the same, in virtue not only of their size but of the simple forcefulness of their historiated initials and rude but monumental figures, they are invested with a ponderous distinction and compelling power which goes far to redress the geographical balance of European book illumination.

The early folio-size Umbro-Roman Bibles and kindred manuscripts acted as the foundation stones of all Romanesque miniature painting in Central Italy. Following Rome, the great commercial centers of Tuscany—Florence, Siena, Pisa, Pistoia and Lucca—made their mark in the history of the Italian miniature with Bibles, Passionals and other manuscripts, mostly of very large dimensions. E. B. Garrison has been engaged for several years in the arduous task of setting order in this vast proliferation of illuminated books, and thanks to his efforts we are beginning to distinguish the lines of development and achievements of the various schools. As regards the situation in the provinces north of the Apennines, we are not so well informed. Bologna and Venice do not seem to have acquired any real significance as centers of book production until the second half of the 13th century, although the scholarly achievements of Bologna university and the commercial prosperity of Venice from the 12th century on might have led us to expect an earlier flowering of art in these great cities. In Northern Italy, where the illuminators of Milan and Ivrea had produced outstanding works as early as the year 1000, the Romanesque period itself comes as something of a disappointment, for in the light of the exhaustive research work of Pietro Toesca it seems rather unlikely that we shall ever come upon any so far undiscovered manuscripts from which we could infer the existence of really important schools of illumination in 12th-century Lombardy. The explanation may well be that during this period this part of Italy was particularly hard hit by the incessant strife between Guelphs and Ghibellines.

That Southern Italy, on the other hand, played an important part in the evolution of the illuminated manuscript has been made clear by the paleographical researches of E. A. Lowe. South Italian texts are easily recognizable, since most of them are written in a peculiar "national hand," the so-called *scriptura beneventana*, dating from the 8th century. Another speciality of the South Italian scriptoria was the production of Illustration page 147 liturgical Exultet Rolls, adorned with pictures and initials, for use at the festival of Easter. Closely studied several decades ago by Emile Bertaux, they have now been made available to students in a complete illustrated edition published by Myrtilla Avery. In the course of their researches many scholars past and present have been drawn to St Benedict's monastery at Monte Cassino, spiritual capital so to speak of Southern Italy, where, under the auspices of the art-loving abbot Desiderius (1058-1087), there was a remarkable flowering of book illumination and many other forms of art. Special importance attaches to the abbacy of Desiderius in view of his close artistic contacts with Constantinople, of which there is explicit mention in contemporary documents.

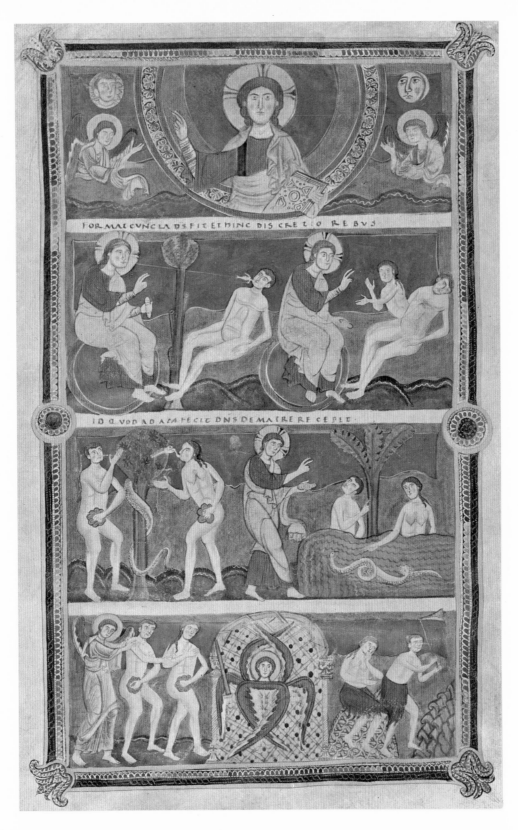

PANTHEON BIBLE. THE CREATION AND FALL OF MAN. ROME, FIRST HALF OF THE TWELFTH CENTURY.
(17 7/8 × 11 3/16″) VAT. LAT. 12 958, FOLIO 3 VERSO, BIBLIOTECA APOSTOLICA, VATICAN.

But it was not only in the region of Benevento, but throughout Italy, that miniature painting was fertilized and stimulated by Byzantine influences. And since Byzantine art was a decisive factor in the development of Romanesque illumination in general, the importance of the position of Italy, as the geographical link between East and West and the channel through which new inspiration from the Greek art world flowed unceasingly into Europe, can hardly be overestimated.

A Byzantinizing trend is clearly present in the illuminated manuscripts which were produced in Sicily, at Palermo and Syracuse, during the rule of the Norman kings, and which Hugo Buchthal was the first to bring to notice. It is also to Buchthal's researches that we owe our knowledge of the strongly Byzantinizing schools of painting that flourished in the Holy Land at the time of the Latin domination of that country. A group of manuscripts centering on the Psalter of Queen Melisende can safely be assigned to Jerusalem itself, where a scriptorium under the management of the Augustinian Canons of the Holy Sepulchre produced costly liturgical manuscripts for the court. In the 13th century, as a result of the changed political situation, the center of gravity shifted to Acre, the military base of the Crusaders at the foot of Mount Carmel. These two schools, which needless to say were deeply permeated with Byzantine influences, are of special interest as representing the farthest outpost ever reached by Latin book illumination in the East.

In France, too, the renewed activity of the southern schools is a distinctive feature of the Romanesque period. True, the old centers of Carolingian miniature painting between the Loire and the Meuse retained a certain pre-eminence as late as the 12th century, and such celebrated ones as Fleury (Saint-Benoît-sur-Loire), Tours, Paris, Metz, Reims, Corbie, Saint-Vaast (at Arras), Saint-Amand and Saint-Bertin (at Saint-Omer) kept something of their ancient luster in the age of Romanesque illumination. From the 11th century on, however, they shared their privileged position with a whole galaxy of Southern French scriptoria: Limoges, Moissac, Albi, Saint-Gilles and others. The creations of these Southern French illuminators are by and large of such high quality that in one instance a single manuscript, the Beatus Apocalypse of Saint-Sever, in Gascony, has sufficed to make this monastery world-famous.

Mention must also be made of Burgundy, the province where the reform movements originated which had so decisive and stimulating an influence on monastic life and thereby on art; an influence that was not confined to Burgundy but extended far afield. Cluny under the great abbots St Odilo (994-1048) and St Hugh (1048-1109), each of whom held office for over half a century, Saint-Bénigne of Dijon under the abbot and reformer William of Volpiano (991-1031), and Cîteaux under its third abbot Stephen Harding (1108-1133)—all three can claim a leading place in the history of book illumination. Until now, however, the only school that has been adequately studied and appraised (in the illustrated publications of Charles Oursel) is that of Cîteaux.

At Verdun, despite the activities of Richard of Saint-Vanne (1004-1046), another eminent leader of the reform movement at the beginning of the Romanesque period, no school of painting of any real consequence emerged. It was rather in the Flemish

Illustrations pages
153, 156, 185, 187, 194

Illustration page 179

Illustration page 132

Illustrations pages 188-189

Illustrations pages
155, 202, 203

and Northern French abbeys at Liége, Stavelot, Lobbes, Saint-Omer, Arras, Corbie and Saint-Amand that Richard's revivalist zeal fanned the failing flame of art. The influence of the East French reform movement spread as far as Normandy, where both William of Volpiano and Richard of Saint-Vanne found a fruitful field of action. To them was due the foundation, in the 11th century, of the new monastic schools of painting at Fécamp, Mont-Saint-Michel, Jumièges, Saint-Evroult and the abbey of Saint-Ouen at Rouen. In the second half of the 11th century, under the rule of Lanfranc and Anselm, the Norman monastery of Bec became one of the foremost seats of learning in Europe and a leading center for the production of manuscripts, of which unfortunately so far there are only two notable examples available (Paris, Bibl. Nat., lat. 2342, and Leyden, Univ. Libr., BPL 20) giving an idea of the achievements of this workshop.

During the Romanesque period the artistic activity of the monasteries was more than ever dependent on the personalities of the abbots in charge of them. The journeys they undertook and the relations they maintained with other great men of the day often go far towards explaining the changes and stylistic innovations we can observe in the manuscripts produced under their auspices. Scholars have still much ground to cover before they can fully elucidate the relations between the development of miniature painting and political conditions local as well as general. But today at least we are beginning to realize what men like Count Oliva (1008-1048), lay abbot of Santa Maria of Ripoll, and his friend Abbot Gauzlin of Fleury (1005-1029), step-brother of King Robert the Pious, meant for the scriptoria that flourished in their respective abbeys. Other important names in the history of Romanesque book illumination are those of Abbots Odbert of Saint-Bertin (986-1007), Adelard of Saint-Germain-des-Prés in Paris (1030-1060), Alvisus of Anchin (1111-1131), Wedricus of Liessies (1124-1147), and Prior Manasse of Reims (from 1096 Archbishop), to mention but a few of many. The outstanding example of an art-loving prelate in the 12th century is the famous Abbot Suger of Saint-Denis (1122-1151). Strange to say, however, scholars have so far been unable to associate a single illuminated manuscript with Suger's name, and even in his own account of the memorable achievements of his administration he makes no mention of any manuscript executed for Saint-Denis. On the other hand, his great contemporary and rival, St Bernard of Clairvaux (1091-1153), who apparently had little taste for fine art and indeed stigmatized it as an unnecessary luxury, is traditionally believed to have possessed a Bible richly decorated with historiated initials (Troyes, Bibl. Munic., MS 458). The abbey he founded at Clairvaux has also bequeathed us some fine manuscripts; as a rule, however, in compliance with the ascetic ideal of the Cistercians, they are devoid of miniatures done in gold and color.

The monasteries named above are but a very few of those in which the work of copying and illuminating manuscripts was carried on with unremitting zeal. So intense was the spiritual life of France in the 12th century that it soon became the cynosure of the whole of Europe. As active seats of learning, the cathedral schools of Chartres, Laon and Paris overshadowed the educational centers of neighboring lands, and even before the middle of the 12th century the University of Paris began to exercise a magnetic attraction on all who wished to share in the higher education of the age. Under the auspices of the great university new scriptoria arose which diffused the writings of famous Schoolmen—Hugh of St Victor, Peter Lombard, Abelard and others—in manuscript copies, many of them, though unillustrated, of great artistic merit. The study of their bindings has led to the assumption that a whole group of biblical manuscripts with scholastic commentaries, whose leather covers are blind-stamped with figures and decorative patterns, may be products of the French capital, and since several also contain painted ornamental letters, we have here perhaps a means of enlarging our knowledge of the style of the Parisian ateliers round about 1150 and thereafter.

But even before Paris became its major art center, France had taken the lead in the field of book illumination. While at the beginning of the Romanesque period French illuminators were still drawing inspiration from the art of neighboring lands, by the end of the 11th century the balance had shifted and they now began to exercise an influence ranging beyond the frontiers of France.

It is in Spain and England that we see this process most clearly at work. The isolated position of their country beyond the Pyrenees had enabled the Mozarabic illuminators to develop a primitive but highly original style, and very probably Southern French miniature painting in the early 11th century owed something to Spain, anyhow as regards its color. The interest shown by French artists in the Beatus Apocalypse goes to prove that some sort of contacts had been established with the South. As we have already mentioned, a famous copy of this manuscript was made about the middle of the Illustration page 132 11th century at the monastery of Saint-Sever in Gascony (Paris, Bibl. Nat., MS lat. 8878). On comparing the miniatures in this manuscript with the Mozarabic originals, however, we cannot fail to notice that, stylistically, the French Apocalypse already outdoes the copies produced in Spain. And once the Reconquista had thrown Spain open to the rest of Europe, the initiative lay definitely with the French and the stream of influence began flowing from France southward. The Visigothic script was replaced by the French minuscule, and along with this came a new style of ornament and new imagery. From a purely artistic point of view, however, we may well question if there was any real gain. Losing its former independence, the Spanish miniature henceforth followed more or less in the wake of the schools of Southern France, which in their turn became more and more dependent on the art of the North. From now on, Spanish book illumination wears a curiously provincial air and, broadly speaking, counts for little in the general evolution of this branch of art. True, the Spanish temperament still finds expression in certain idiosyncrasies of design, but the Romanesque illuminators of Spain no longer rank as truly creative artists as compared with the Mozarabic illuminators of an earlier day, and hence we see no need to linger on the productions of the Spanish schools during this period.

In the North, also, French miniature painting extended its sphere of action, as a result of the Norman conquest of England in 1066. Here, however, the position differed from that in the South—and this for two reasons. For one thing, the natural tendencies of the Anglo-Saxon miniature were never completely submerged by the art of the invaders and, secondly, Norman art itself was from the very start strongly impregnated with Anglo-Saxon stylistic elements. Recent English research work has given support to the view that what happened after the Conquest was that a higher standard of indigenous art yielded to a lower, imported one. But on the other hand, it cannot be denied that Norman miniature painting was more deeply imbued with the Romanesque spirit than was Anglo-Saxon painting and for this reason richer in promise for the future. Be this as it may, the fact remains that the art of the Norman illuminators steadily gained ground in English monasteries and for a while it looked as if England were destined to become a Norman province artistically as well as politically. But the event was otherwise; once again English miniature painting proved capable of asserting its superiority and independence, while in the course of the 12th century the Norman scriptoria came more and more under English influence or else sank to a merely provincial level. Here we have, in many ways, a repetition of the relations that had existed in pre-Carolingian times between the art centers of Ireland and those of Northumbria. The bonds between the English scriptoria and those in the Northern French provinces of Artois and the Ile-de-France were steadily consolidated, and though there was a constant give-and-take of influences across the Channel, it is an indubitable fact that in the great majority of cases the English schools gave more than they received.

We are indebted to the eminent paleographer N. P. Ker for a comprehensive account of the leading scriptoria, and his survey of the extant medieval manuscripts produced in England, classified according to the libraries from which they emanate, has been of invaluable service to the art historian and cleared the ground for further research work in this field.

In the Romanesque period, as in Anglo-Saxon times, the most active scriptoria were situated in the South of England. Both Canterbury and Winchester, leading Illustrations pages 166, 168, 175, 176 centers of Anglo-Saxon illumination in the 10th and 11th centuries, maintained their lead after the Conquest and throughout the period covered by the present work. But two new schools, those of St Albans and Bury St Edmunds, now came to the fore, Illustration page 171 and there were other active centers at Rochester, Malmesbury, Hereford, Sherborne, Winchcombe and London. Curiously enough, the newly founded Cluniac and Cistercian monasteries, such as St Andrew's of Northampton, Lewes Priory and Fountains Abbey, seem to have played no really outstanding part in the development of Romanesque illumination in England.

On the whole, the center of gravity was still located mainly in the South. Wales, Scotland and Ireland hardly counted, and even Northumbria produced relatively few works of any marked originality. And now it has been proved conclusively that most of the manuscripts with illuminations presented by Bishop William of St Carilef (1081-1096) to St Cuthbert's cathedral were actually imported ready-made from Normandy after the bishop's exile in 1088-1091, Durham has lost much of its significance as a creative center of English Romanesque illumination. Nevertheless, there certainly existed an active school of illuminators at Durham, as also at York, whose cathedral library unfortunately was destroyed as a result of successive fires.

The interrelations between the French and German schools of illumination were very different at the end of the Romanesque period from what they were at the beginning. In the early part of the 11th century we find a flow of influences from East to West, though there is no denying the fact that German models were generally less appreciated in France than Anglo-Saxon ones. Seemingly with a view to avoiding any semblance of subservience to the German emperor, both Gauzlin at Fleury and William of Volpiano at Dijon made a point of importing craftsmen not from the Ottonian schools located on the Rhine but from Lombardy—thus availing themselves of the Ottonian style through indirect channels. German influence makes itself felt as far afield as Normandy in the treatment of the ornaments of initial letters (e.g. MS 97, Bibl. Munic., Avranches). But

Illustration page 188

the greatest conquest of Ottonian art in France was Cluny, where the golden rinceaux characteristic of the German style were acclimatized in the second half of the 11th century. Soon, however, the tide set in the other direction; the miniature painting of Swabia, which effectively inaugurated the Romanesque style in Germany after the outbreak of the struggle over investiture, mainly derived from Cluny. The most active Swabian art centers were the reformed monastery of Hirsau and the many new Cluniac-minded monasteries established under its auspices in the diocese of Constance: Zwiefalten, Weissenau, St. Blasien, Einsiedeln and Engelberg, to name but the most outstanding ones. Not far from the Lake of Constance was the family monastery of the Guelphs,

Illustration page 197

Weingarten, which under Abbot Cuno (1109-1132) and above all under Abbot Berthold (1200-1232) produced a group of very fine manuscripts; those of both periods, as Hanns Swarzenski has proved, owe much of their splendor to the influence of the sumptuous Anglo-Saxon and Flemish gospel books donated to the abbey by Countess Judith of Flanders (1032-1094). Connected, it would seem, with the Swabian-Swiss art group is the miniature painting that flourished in Alsace, in the monasteries at Murbach and, under the rule of the Abbess Herrad of Landsberg (1167-1195), on the Odilienberg —although it is difficult to unravel all the strands of influence intermingled in this art.

Germany in the 12th and 13th centuries never forgot the great days of the Ottonian empire, and this is why miniature painting on the Rhine and eastward displays a retrospective trend not to be found, anyhow to the same extent, in other countries. As late as the mid-13th century a manuscript was written in Mainz with gold ink, in imitation of the Gospel Books of the Ottonian emperors (Aschaffenburg, Schlossbibl., MS 13), and both in Bavaria and at Salzburg we find miniature painting advancing almost without a break from the late Ottonian style to Romanesque forms. The most inter-

Illustration page 167

esting developments took place at Salzburg, which now became the leading center of South German illumination and whose rise to this position forms the subject of an authoritative monograph by Georg Swarzenski. Around Salzburg were grouped a number of newly founded or newly reformed monasteries, such as Admont, St. Florian and Mondsee, all with excellent scriptoria whose productions have to a large extent survived, and there were also active workshops at Klosterneuburg, Zwettl and Heiligenkreuz. Indeed, at no other time did miniature painting flourish so luxuriantly in the part of Europe now known as Austria as in the Romanesque period. Bavaria, with the monasteries of Prüfening (near Regensburg) and Scheyern, and Franconia with Bamberg and Würzburg, tried to keep pace with Austria in the production of illuminated manuscripts. Some cities, such as Cologne, Mainz, Trier and Regensburg, which had been the headquarters of important schools of painting in Ottonian times, went on producing illuminated manuscripts (though of a somewhat inferior quality) in the 12th century. As for the old "state abbeys" of St Gall, Reichenau and Echternach, where so many of the most sumptuous Carolingian and Ottonian manuscripts had seen the day, they had fallen on a decline and become relatively sterile in the Romanesque period. The truly creative work was done chiefly in those monasteries which had been activated by the spirit of the Cluniac reform: München-Gladbach, Prüm and Maria Laach, amongst others. Also, one of the Premonstratensian abbeys, that at Arnstein in the Rhineland, produced some richly illuminated manuscripts (now in the British Museum) pointing to the existence there of an active and flourishing atelier.

Saxony and Westphalia, whose chief centers were located at Korvei, Hildesheim, Halberstadt, Helmarshausen and Goslar, comprised a region with a distinctive style of its own. Its evident connections with the West are ascribed by Albert Boeckler mainly to the mediation of Wibald, the powerful abbot of Stavelot (1130-1158) and, from 1146 on, also abbot of Korvei. Georg Swarzenski and Franz Jansen have particularly stressed the importance of Helmarshausen, as being a monastery under the direct patronage of Henry the Lion, "uncrowned king of North Germany" (1129-1195). It was from Helmarshausen that the Westphalian style made its way into Scandinavia, as evidenced by the school of Lund.

The 13th century witnessed the rise of the so-called Thuringian-Saxon school, first studied systematically by Arthur Haseloff. This school began under the patronage of Landgrave Hermann of Thuringia (d. 1217) and his family. The mannerist "jagged-fold" Illustration page 169 style which it introduced into German miniature painting was imitated not only in North Germany but also along the Rhine, the Main and the Danube, as has been demonstrated by Hanns Swarzenski in his corpus of 13th-century miniatures from this region. Where exactly the Thuringian-Saxon ateliers were located remains an open question. The "ducal" monastery of Reinhardsbrunn has been suggested, and Hildesheim is another possibility, while affiliated ateliers may have been active at Goslar and Erfurt about the middle of the century.

By and large, Romanesque miniature painting in Germany testifies to the slowly but steadily increasing influence of the West—of France, Lorraine and England. Indeed, Western influence penetrated even as far as Bohemia; thus the lavishly illuminated manuscripts grouped around the Vyšehrad Gospel Book in Prague—as early as about 1080-1090—have many points of stylistic contact with the Cluniac art of about the same period. A new and stronger link with the West was created when Bishop Heinrich Ždik invited Premonstratensian monks from the Eifel district of the Rhineland to settle in the monastery of Strahow near Prague. From now on, as Albert Boeckler has demonstrated, Bohemian book illumination became affiliated to that of the Rhineland and, Illustration page 204 in particular, to that of Cologne.

As regards Flanders, its position midway between France, England and Germany is reflected in its adoption of elements derived from all three countries. Despite the fact that some had been founded in the early missionary days, the monastery schools of the Meuse and Scheldt regions play a relatively small part in the history of Carolingian book illumination; not until the 11th century can we speak of a distinctively Flemish style. The flowering of Flemish illumination falls into two phases: an Early Romanesque-Ottonian period to begin with; then, about the middle of the 12th century, a period that may be described as High Romanesque. Both, it seems, were connected with monastic reforms, the earlier with the movement set on foot by Richard of Verdun, the later with the Cluniac reform and its impact on monastic life in Flanders. In both cases Liége appears to have been the most active center of book production, but the monasteries of Stavelot, Saint-Trond, Lobbes, Floreffe, Ghent and Saint-Omer also maintained scriptoria. The most notable achievements of Flemish miniature painting, those of the so-called Mosan School, datable to about the middle of the 12th century, were obviously related to contemporary goldsmiths' work, which was at its prime in Flanders precisely at this time. To André Boutemy, one of the experts in this field, we owe a comprehensive survey of the Flemish and Northern French schools of miniature painting, besides several valuable articles dealing with various aspects of the subject.

Illustrations pages
149, 159, 180

Illustration page 165

Thus, to whatever part of Europe we direct our gaze, we find a steady output of illuminated books in progress during the Romanesque period. Stylistic idiosyncrasies —some clearly marked, others perceptible only to the expert eye of the trained specialist—enable us to group the manuscripts according to countries; in certain favored cases according to localities and schools. Explicable to some extent by the different art traditions from which they stem, these local characteristics were gradually submerged by the rising tide of a style that was now becoming international. This development was more than the mere matter of a miniature painter's familiarizing himself with the art of others and assimilating it. Everything, indeed, points to the fact that in the 12th century illuminated manuscripts circulated much less than in the past; it was, rather, the artists themselves who traveled more widely and more frequently. And since the itinerant artists were often mural painters as well as illuminators, it may well be that it was the greater stylistic homogeneity of wall painting which, in the Romanesque period, ended up by imposing a similar uniformity on the "minor" art.

Principal Types of Manuscripts

The foregoing survey of the leading centers of production has made it clear that Romanesque book illumination rested on a broader geographical basis than Early Medieval illumination. Instead of a restricted number of ateliers working largely for export, such as we met with in the Carolingian and Ottonian periods, we now find a multitude of scriptoria, each of them catering primarily to its own requirements. The result was a striking increase in the total number of manuscripts produced. Today almost every public library with manuscript collections possesses more books from the

Romanesque period than from all the preceding centuries together. Though no exact statistics are available on which to base our estimate, we venture to say that, were all medieval manuscripts containing miniatures stacked in ascending chronological order— that is to say with the earliest at the bottom—we should find that the structure formed an inverted pyramid, whose point consisted of the few surviving Late Antique manuscripts, while from the 12th century on its dimensions began rapidly to expand.

When we seek to know the reason for the steep rise in the production of illuminated books that set in with the beginning of the Romanesque period, the obvious explanation is probably the correct one: that the general demand for such works had become greater than ever in the past. True, we can form only a vague idea of the uses to which a monastery library was put in the early Middle Ages, but it would seem that, generally speaking, the reading of books was a practice confined to the more scholarly minded and cultured monks. But from the 11th century on, at Cluny and in monasteries subject to the Cluniac reform, it became the rule for each monk to borrow one book a year from the monastery library, and he had to confess his sin if, at the end of the year, he had failed to study the book thoroughly from cover to cover. Moreover, we may be fairly sure that there were also a good many monks of a studious turn of mind who read far more than one book a year.

That in religious circles there was now an increased demand for literature of every conceivable kind may be accounted for by the general improvement in the educational standards of the age. For the Church had come to realize that the source of its power and influence lay in its superior intellectual attainments, and when under the leadership of Hildebrand (subsequently Pope Gregory VII) the Papacy made bold to break its alliance with the secular power in the second half of the 11th century, it did so with the fully justified assurance that the spiritual forces at its command outweighed those of any earthly monarch, even the Holy Roman Emperor. The same ideology can be seen to underlie Romanesque miniature painting, and, had the beginning of the new age to be traced back to a single event, none would answer the purpose better than the Declaration of Independence of the Church at the outbreak of the struggle over investiture. In some Carolingian and Ottonian illuminated manuscripts a monarch (representing the State) and a Father of the Church (representing the Church) are shown side by side, equally majestic and imposing. In Romanesque manuscripts, on the other hand, portraits of monarchs are both extremely rare and unimpressive, whereas those of the Fathers of the Church—in the guise of ideal likenesses of contemporary prelates—furnish one of the Illustrations pages 199, 204 artists' favorite themes and are presented with the utmost splendor.

Thus now far more than ever before the Church had taken book illumination into its own hands—a change that was symbolized by the fact that henceforth such manuscripts as the registers of monasteries and churches in which titles to property and legal records figure among the texts were embellished with decorations. Examples are *El libro de los Testamentos* at Oviedo, written and illuminated for Bishop Pelayo between 1126 and 1129; the cartularies of Mont-Saint-Michel (Avranches, Bibl. Munic., MS 210) and Saint-Pierre of Nevers (Paris, Bibl. Nat., lat. 9865); the Sherborne Lectionary containing an inventory of the cathedral treasure (London, Brit. Mus., Add. 46487); the Confraternity Book from Korvei (Münster, Staatsarchiv, Cod. I. 133); the so-called Golden Book from Prüm (Trier, Stadtbibl., Cod. 1709), all dating to the 12th century.

The increased interest in knowledge and education distinctive of the Romanesque period led to a marked change in the nature and function of books. The men of the early Middle Ages had regarded all sacred books, and more particularly texts of Holy Scripture, as vessels of divine wisdom and these were treated far too reverently to be commonly used and read; it was enough for the pious simply to gaze on them from a respectful distance. The beautifully written, gorgeously illuminated Gospel Books were used only on the most solemn feast days when readings from them were given at divine service, during which they were displayed, with befitting pomp and circumstance, like sacred reliquaries, on the altar. During the Romanesque period, however, the distance between men and Holy Scripture was reduced and from now on considerably less attention was devoted to the production of service books. Romanesque illuminators employed most of their time and energy on the making of Bibles, Passionals and copies of the homilies of the Fathers of the Church and these, unlike the Mass and Gospel Books, were not for use in the church service proper. They figure in the library catalogues of the monasteries as ordinary books and were intended for private study or for reading aloud at meal times. In the latter case they were at the same time meant to serve as showpieces, for when they lay open on the reading desk in the refectory, the monks were free to enjoy the pictures and ornamentation. And not only the monks themselves, but also visiting ecclesiastics and laymen—more and more numerous in this age of the great pilgrimages—could see and admire the manuscripts on view in the monastic refectories. Such books were the pride of their owners and not infrequently excited the envy and covetousness of outsiders. When King Henry II of England heard that the monks of St Swithun's at Winchester had a particularly handsome Bible in their refectory, he compelled them to cede the book to Witham Abbey, which he had founded. It was not until several years later, when a monk from Winchester visited the Abbey and recognized the manuscript, that it was returned to its rightful owners.

Whereas the miniatures of the early Middle Ages were made for the satisfaction of a privileged few, dignitaries of the Church and Court, Romanesque miniature painting—more democratic in spirit—was meant to appeal to a larger public and to act as a source of pleasure and edification for the whole Christian community. This was one of the reasons for the great size of the vellum pages and their lavish ornamentation. Jerome in his day inveighed against the large de luxe manuscripts which he described as "burdens rather than books," but his fellow countrymen of the 12th century did not share his views. The Italians even imposed on miniature painting their innate taste for spectacular effect and the grandiose forms of the ornamental letters in their *bibbie atlantiche* often have an epigraphic spareness, while figures too are given a monumental quality. After these large folio Bibles came the no less enormous Antiphonaries of the 13th century, whose size was determined by the fact that text and musical notation had to be read at a certain distance by singers assembled round the lectern. Some Italian miniatures,

EXULTET ROLL. READING OF THE ROLL AND THE EARTH IN SUMMER DRESS. BARI, ELEVENTH CENTURY.
(24⅜ × 15⅜″) CATHEDRAL ARCHIVES, BARI.

Illustration page 147
notably those of Exultet Rolls made by South Italian illuminators, were even intended to be displayed to the entire congregation. When on Holy Saturday, after blessing and lighting the Paschal candle, the deacon intoned the old hymn *"Exultet iam angelica turba,"* he held up the roll in front of him with both hands, level with his chest, and, as he read, let it slowly unfurl itself over the edge of the lectern in full view of the assembled parishioners, so that all the pictures figuring in the text passed one by one before their eyes. For this reason, the pictures in many such rolls were painted upside down as regards the text, so as to enable the congregation to see them in the right position. Up to a point, we have in these Exultet Rolls a curiously exact anticipation of the technique of our present-day cinema.

Illustrations pages 185, 187, 194

Illustration page 149

To the category of showpieces also belong the de luxe editions of certain lives of saints, which became very popular in the 11th and 12th centuries, particularly in France and England. These are the so-called *libelli*, manuscripts with relatively few pages, which relate the life, martyrdom and miracles of a saint not only in words but also in a cycle of pictures mostly of full-page size. In celebration of the local patron saint Amandus three manuscripts were written and illuminated at different times in Saint-Amand (Valenciennes, Bibl. Munic., MSS 500, 501, 502) and the earliest (MS 502) and the latest (MS 500) of these contain biographical picture cycles. Equally famous are the illustrated Lives of St Radegonde (Poitiers, Bibl. Munic., MS 250), of St Aubin (Paris, Bibl. Nat., nouv. acq. lat. 1390), of St Omer (Saint-Omer, Bibl. Munic., MS 698), of St Quentin (Saint-Quentin, Basilique), of St Edmund (New York, Morgan Library, M. 736) and of St Benedict and St Maur (Vat. lat. 1202). Two Lives of St Cuthbert of Durham are extant, one of the early, the other of the late 12th century (Oxford, University College Library, MS 165, and London, Brit. Mus., Add. 39 943). Situated on the borderline between Romanesque and Gothic is the illuminated roll with scenes from the life of St Guthlac of Croyland (London, Brit. Mus., Harl. Roll Y. 6), which was probably intended to be displayed (horizontally) to worshippers on feast days.

Illustration page 149

In all these manuscripts we can sense the artists' naive joy in story-telling, and the pictures have an irresistible appeal for even the most sophisticated modern eye. We reproduce a typical example: the tale of the disobedient servant of St Audomarus (or St Omer, as he is known in France). The story is that, on a Sunday, against his master's orders, the man had boarded a small boat at Boulogne and gone for a sail, whereupon a storm drove him straight across the Channel to the heathen English coast. Terrified, he invoked his saintly master's succor. The wind promptly turned and, using his cloak as a sail, the servant came safely back to port, where he threw himself at the saint's feet and begged forgiveness for his disobedience.

Many cycles of saints' lives were obviously planned with an eye to their propaganda value, as when we are shown the evils that befall those who dare to lay impious hands on the lawful property of a monastery. Similarly we often find wicked princes meeting with the punishment they merit. In the Life of St Edmund the old Danes come off very badly indeed—a theme that no doubt was much appreciated in Norman England, after its "liberation" by the Conqueror from the Viking occupants.

LIFE AND MIRACLES OF ST AUDOMARUS. ST AUDOMARUS AND HIS DISOBEDIENT SERVANT. SAINT-OMER, SECOND
HALF OF ELEVENTH CENTURY. (7×4 ¹¹/₁₆″) MS 698, FOLIO 10 VERSO, BIBLIOTHÈQUE MUNICIPALE, SAINT-OMER.

ST GREGORY'S MORALIA IN JOB. INITIAL I AND JOB AND HIS WIFE. ROME, LATE ELEVENTH CENTURY. (20³/₁₆×13″) BIBL. 41 (B. II. 16), FOLIO 231, STAATSBIBLIOTHEK, BAMBERG.

Francis Wormald has made an authoritative study of these *libelli*, in which he draws attention to their true purport and significance and shows their intimate connection with the cult of the patron saints of great Benedictine monasteries as practised by the ever increasing hosts of pilgrims. Like the large Passionals, they were almost certainly used for readings in the refectories; indeed we know from the records that in the 15th century a copy of the *Vita et Miracula sancti Eadmundi* was still preserved *in pulpito refectorii*, i.e. in the lectern of the refectory at Bury St Edmunds.

Readings were also made from Bibles, lives of the saints and patristic writings, but it is not always easy to say whether such books were primarily intended for the instruction of the assembled monks or as objects of study and meditation by individual readers. Almost every monastic library owned a complete set of the Bible commentaries by the Church Fathers and a wide selection of the more recent theological treatises. Not only in the newly founded monasteries but also in ancient ones whose origins went back to pre-Carolingian times and which had long possessed the standard works of the Fathers, the 12th century was a period of great activity in the production of patristic texts—one reason being, no doubt, that the pre-Carolingian handwriting had become difficult for the average monk to read.

The keen interest taken in the exegetical writings of the early and later Churchmen was largely based on the theory promulgated by scholastic theologians—that of the "double meanings" present everywhere in Holy Scripture. On this view, the Bible text, when perused by the common reader, transmits the Christian message of salvation only in the *letter*, that is to say on its most obvious plane, but it also has a deeper, underlying significance that can be apprehended only by those who, by the operation of divine grace, can penetrate behind the veil of words. This special grace had been bestowed on the Church Fathers, and they recorded their inspired discoveries in commentaries on each book of Holy Writ. Following their example, later theologians also applied themselves to interpreting the Scriptures *figuraliter* rather than *litteraliter*.

Since this growing body of exegetical literature threatened to assume the proportions of an avalanche, attempts were made to make abridgements of the most helpful commentaries in the form of excerpts or glosses. In cathedral schools and universities a practice developed of inscribing these in the margins of the Bible text, in smaller characters. For technical reasons, the marginal notes were written out in full only in the case of certain books, such as the Psalms and the Epistles of St Paul, in which exegeses of this order seemed particularly necessary. Hence the appearance of a new type of manuscript equipped with "critical apparatus" and it, too, has its importance in the history of miniature painting, since manuscripts of this kind were produced by some of the leading university workshops in France towards the end of the 12th century, and influenced the Early Gothic style. Among the manuscripts given to Canterbury by Thomas Becket's secretary Henry of Bosham were some noteworthy specimens of this new type of book.

Although there was little or nothing in their subject matter to inspire an artist, the theological treatises of the Romanesque period were frequently adorned with remarkably handsome initial letters. In this respect French illuminators were following a tradition that went back to Merovingian times, when monasteries made a point of possessing richly illuminated editions of the patristic Bible commentaries. In some English 12th-century manuscripts we find initials containing fish motifs—which goes to show that English illuminators, too, sometimes worked from Merovingian models. Now and again a full-size miniature is inserted so as to lend more interest to the manuscript. Sometimes the patron saint of the monastery is pictured receiving the book from the abbot or the scribe, and sometimes a portrait of the author of the text figures on the title page. Particularly popular in this respect were St Jerome, St Augustine and St Gregory the Great. In full ecclesiastical attire, and with a typically Romanesque *eloquentia corporis*, Illustration page 199 they greet us on the opening pages of their writings, effortlessly filling the entire picture surface with their portly presences.

Illustration page 150 Miniatures bearing directly on the text itself are comparatively rare; hence the exceptional interest of three illuminated manuscripts of St Gregory's *Moralia in Job*, each containing a cycle of scenes of Job's life. All three differ from each other. In the oldest, a Roman work of the late 11th century (Bamberg, Staatsbibl., Bibl. 41), almost immobile figures are spaced out in the margins; the second (Paris, Bibl. Nat., lat. 15 675), made about 1150 in the Cambrai region, contains a narrative sequence of pictures placed at the beginning of the book; whereas in the third, a Late Romanesque German manuscript of ca. 1250 (Herzogenburg, Stiftsbibl., MS 95), all the scenes figure in the historiated initials. It was also in the Romanesque period that the practice began of illustrating Augustine's *De Civitate Dei*; in the earliest copies we again find an iconography having no very obvious bearing on the text and differing from book to book. Mention may be made of an English manuscript of about 1100 (Florence, Bibl. Laur., Pluto XII. 17), a Spanish of about 1150 (Tortosa, Cathedral Library), a North German of the second half of the 12th century (Pforta, Bibliothek der Landesschule, A. 10) and a Bohemian manuscript of about the same period (Prague, Metropolitan Libr., A. 7). In England the *Meditationes* of St Anselm were also given illustrations and here, too, there are many discrepancies in the iconography followed by the artists who worked on the various manuscripts: Verdun, Bibl. Munic., MS 70; Oxford, Bodl. Libr., Auct. D.2.6; Admont, Stiftsbibl., MS 289. (Otto Pächt, however, after a careful study of them, has succeeded in detecting certain iconographical concordances.)

In the initials of Bible commentaries we occasionally find figures and narrative scenes directly relating to the text; the verbal imagery of the Psalms in particular was apt to fire the artists' imagination. For example, in a large Augustine manuscript of the late 11th century (Valenciennes, Bibl. Munic., MS 39), in the initial letter on the first page of the commentary on Psalm XXXVIII *("Dixi custodiam vias meas ut non delinquam in lingua mea")*, we see an old man with his forefinger raised and pointing to his mouth. This scene is the earliest instance of a motif which afterwards was commonly used in Gothic Psalters. The same method was followed some ten or twenty years later by the artist who decorated the initials of the Albani Psalter at Hildesheim with a complete cycle of illustrations, at once inspired by the literal meaning of the words and persistently reflecting the spiritual anguish of a pious Christian fearing for his soul's salvation.

But in the St Augustine manuscript at Valenciennes we find another type of initials with figures having no obvious relation to the text and motifs pagan in conception which seem, rather, to clash with its religious content; this is in fact the type of initial most frequently employed in theological manuscripts of the Romanesque period. As an example, we reproduce an initial "D" in which the outlines of the letter are composed Illustration page 153 of the interlocked bodies of a large dragon and a basilisk, while in the interior field is a second dragonlike monster about to close its jaws on the head of a young man who, seemingly quite unaware of impending danger, bestrides yet another fabulous creature, steadying himself by gripping the bodies of the two dragons on either side.

Here we are plunged into the world of Romanesque fantasy, of *Caprichos* peopled with comical or terrifying creations of the artist's Goyesque imagination: the goblins, dragons, monsters, acrobats, hunters and fighting men inhabiting the initials and their ramifications. These artists' capacity for inventing new motifs and combinations of Illustrations pages 156, 177 them is literally inexhaustible; never do they repeat themselves. As in pre-Carolingian ornamentation, animals are sometimes interlaced in lacertines, sometimes one grows out of another's body. There is a wealth of hybrid forms, intermingling plant and animal elements. It is as if the barriers between the animal and vegetable kingdoms had been cast down, and plants could turn into animals, animals into plants, at random.

The Romanesque dragon itself is a composite creature of this type, partly dog, partly bird, partly lizard, with a tail that sometimes ends in a tuft of leaves or a spiral frond.

Whether the figures form part of the letters themselves or move freely within them, they always seem to belong to a world of elemental ferocity. They grapple, locked in savage conflict, or rush wildly at one another with snapping beaks or bared teeth. Whenever a chance presents itself of biting and clawing each other, wrestling and fighting at close quarters, interlocked, they never fail to take it. Dragons lie in wait for their human prey, who promptly round on them with swords or spears. But the battle is never really won and —strangest of all—the victims show no

ST AUGUSTINE'S COMMENTARIES ON THE PSALMS. INITIAL D. SAINT-AMAND, LATE ELEVENTH CENTURY. (5½×3½″) MS 39, FOLIO 77, BIBLIOTHÈQUE MUNICIPALE, VALENCIENNES.

Illustration page 177

signs of suffering. They seem quite indifferent when a beast of prey sinks its teeth into their flesh, nor do the dragons show the least dismay when their neck is run through with a sword and blood flows in scarlet torrents from the wound. In fact we are often reminded of the sham fights of the circus, the antics and tricks of animal-tamers, sword-swallowers and acrobats. (In this connection it is of interest to note that some Romanesque initials actually contain figures of acrobats.) Other motifs derive from the coarse ribaldry of animal fables and popular proverbs, as when in several English historiated initials we see an aged cripple handicapped by a wooden leg, vainly trying to shear a leaping hare. Another singular feature of Romanesque art in general is that the figures are sometimes naked; hitherto nude bodies had figured only in representations of the dead and in illustrations of special themes, such as that of Adam and Eve. Indeed the presence of a streak of eroticism in many of these compositions is undeniable.

Thus the historiated initial, as used in copies of the edifying writings of the theologians, gave access to a whole world of imagery whose effect is anything but edifying —an ambivalent, half-scrurrilous, half-masochistic world of apparently quite amoral creatures whose presence in these Christian books may seem an anticipation of the "Temptation of St Anthony" as depicted three centuries later by that belated Romanesque artist Hieronymus Bosch. Moreover, such themes were employed not only in manuscripts but also in church architecture. That in the 12th century one man at least felt bound to take exception to their presence is proved by a famous passage in the writings of St Bernard, founder of Clairvaux, who in his condemnation of the sculptures decorating the cloisters of Cluniac monasteries gave a whole catalogue of the Romanesque "monstrosities, with their deformed beauty and beautiful deformity. To what purpose are those unclean apes, those fierce lions, those monstrous centaurs, those half-men, those striped tigers, those fighting knights, those hunters winding their horns?" (*Apologia ad Wilhelmum*, Migne, Patr. Lat. CLXXXII, col. 914).

From this it is only a step to concluding that the Romanesque "capricho" was devoid of any didactic or symbolic significance. Meyer Schapiro, who has approached this problem in a magistral study of the esthetic conceptions of the Romanesque period, is right to a certain extent in defining them as "an example of a pagan life-attitude which will ultimately compete with the Christian, an attitude of spontaneous enjoyment and curiosity about the world, expressed through images that stir the senses and the profane imagination."

Yet it is hard to believe that the Church—which evidently took a different view from that of St Bernard—would have opened its books and places of worship to these queer imaginings, had they not somehow formed an integral part of its own vision of the universe. Even if these bizarre figures, their combats and their antics defy explanation, taken separately, the fact remains that as a whole they speak a language which is perfectly clear. They spring from an underworld into which the light of divine grace has never penetrated, regions whose existence, however, is so to speak a necessary complement to the realm of man's salvation. Kept in leash by the set forms of the initial letters, these monsters form the dark, demonic background against which the light of divine

POST

IMPLETŪ

REDEM

PTIONIS

humane misteriū·uerbo dei in assūpto ho
mine apparente·et ueritatis sue splendori
bꝫ mundanas tenebras illustrante·aplice doc

PASSIONAL. INITIAL P. CITEAUX, CA. 1125. (9 1/16 × 4 1/4 ") MS H. 30, FOLIO 165.
BIBLIOTHÈQUE DE L'ÉCOLE DE MÉDECINE, MONTPELLIER.

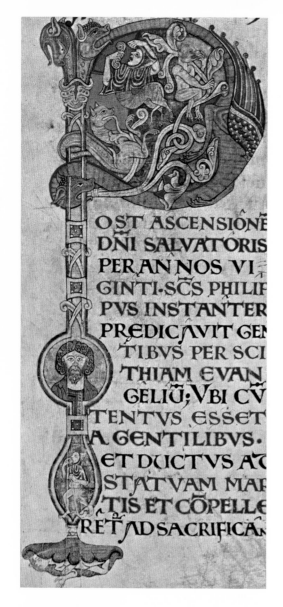

revelation seems doubly radiant. Their function here is the same as that of the devilish monsters that on Romanesque church portals peep out from under the saints' feet. Similarly, in a large ornamental initial from a Cistercian Passional (illustration page 155), we see a dragon acting simultaneously both as a pedestal for a standing saint and as an essential decorative element of the letter. Long before this, in his palace at Constantinople, the Emperor Constantine the Great had had himself represented triumphing over the Serpent of Evil with the help of the holy monogram of Christ, and, when all is said and done, the Romanesque dragon initials are nothing other than a revival and extension of this concept in a wider context.

After the Church intensified her campaign against simony, the marriage of priests and worldliness in general in the second half of the 11th century, the moral problems of the day acquired a new immediacy. The age-old conflict between Good and Evil was now a theme which bulked larger than ever before in works of art of all descriptions. Every circumstance of the human situation was implicated in the struggle between Heaven and Hell, everything became "moralized," and Romanesque initial letters show us that even ornamentation was affected by the increased rigor of the ethical prescriptions of the Church—without, however, quite abandoning that spirit of playful, fancy-free extravagance without which no creative art can live. All the imagery that took shape within the ornamental letters remained, as it were, on the brink of the crater, but what the volcano itself —i.e. the jaws of Hell—actually looked like was also represented in Romanesque manuscripts, and nowhere better than in the English. In one of the scenes of the Last Judgment in the Psalter of Henry of Blois, bishop of Winchester, dating to the middle of the

Illustration page 157 12th century, we see an angel locking the door behind the Damned and it is certainly not by chance that the mouth of the huge beast that is gulping them down in a serried mass suggests a Romanesque initial letter carried to its most monstrous limit—a super-initial!

The urge to "moralize" gained ground everywhere in the Romanesque period and came to pervade virtually every field of knowledge. Heaven and earth no less than human existence—astronomy, zoology, botany and geography no less than history— were viewed from the standpoint of the doctrine of salvation. In the so-called Bestiaries the peculiarities of different animals were interpreted as symbols for events recorded in

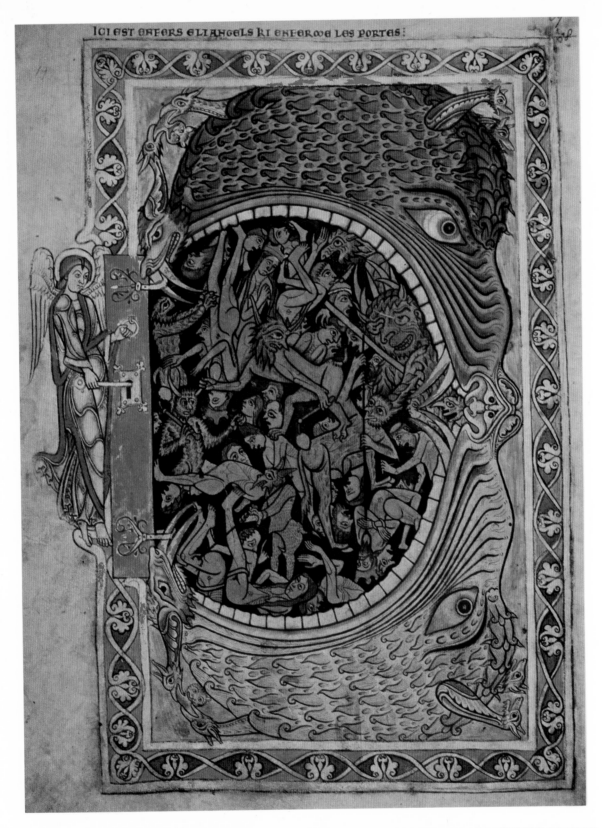

PSALTER OF HENRY OF BLOIS. ANGEL LOCKING THE DAMNED IN HELL. WINCHESTER, MID-TWELFTH CENTURY.
($12 \frac{5}{8} \times 8 \frac{7}{8}$″) COTTON MS NERO C. IV, FOLIO 39, BRITISH MUSEUM, LONDON.

the Bible, and a corresponding virtue or vice was assigned to each. But though allegorically an animal might symbolize the Resurrection of Christ or His death on the Cross, literally it remained a lineal descendant of pagan animal imagery and as such was stylized—exactly like the figures in the ornamental initials of manuscripts—in quaint or terrifying shapes. In short, as C. R. Dodwell has pointed out with reference to the manuscripts of the Canterbury School, there was a continual exchange of ideas between the natural history illustrations and the "caprichos" of the historiated initials.

How far this moralizing tendency could be pressed is shown most clearly by the encyclopedias of the Romanesque period, whose chief interest for us here lies in their illustrations. Two such works were compiled north of the Alps in the 12th century: the *Liber Floridus* of Lambert, a canon of Saint-Omer, finished before 1120, and the *Hortus Deliciarum* of Abbess Herrad of Landsberg (1167-1195). The original manuscript of Lambert's work still exists (Ghent, Univ. Libr., Cod. 1125), as well as many copies, one of them dating to the second half of the 12th century (Wolfenbüttel, Herzog-August-Bibliothek, Gud. lat. 1). The *Hortus Deliciarum*, unfortunately, perished by fire in 1870 during the bombardment of Strasbourg and is known today only from drawings which, though they do not reproduce the entire manuscript, give us a fairly complete idea of the miniatures which originally figured in it.

Illustration page 159

Anything but a methodical minded man, Lambert of Saint-Omer composed his book very much like a bouquet of flowers plucked at random, with little regard for the order in which one section followed another. Herrad of Landsberg, on the other hand, used the Bible story as an "Ariadne's clew" serving to guide the reader through the maze of diverse facts, with the result that most of her encyclopedia could be described as a variety of Moralized Bible. Both Lambert and Herrad—and this is typical of the Romanesque mentality—combine a broad universal vision with a special interest in their home surroundings: the town of Saint-Omer and his family, in the case of Lambert; the nunnery on the Odilienberg of which she was abbess, in the case of Herrad. Both included their own likenesses, Herrad even adding a group portrait of the nuns under her charge, for whose instruction she had written the book.

Lambert did not merely name his work a "book of flowers" in the figurative sense of an anthology, but also adorned it with several botanical illustrations. Two of these, exactly balancing each other, fill facing pages. Thus on the lefthand page we see a stylized tree whose branches also end in strongly stylized leaves all of which are differently patterned, and each, according to its inscription, represents the foliage of some "noble" tree or shrub: pine, terebinth, rose, box, cedar and the like. The twelve species of tree thus depicted correspond to twelve virtues, which are symbolized by female portraits in medallions attached to the branches. On the treetrunk below is *caritas* or neighborly love, mother of all the virtues. The picture as a whole is therefore an allegory of the "good" tree *(arbor bona)*, resplendent in full color and symbolizing the Christian Church *(ecclesia fidelium)*. Then, on the righthand page, comes the "evil" tree *(arbor mala)*, virtually monochrome, which represents the Synagogue. Its leaves are all alike for it stands for a single species: the withered fig-tree on which, in the words of Christ, "no

Illustration page 159

fruit grow" (Matthew XXI, 19) and to whose roots, according to the prophecy of John the Baptist, "the axe is laid" (Matthew III, 10)—though here, for the sake of symmetry, *two* axes are employed. In the barren leaves of this tree are empty medallions with inscriptions bearing the names of the vices, each of which parallels a corresponding virtue on the opposite page; this "evil" treetrunk is inscribed *cupiditas sive avaritia*, i.e. greed, mother of all the vices. In a highly "intellectualized" picture of this kind the author seems to be asking more of the visual arts than they can properly be asked to give. The result, nevertheless, is a composition that not only gratifies the moral sense, but also appeals to an eye sensitive to decorative values.

The allegorical trend of thought that makes itself felt so strongly in the illustrations of the *Liber Floridus* is less pronounced in the *Hortus Deliciarum*. Not that it is absent; on the contrary, here too are compositions constructed radially around a focal point

LIBER FLORIDUS. TREE OF GOOD AND TREE OF EVIL. SAINT-OMER, BEFORE 1120 (EACH PAGE: 12×7 ⅝ ″) COD. 1125, FOLIOS 231 VERSO AND 232, BIBLIOTHÈQUE DE L'UNIVERSITÉ, GHENT.

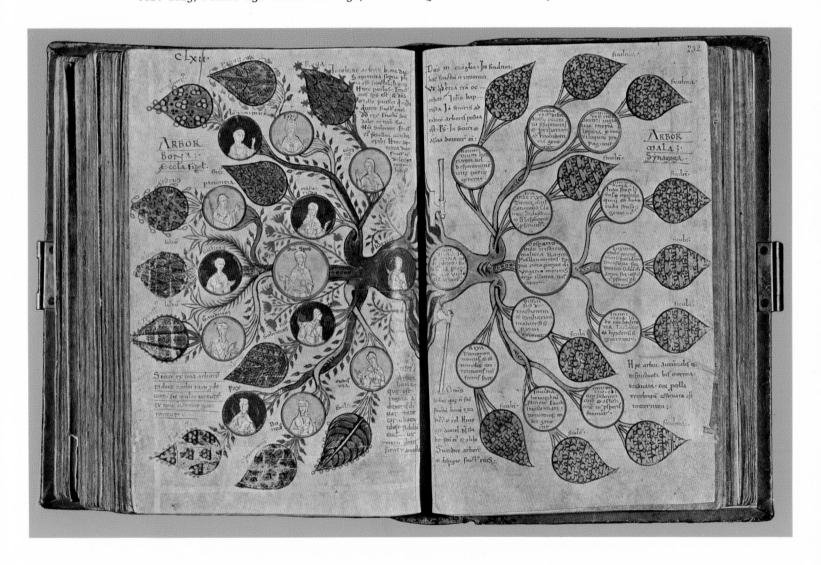

and illustrating an abstract concept in graphic form, but on the whole it is "historical" scenes from the Old and New Testaments that predominate, in conformity with the epic character of the sacred narrative. Many of these scenes are highly interesting iconographically, since they speak for a close acquaintance with Byzantine art, but there are also pictures which give the impression of original compositions. As with Lambert, the Vices and Virtues are depicted facing each other, though not schematically in medallions but in the dramatic form—derived from Prudentius—of a pitched battle between Amazons armed with the most up-to-date weapons and tilting with each other like knights in the lists. Although Herrad—who was well placed to know the frailties of her own sex—had no trouble in mustering a numerically superior host of female Vices, in the end, as was but fitting, the Virtues win the day.

Towards the close of the book the compositions become larger and bolder. In the original some of the Apocalyptic scenes must have produced a truly monumental effect. It has been calculated that the "Garden of Delights" originally contained 340 scenes with several thousand figures. It is safe to say that with the destruction of this manuscript we lost one of the masterworks of medieval book illumination. Today, except for the drawings made from them, we possess but a single token of the high artistic quality of these miniatures: a strip of vellum over two feet long with scenes from the life of John the Baptist (London, Brit. Mus., Add. 42497), which without any doubt originated from the same atelier as the *Hortus Deliciarum*. When attention was first drawn to it, it was thought to be a surviving fragment of Herrad's "encyclopedia," since we know that a few pages were detached from the manuscript before the fire. But Rosalie Green, leading authority on the problems connected with the *Hortus*, has discovered that this piece of vellum must have been a flabellum—i.e. a fan used for keeping flies from the sacred elements on the altar.

Abbess Herrad of Landsberg was not the only German woman of her day who has bequeathed to us a panoramic vision of the world at large, as seen through medieval eyes. St Hildegard of Bingen (1098-1179) was in no wise her inferior as regards the scope and depth of her erudition. Although she never received any formal schooling, she was a living encyclopedia, deeply versed, through divine inspiration, not only in the natural sciences but in the arcana of dogmatic theology. She even invented a secret language of 920 new words and—like Bernard Shaw in a later age—advocated a thoroughgoing reform of the Latin alphabet. She was also a seeress and, like Herrad, enlisted the help of art in making the revelations of her "inner eye" more accessible to others. The first series of her visions, set down in a book which she called *Scivias* (perhaps an abridged form of Latin for *Scitote vias* [*Domini*], i.e. "Know the ways [of God]," but more probably a word belonging to her private language), existed until the recent war in a manuscript copy containing many miniatures at Wiesbaden (Landesbibl., Fol. 1); its present whereabouts is unknown. A second series, entitled *Liber divinorum operum*, is known by way of an illuminated manuscript at Lucca (Bibl. govern., MS 1942), which dates, however, only from the early 13th century. Both cycles contain pictures charged with mystical significance, some of them positively surrealistic in effect. Each illustration in the Lucca manuscript is accompanied by a smaller miniature resembling a postage stamp, in which we see the prophetess writing down her visions. (This, incidentally, she never actually did, but left it to her father confessors.)

The women of the 12th century, and German women in particular, were filled with a thirst for culture. For their benefit, at the request of an abbess named Theodora, the monk Conrad of Hirsau, pupil of the great monastic reformer William of Hirsau, wrote a *Speculum Virginum* in twelve chapters, each of them prefaced by an allegorical drawing. "Young ladies—wrote the author in his preface—take pleasure in looking at themselves in the mirror to see if they are comely; held up to them here, however, is a mirror which will help them to see more clearly how to please the Heavenly Bridegroom." The text and drawings give a symbolic picture of the system into which the Christian dogma of salvation had been condensed by the theologians. At one point, for example, we see the trees of the four cardinal virtues being watered by the four Evangelists, the four Fathers of the Church, and personifications of the four Rivers of Paradise; all these streams flow into the well of Wisdom in the center of the picture, beneath the symbol of the Virgin carrying the Child, incarnation of the Word of God. Other drawings are more pointedly moralistic in intent. Thus we see the Ladder of Virtues up which the maidens are climbing, undeterred either by the loathsome dragon lurking at its foot or by a fierce Ethiopian halfway up who is brandishing a big knife, while at the summit we see the Heavenly Bridegroom waiting to greet them.

The oldest manuscript we have of the *Speculum Virginum* (London, Brit. Mus., Arundel 44) was probably executed in Swabia during the author's lifetime or shortly afterwards. How popular the book became not only in German but also in French monasteries is evidenced by the fact that no less than three copies were made towards the end of the 12th century (Berlin, Staatsbibl., Phill. 1701, stemming from Igny; and Troyes, Bibl. Munic., MSS 252 and 413 from Clairvaux); the drawings in these are exceptionally fine. Occasionally, too, we find the writings of St Bernard himself embellished with moralizing miniatures, as in the Douai manuscript (Bibl. Munic., MS 372), which contains a Ladder of Virtues.

At the beginning of the *Speculum Virginum* is the picture of a tree adorned with Illustration page 162 rinceaux and half-length portraits. It is charged with a symbolic meaning even more vital than that of the trees in the *Liber Floridus*, since it demonstrates Christ's descent from the House of David, the unbroken genealogical line linking the Old and the New Testament. From the head of Christ sprout forth as leaves the seven gifts of the Holy Ghost. In this particular case Christ's ancestry is carried as far back as Boaz; usually, however, it is represented as beginning with the grandson of Boaz, Jesse, according to the prophecy of Isaiah (XI, I): *Egredietur virga de radice Jesse*—"And there shall come forth a rod out of the stem of Jesse, and a Branch shall grow out of his roots." Such a composition is generally known as a Tree of Jesse, and though the earliest examples of it are to be found in illuminated manuscripts, it is probable that we owe its fully developed canonical form to the monumental arts. Emile Mâle surmised that Abbot Suger of Saint-Denis was the originator of the theme, but the exhaustive research

CONRAD OF HIRSAU'S SPECULUM VIRGINUM. THE ANCESTORS OF CHRIST. CLAIRVAUX, LATE TWELFTH CENTURY. (13×7¹/₁₆″) MS 252, FOLIO 2 VERSO, BIBLIOTHÈQUE MUNICIPALE, TROYES.

work of Arthur Watson has not confirmed this view. The "Tree of Jesse" motif is about a generation older and to all appearances should be related to the cult of the Virgin whose rise to favor in England and France can be traced to the early 12th century.

In the Middle Ages the relationship between the Old and the New Testament was one of the most closely studied problems of biblical exegesis. Different approaches were gradually systematized into the so-called typological method, according to which every notable event in the New Testament had one or more prefigurations in the Old. By the 12th century this method had come into vogue in art. As far as book illumination is concerned, it was practised by two schools in particular, the Flemish and the North German. The enamelists of the Mosan School combine typological parallels with motifs from the Bestiary, while in the Gospel Books of Averbode (Liége, Bibl. Univ., MS 3) and Saint-Trond (formerly London, Chester Beatty and Eric G. Millar Collections, now New York, Morgan Library, M. 883) there are miniatures that look almost like imitations of the sculptures and enamels of such artists as Godefroid de Claire. The most notable works of this type in Germany are the miniatures in the Ratmann Missal at Hildesheim and in another related Sacramentary in the library of Count Fürstenberg at Stammheim. Here the miniatures are inserted in a frame with square fields in the corners—a layout which anticipates that of the *Biblia pauperum* ("Poor Men's Bible") and the *Speculum humanae salvationis* (Mirror of Human Salvation). Prophets carrying banderoles whose inscriptions relate to episodes of the New Testament also figure in this type of illustration. In the Gospel Book of Henry the Lion (formerly Gmunden, Library of the Duke of Cumberland) they are posted at the corners of the frames as witnesses to the incidents in the life of Christ two scenes of which figure in each miniature. To an ever increasing degree, the work of art came to be the product of a close collaboration between the painter and his theological advisers, whom one can almost picture looking over his shoulder as he plied his brush.

Admirable in their kind as are the typological sequences described above, the fact remains that the Romanesque illuminators' greatest achievements were in the field of Bible illustration. No one has yet set about the arduous task of collating all the extant Romanesque Bible manuscripts containing miniatures; and anyone who does so will find he has to cope with a well-nigh incredible number of works, since in the 12th century almost every monastery in Western Europe must have possessed one or more complete Bibles, newly copied and illuminated. And since these manuscripts can be fairly evenly distributed over the whole period, it is not too much to say that the history of Romanesque illumination might be based almost entirely on the evidence of these great Bibles.

Unlike Carolingian Bibles, most of which consisted of a single volume, Romanesque Bibles usually ran to anywhere from two to five folio volumes. Actually, this change had become indispensable owing to the larger scale of the Romanesque minuscule. The fewer the volumes, the larger the page format became, with a proportionate increase in the size of initials and miniatures. The trend of the age was towards monumentality and led (to take an example from the goldsmiths' art) to the making of the large reliquary shrines shaped like sarcophagi produced in the Mosan and Rhenish regions. In the field of book illumination it resulted at times in a veritable *folie des grandeurs*, against which the Gothic ateliers decisively reacted in the following century. Sometimes the ornamentation of the huge Romanesque Bibles proved to be a task exceeding the powers of a single monastic workshop, and necessitated the co-operation of a number of artists working in relays. Such was the case with the finest of all Romanesque Bibles, that in Winchester Cathedral, in which, even so, many historiated initials were left unfinished—a circumstance that has the advantage of enabling us to study the painters' technique in its successive stages. True, the largest Bible of all—the Codex Gigas (Stockholm, Royal Library, A. 148), a manuscript so heavy that two men are needed to lift it—was produced in a single run of work but, as legend has it, only with the help of the Devil, whose effigy, as a matter of fact, we find depicted on a monumental scale at the end of the manuscript.

While the text of the Carolingian Bibles was based on the revision of the Vulgate carried out by Alcuin at Charlemagne's bidding, there are no indications that any similar revision took place in the Romanesque period, unless it be that the text of the Umbro-Roman Bibles represents a new version sponsored by the Roman Curia. In general it was left to each monastery to act on its own initiative. Thus when Stephen Harding, third abbot of Cîteaux, wished to provide his congregation with a "standard" edition of the Holy Scriptures, he called upon Jewish scholars to correct the Latin translation of the Old Testament in the light of the original Hebrew version. Generally, however, the *textus receptus* was accepted without demur, one reason being, perhaps, that contemporary theologians were more interested in the symbolical than in the literal meaning of the text. On this view, the scribes copying a Bible were concerned only with the raw material, as it were, of the divine revelation, and it was just this attitude that gave them a certain freedom in the outward presentation of the manuscripts, which, both textually and typographically, varied very widely. Little by little the text itself lost something of its sanctity and came increasingly to be regarded as an historical document. Thus in the Floreffe Bible (London, Brit. Mus., Add. 17 737/38) we find the Old Testament preceded by historical tables, supplementing the data furnished by the Bible itself and summarizing the story of mankind up to the time of the making of the manuscript. The logical conclusion of this process was the *Historia scholastica* of Petrus Comestor (d. 1178), in which incidents recorded in the Bible, arranged in chronological order, are intercalated among those of pagan history. Later translated into French and known by the name of "Bible historiale," this compilation all but supplanted the usual Bible text over a considerable period.

These are facts we need to bear in mind when we study Bible illustrations of the Romanesque period. We can sense the artist's pleasure when he lingers over the dramatic events of Jewish history which illustrate the omnipotence of God and the vagaries of human destiny; and by the same token his reluctance to omit a battle-piece or a beheadal whenever this could be included. But cycles of illustrations, in the form of a running accompaniment to the biblical text, are wholly lacking. The pictures are almost invariably placed at the beginning of each Book, either as vignettes in separate frames or enclosed in the initials. In the former case the artists generally make use of the empty space left by the scribes between the end of one Book and the beginning of the next. Only in exceptionally sumptuous Bibles do we find half- or full-page miniatures, mostly arranged in strips of scenes forming a continuous narrative sequence.

Illustrations pages 166-168, 176, 180

Illustration page 137

Not all the Books of the Bible lent themselves to illustrations of this sort, but even so the artists could generally fall back on another kind of picture, viz. author portraits. These were always appropriate for Books of which the writers' names were known —Solomon, David, the major and minor Prophets, Evangelists and Apostles. It was the combination of these two methods of illustration that enabled the Romanesque artists to adorn each Book of the Old and the New Testament with an appropriate picture.

The practice of including portraits of the authors was systematically followed for the first time by the makers of the great Italian Bibles. On the model of certain Greek manuscripts of the prophetic books, they mostly represent the biblical writers as full-length standing figures holding scrolls. To begin with, these were painted above or beside the initial letters; subsequently, however, the tendency was to integrate the figures into the initial. In the oldest Bibles the scrolls held by Prophets and Apostles are left blank. When, about 1100, they were given inscriptions—as in the Roman Bible of Santa Cecilia in Trastevere (Vatican, Barb. lat. 587)—these consist of passages extolling God's omnipotence and the supremacy of the Church—as was appropriate for Bibles produced under the auspices of the Roman Curia. Narrative scenes were at first very rare in Italian illustrated Bibles, the only exception being a group of scenes of the Creation, Illustration page 137 which appear in the Roman picture cycles almost from the start. In the course of the 12th century, however, doubtless under Northern influence, historiated initials were introduced, while, conversely, the practice of including author portraits made its way from Italy to the countries north of the Alps. In French illustrated Bibles attempts were made at an early date to infuse movement even into author portraits by representing the Prophets, whenever an opportunity arose, in a dramatic or characteristic situation —as when we are shown Jonah being thrown into the sea or vomited forth by the whale; Amos tending his flocks; Isaiah brutally sawn in two, and so forth.

Most illuminated Bibles of the Romanesque period are such highly individual creations that they do not always lend themselves easily to classification according to

AVERBODE GOSPEL BOOK. TYPE AND ANTITYPES OF THE CRUCIFIXION. MOSAN SCHOOL, MID-TWELFTH CENTURY. (EACH PAGE: 11×7⁷/₁₆″) COD. 3 (363), FOLIOS 86 VERSO AND 87, BIBLIOTHÈQUE DE L'UNIVERSITÉ, LIÉGE.

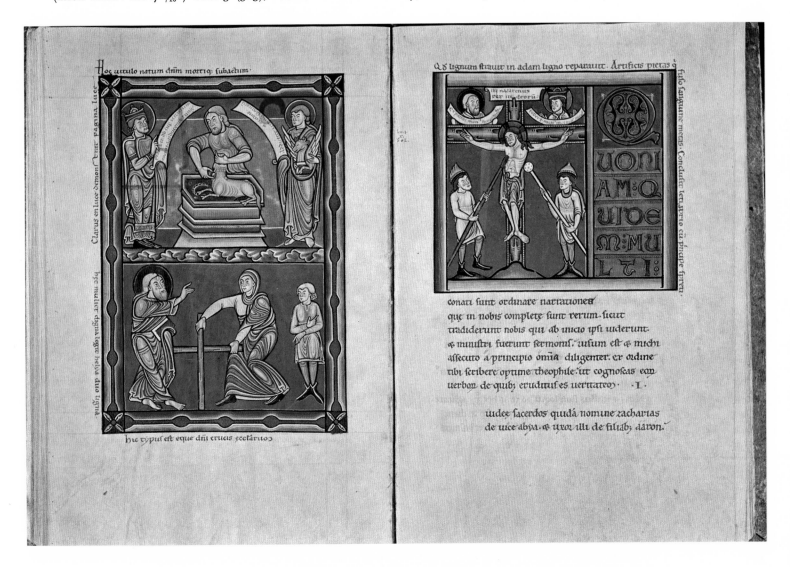

schools. The largest and also the most homogeneous category is represented by the Italian folio Bibles of which mention has already been made. Sometimes indeed they give an impression of being rather stereotyped and tedious, but thanks to the research work of E.B. Garrison we now begin to see that under a superficial sameness there are undeniable differences due partly to their places of origin and partly to the time when they were made.

Of the earlier Bibles, those dating to the 11th century, almost every one constitutes a milestone in the development of Romanesque miniature painting. The oldest French Bibles—the so-called First Bible of Limoges (Paris, Bibl. Nat., lat. 5) and the Cluny Bible commissioned by St Odilo (Paris, Bibl. Nat., lat. 15 176)—make use only of ornamental initials. But already before the middle of the century a quite amazing wealth of allegory had been included in the Catalonian Bibles now in Paris (Bibl. Nat., lat. 6) and at the Vatican (Vat. lat. 5729). The Saint-Vaast Bible (Arras, Bibl. Munic., MS 435) represents an early effort to add illustrations to lavish ornamentation. Another masterwork of 11th-century Romanesque Bible illustration is Illustration page 191 the two-volume Bible at Pommersfelden (Schlossbibl., Cod. 333-34), which, according to an inscription restored in the 12th century but left unchanged, was presented by a certain Canon Hongarus to the church of St Castor in Coblenz when Udo was archbishop of Trier —which means that it was made before 1077, an astonishingly early date for this manuscript. Two Bibles in which the pictures are systematically incorporated in the initial letters bear the signature of a monk named Goderannus, the first made in 1085 at Lobbes Illustration page 180 (Tournai, Grand Séminaire), the second in 1097-1098 at Stavelot (London, Brit. Mus., 28 106/07). Roughly contemporary with these are the Carilef Bible at Durham (Cathedral Library, A.II.4) and the Bible of Saint-Pierre de Redon at Bordeaux (Bibl. Munic., MS 1), both presumably the work of Norman artists. In Southern France the finest Bible manuscripts hail from Limoges and are datable to ca. 1100 (Paris, Bibl. Nat., lat. 8, and Saint-Yrieix, Bibl. Munic.); their style is High rather than Early Romanesque.

Bible manuscripts were produced in ever greater numbers in the 12th century, two of the chief centers of production being Salzburg and the South of England. The Bibles from both sources contain illustrations whose size much exceeds the usual scale of miniature paintings. Three outstanding works from Salzburg are the Walters Bible (Michelbeuern, Stiftsbibl., Cod. I), the Gebhardt Bible from Admont (Vienna, Nationalbibl., Ser. nov. 2701-02) and the Gumpert Bible from Anspach (Erlangen, Univ. Bibl., Cod. 121). Three equally fine works produced in England are the Lambeth Bible (London, Lambeth Palace, MS 3, and Maidstone Museum, MS P. 5), the Bury Bible (Cambridge, Corpus Christi College Library, MS 2) and the Winchester Bible (Winchester Cathedral Library). In the

Illustration page 167

Illustration page 168

Illustrations pages 166, 176

GEBHARDT BIBLE FROM ADMONT. MOSES RECEIVING THE TABLES OF THE LAW. SALZBURG, TWELFTH CENTURY. (EACH PAGE: 22 3/8 × 15 15/16″) SER. NOV. 2701, FOLIOS 68 VERSO AND 69, NATIONALBIBLIOTHEK, VIENNA.

full-page scenes of the last-named, it would seem that a change of plan supervened in the course of the work, which was never completely finished. Indeed, the most beautiful and meticulously executed full-page miniature (New York, Morgan Library, M. 619) was never actually incorporated in the manuscript; that none the less it escaped destruction is probably due to the high artistic quality of its scenes of the life of David.

LAMBETH BIBLE. INITIAL R AND THE STORY OF RUTH. CANTERBURY, MID-TWELFTH CENTURY. $(8\,^3/_8 \times 8\,^{13}/_{16}{}'')$
MS 3, FOLIO 130, LAMBETH PALACE LIBRARY, LONDON.

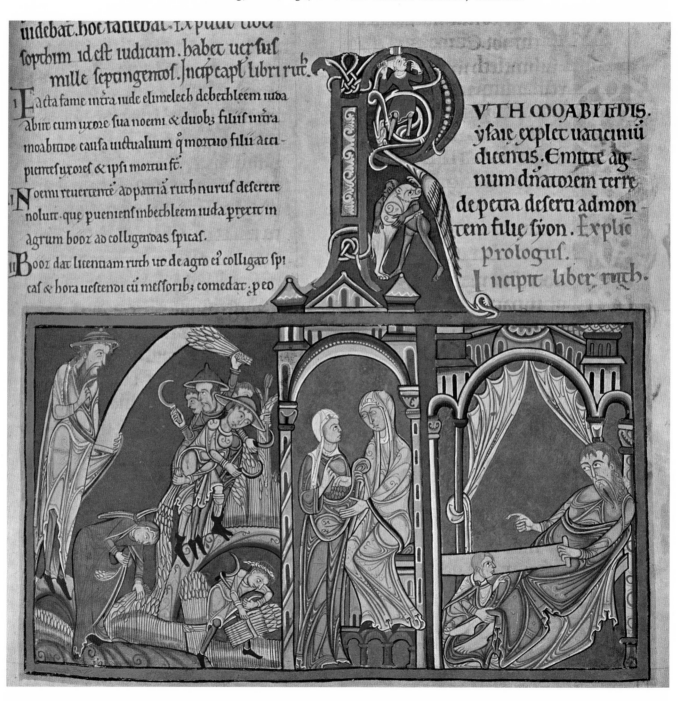

PSALTER OF ST ELIZABETH. CALENDAR FOR JULY. THURINGIAN-SAXON SCHOOL, BEFORE 1217. (7¼×5″)
CODICI SACRI 7, PAGE 8, BIBLIOTECA COMUNALE, CIVIDALE.

Also in France, towards the close of the Romanesque period, we find a notable series of magnificently illuminated Bibles which may be grouped around the Souvigny Bible (Moulins, Bibl. Munic., MS 1); these were brought together for the first time in 1954 at the exhibition of pre-Gothic miniature painting organized by Jean Porcher at the Bibliothèque Nationale, Paris. To the same group also belong (as pointed out by Meyer Schapiro) the supplementary Evangelist portraits added to the Odilo Bible (Paris, Bibl. Nat., lat. 15 176). Given the places of origin of most of these manuscripts, they can safely be attributed to a school active in Burgundy or its vicinity.

Illustration page 174

Turning to the north of France, we find yet another group of Bibles, finest of which is the Manerius Bible now in Paris (Bibl. Sainte-Geneviève, MSS 8-10), named after the scribe who copied it. Manerius—who, with a typically medieval addiction to far-fetched etymologies, boasted that his name derived from the Latin *manu gnarus* ("skilled of hand")—was according to his own statement a native of Canterbury. There is no question, however, that the scene of his labors was not England, but Northern France. It is still an open question whether he resided in Paris, Pontigny, Sens or at St Bertin's Abbey at Saint-Omer (similar manuscripts are known to have originated from all these places). In the Manerius Bible the Romanesque style attains a maturity that is already verging on the Gothic. All the same its monumental format and the artist's manifest delight in eye-pleasing "caprichos" justify us in including it among the manuscripts properly described as Romanesque.

Bibles are to Romanesque illumination what Psalters were to be to Gothic. The golden age of Psalter illustration lies in the 13th century, but its beginnings go back to the 12th. The Psalter was the first liturgical book intended for the use of laymen and as such the precursor of the Book of Hours. Richly ornamented private Psalters had been produced already in the Carolingian and Ottonian epochs, but always for the personal use of great dignitaries of Church and State. Now, however, a new clientèle appeared on the scene: that of the ladies of the nobility. The illuminated book became one of the most cherished possessions of every woman of high birth, a visible sign both of her rank in life and of her piety. Psalters of this type can scarcely have come into vogue before 1100; were it otherwise, we should find not Gospel Books alone historically associated with the names of such women as St Margaret of Scotland (d. 1093), or the Countesses Judith of Flanders (d. 1094) and Matilda of Tuscany (d. 1115). As it is, the earliest example of a de luxe Psalter in the possession of a pious gentlewoman is no

Illustration page 171

doubt the Albani Psalter at Hildesheim, which was originally owned by a famous English lady of Danish extraction, named Christina, who had settled as an anchoress in the vicinity of St Albans. With its magnificent illustrations and historiated initials, it ranks as one of the masterworks of Romanesque book illumination in England. Similar in style are the Psalter from Shaftesbury Abbey (London, Brit. Mus., Lansdowne 383), made for a high-born nun, whom we see on the opening page kneeling at the feet of the Virgin, and the beautiful Psalter in Copenhagen (Royal Library, Thott 143, 2°), which, very soon after being made, was taken to Scandinavia where it came into the possession of a relative of the Swedish regent Birger Jarl (d. 1202).

ALBANI PSALTER. THE ANNUNCIATION (FOLIO 3). ST ALBANS, CA. 1125. (7 $\frac{3}{16}$ × 5 $\frac{5}{8}$ ")
TREASURE OF ST GODEHARD'S, HILDESHEIM.

There is no question that England played a decisive part in the creation of the de luxe Psalter for private use, and we need not be surprised at the fact that, as shown by Francis Wormald, the calendar saints in the Psalter of Queen Melisende of Jerusalem (London, Brit. Mus., Egerton 1139) derive from an English prototype. Two small royal Psalters in London (Brit. Mus., Lansdowne 381) and Baltimore (Walters Art Gallery, w. 1) were produced at Helmarshausen for female members of the Guelph family, and here again dynastic connections lead us back to England. After the production of private Psalters had become the distinctive speciality of French and English illuminators in the 13th century, a steadily increasing number of German Psalters made their appearance, as a glance at the corpus of Late Romanesque miniatures on the Rhine, Main and Danube, edited by Hanns Swarzenski, clearly shows. The Thuringian-Saxon school of Illustration page 169 painting also specialized in Psalters, finest of which are the Psalter of St Elizabeth at Cividale and the so-called Landgrave Psalter at Stuttgart.

Characteristic of the de luxe Psalter for private use is its lavish illustration. For one thing, the initials at the beginning of the most important psalms are given exceptionally large dimensions, the most handsomely decorated being the full-page B(eatus vir) which introduces the First Psalm. Sometimes, too, a sequence of full-page scenes of the Life of Christ is intercalated between the calendar and the psalms, these being no doubt intended to provide the reader with themes of pious meditation. In the choice of scenes we find a predilection for incidents from Christ's Childhood and Passion. This means, of course, that besides Christ the Virgin is given a leading role—another indication of the steady growth, during the Romanesque period, of the new cult of the Madonna, chief promoter of which in England was Anselm, elected Abbot of Bury St Edmunds Illustration page 171 in 1121. Nor is it by chance that in the picture of the Annunciation in the Albani Psalter the Virgin herself is shown with a book, no doubt a private Psalter, in her lap.

In some Psalters, the life of David is illustrated alongside the life of Christ, and in certain cases we even find a full-length biblical sequence from the Creation to the Last Judgment. Some highly interesting fragments of such Bible cycles—painted at Liége about the middle of the 12th century, to judge by the style—are preserved in Berlin (Kupferstichkabinett, 78.A.6), Liége (Wittert Collection) and London (Victoria and Albert Museum) and though this cannot be proved, we are tempted to believe that they originally figured in richly decorated Psalters—masterpieces of Romanesque book illumination known to us only by these few surviving pages.

Romanesque Initial Letters

It must be remembered that the art of book illumination in the Middle Ages was quite as much an affair of ornamentation as one of illustration. From the earliest period on, this ornamentation took three distinctive forms. Firstly the "carpet page," in which the page is entirely covered with decorative patterns; secondly, the ornamental frame or border enclosing a title, frontispiece or picture; and, lastly, elaborate initial letters in which calligraphy and ornament are intermingled.

The first of these, the carpet or pattern page, was virtually obsolete in the Romanesque period. Perhaps the art of the 12th century was too literary minded to devote a whole page of a book to an abstract composition. Even in the blind-tooling on leather bindings we find an ever increasing use of figural as against non-figurative motifs.

Decorative borders were still used as settings for full-page miniatures, and in some cases were of a highly elaborate description. But they now more rarely figured in conjunction with written text. Similarly the title pages in decorative frames which were so much in favor with Carolingian and Ottonian illuminators, are seldom found in Romanesque manuscripts; as a rule the scribe contented himself with writing the title in the same Illustration page 175 column as the text, above the ornamental initial. A favorite practice was to play off the words or syllables of the title against each other by means of alternating colors —usually blue, green and red, a typically Romanesque color combination. Another characteristic of Romanesque title calligraphy, especially in Southern French and Spanish manuscripts, is that of interlocking two or more letters so as to form a monogram. By and large, these practices provided opportunities for scribes (rather than painters) to display their talents.

Among the ornamental letters, too, we find a type of outline initials in red, blue and green which no doubt were executed for the most part by expert calligraphers. They are often embellished with graceful arabesques of foliage and tendrils, and it was out of these that the so-called fleuronné ornamentation of the Gothic period developed. Fine examples are to be found in Northern French and English manuscripts. As a rule, however, the Romanesque ornamental letter is a plastically realized composition calling for the services of an experienced painter, not a mere calligrapher. Contemporary records inform us that in the larger scriptoria there were lay brothers who specialized in the execution of ornamental capital letters, and indeed it is evident that the more elaborate historiated initials must have been the work of highly skilled professional artists.

Canon tables figure both in Gospel Books and Bibles, and are usually very lavishly decorated with ornaments and figures, sometimes to the point of overcrowding. In the Manerius Bible the arches above the canon tables enclose Gospel scenes, and, above Illustration page 174 these again, the artist has given rein to his fancy in a series of amusing scenes stemming from Bestiaries and similar sources. Though in such cases the architectonic values of the canon arches remain intact, it often happens that they are all but submerged by a plethora of decorative motifs—a sign of decadence behind which we can sense a lack of genuine respect for the theological function of the tables. On the other hand, the later Romanesque period witnessed a serious attempt to revitalize the study of the concordances between the Gospels, made by Zacharias, styled "Chrysopolitanus," a Premonstratensian friar from St Martin's monastery at Laon, and some fine illuminated copies of his work were executed around 1200.

Characteristic of Romanesque initials, too, is the way the ornamental forms tend to proliferate; so much so that they do not merely encroach on the bodies of the letters, but even tend to smother them. There are cases in which the basic alphabetical form

MANERIUS BIBLE. EUSEBIAN CANON TABLES: CHRIST HEALING THE PARALYTIC AND THE DEMONIAC. PARIS (?),
LAST QUARTER OF TWELFTH CENTURY. (4 ¼ × 9 ³/₁₆″) MS 10, F. 127 V., BIBLIOTHÈQUE SAINTE-GENEVIÈVE, PARIS.

of the letter can only be deciphered with the utmost difficulty behind the camouflage of
decorations. Sometimes, too, instead of sprouting from the body of the letter, the foliage
forms an independent complex of ornamental motifs within which the lettrines are hung
or intercalated. The initial-painter Sawalo of Saint-Amand was particularly fond of such
arrangements. It is not unusual for the ornamentation completely to submerge the body
of the letter and transform it into a dragon or a vine-shoot. Such is the case with an
Illustration page 175 initial "U" from an English Bible (Oxford, Bodl. Libr., Auct. E. Infra I). In the initial
letters, however, this development does not give the impression of a degeneration to
the same extent as in the canon tables. The former seem to stand up better against the
lavish, all-pervading ornamentalism of Romanesque art.

The dominant motif of initial ornamentation remains the foliage tendril or rinceau,
whose coils of spirals fill up the interiors of letters. But in contrast to the golden rinceaux
of Ottonian art, whose pictorial values are strictly linear, limited to the picture surface,
Romanesque foliage is given three-dimensional form by the use of shaded colors and
more elaborate design; stems are well-rounded and fully plastic, leaves are large and
fleshy, often curling back at the tips. The origin of these leaf-forms may almost certainly

be traced to the "espalier-frame" of Anglo-Saxon illumination (see *Early Medieval Painting*, p. 182); but now these forms are uniformly integrated into the Carolingian-Ottonian spiral rinceau. This new synthesis was chiefly the work of Norman and other North French illuminators of the 11th century, and once they had given the lead, the "Anglo-Romanesque" spiral rinceau gradually penetrated to every part of Europe.

The floral forms terminating the spiral fronds are often of a remarkably intricate structure. Sometimes they consist of a series of calices nested one inside the other; sometimes of petals radiating in all directions and criss-crossing the rinceaux. Especially

BIBLE. INITIAL U AT THE BEGINNING OF THE BOOK OF JOB. WINCHESTER (?), MID-TWELFTH CENTURY. (5 $^{11}/_{16}$×5 ½″) AUCT. E. INFRA I, FOLIO 304, BODLEIAN LIBRARY, OXFORD.

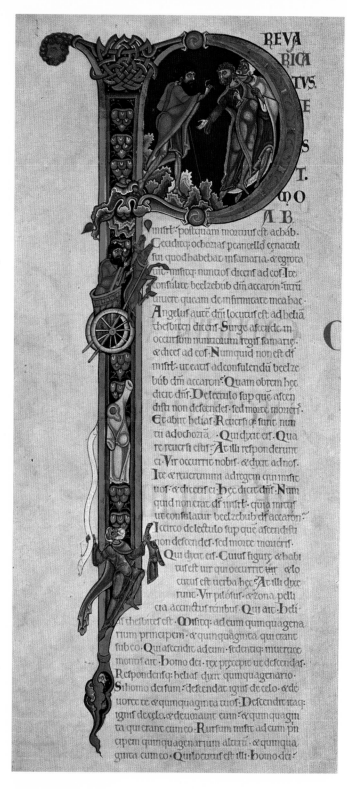

frequent are rose-like motifs inspired by Byzantine floral ornamentation. In the course of the 12th century the central flower tended to become increasingly fleshy and protuberant, until finally it looked almost like an octopus gripping the stems with its widely outspread tentacles. Sometimes, too, we find forms resembling fruit, while others give an impression of being wholly inorganic—metallic rather than floral in effect.

Beside the plant motifs, animals of every sort play an important part in the adornment of Romanesque initials. After being temporarily submerged by the ribbon-like interlaces and foliage of the Carolingians and Ottonians, the fauna of pre-Carolingian illumination makes a reappearance; indeed initials can be found, particularly in French manuscripts, which are composed entirely of animals. But the fish and birds of Merovingian manuscripts are now replaced, for the most part, by quadrupeds and birds; furthermore, human forms are included. All alike are shaped to fit in with the curves of the letters; hence the abundance of dizzy twists and twirls heightening the acrobatic effect of so many Romanesque initials. Most convenient for the draftsman's purpose were the dragons which, supple as lizards, easily adapted themselves to every flexion of the limbs of letters.

Zoomorphic initials are to be found chiefly in Southern French manuscripts, an outstanding early example being the first Bible of Limoges (Paris, Bibl. Nat., lat. 5), with its profusion of elegantly drawn lions, peacocks, dogs and other creatures. But in Northern French and English manuscripts, too, there are initials built up, wholly or in part, of animals or human figures. No one showed more ingenuity in the construction of these figural initials than did the Master of the "Moralia in Job" from Cîteaux (Dijon, Bibl. Munic., MSS 168-170, 173). He had a well-nigh unique knack of adjusting not only single figures but whole scenes to the alphabetical forms of initials, and we even find ornamental initials in which the limbs or bodies of letters —represented now by a tall tree, now by a stretch of marshland—play the part of rudimentary but real landscapes. In some cases he seems to have drawn inspiration from a Byzantine manuscript, for in Greek miniature painting, too, pictorial initials became popular in the second half of the 11th century. The size of the Byzantine initials, however, is always "minuscule," i.e. proportioned to the script. In striking contrast to the Greek dwarf-initials, the figures of the western initials sometimes produce a rather cumbrous effect of "gigantism."

Figural motifs may be inserted in Romanesque ornamental letters for no other purpose than that of lending them vivacity. In the initials of Beneventan manuscripts

we see running dogs tethered by their tails and legs to the interlaces of the ornamental letters, or slinking like weasels through a maze of stems and spirals. Generally speaking, the inhabited rinceau is basic to Romanesque initial decoration. Isolated examples can be found in Carolingian and Ottonian ornamentation, chiefly birds or dog-like lions placed in coils of foliage. But in the ornamentation of Romanesque initials animals appear more frequently and enjoy more freedom of movement: often we see them peeping out at us like squirrels from within the leafage. Also the human figure plays a part in the artists' quest of movement, and it gives them opportunities for indulging their fancy in new and bolder motifs. In the English Bible initial illustrated here (p. 175), the body of a naked running youth is caught in the tanglewood of rinceaux, his outstretched arms and legs jut out like the spokes of a wheel, and emphasize the rotary movement of the spirals.

JOSEPHUS' JEWISH ANTIQUITIES. INITIAL A WITH "CAPRICHOS." CANTERBURY, FIRST THIRD OF THE TWELFTH CENTURY. (5⅞×3⅞″) DD. I. 4, FOLIO 220, UNIVERSITY LIBRARY, CAMBRIDGE.

Illustration page 179

Not only the foliage and spirals but letters themselves now begin to be inhabited by figures climbing up them. Like a living garland, a medley of men and animals capers and gyrates around the bodies of the letters in a frenzied saraband. English and Northern French manuscripts are particularly rich in examples of this form of art. Francis Wormald has aptly described these initials as "gymnastic" and in fact we are vividly reminded of the performances of circus acrobats, despite the fact that the figures are primarily decorative, not representational. What we have here is one of the most characteristic traits of Romanesque art in general. Just as, after the discovery of the laws of perspective, the spatial structure of the picture came to be modeled on that of the stage set, so in Romanesque art we find much that recalls the slender platforms and light scaffolding of a traveling circus, and nowhere more strikingly than in the inhabited initials. Indeed, pursuing this line of thought, we might compare the zoomorphic motifs to the performing animals—dogs, sea-lions and so forth—of a circus, with sometimes a saint, sometimes the initial letter itself, acting the part of animal-trainer!

The life force of the Romanesque historiated initial (and of the circus too) is movement. It was when the peoples of the North came on the scene that this taste for intense, all-pervading animation made itself felt in the art of the Middle Ages. To begin with, it was mainly applied to the abstract elements of insular ornament, such as the spiral, interlace and animal forms; later it was extended to the human figure, as in the drawings of the Utrecht Psalter and in Carolingian art in general. In some respects the Romanesque ornamental letter may be described as a synthesis of the dynamic ornamentation of pre-Carolingian times and the animation of the figures in Carolingian manuscripts. Anglo-Saxon art bulked large in this synthesis, but at the same time the contribution of the schools of Northern France, and in particular those of Normandy, must not be underestimated. The schools of Southern France also made their contribution and, in due course, their achievement mingled with the main stream flowing from the North. And little by little the new French style came to impose itself upon the German, Italian and Spanish schools of illumination.

The figures in a Romanesque initial were not bound to be of an exclusively decorative order—"caprichos" which the artist could handle more or less as he thought fit. Frequently the letters contain portraits of saints or complete biblical scenes, inserted with the twofold purpose of embellishing and illustrating the text. Of such historiated initials we have some early medieval precursors, but it was not until the 11th century that they came into general use. At the very start of the Romanesque movement in France we find a sequence of historiated initials in the Psalter at Boulogne-sur-Mer (Bibl. Munic., MS 20) which Odbert, abbot of Saint-Bertin, illuminated, largely with his own hand, round about the year 1000. Inserted in the capitals—which are still decorated with interlaces of a revived Franco-Saxon type—are small depictions of New Testament episodes, and in some of these we can already sense the artist's effort to adjust the picture elements to the lines of force created by the structure of the letter. Further steps in this direction were taken by the artists to whom we owe the historiated initials in the large Romanesque Bibles. In this context it is particularly interesting to

NEW TESTAMENT. INITIAL L AND ST MATTHEW. REGION OF AGEN-MOISSAC, CA. 1100. (7½×4″)
MS LAT. 254, FOLIO 10, BIBLIOTHÈQUE NATIONALE, PARIS.

STAVELOT BIBLE. INITIAL H: MOSES FOUND BY PHARAOH'S DAUGHTER. MASTER OF THE PENTATEUCH, STAVELOT, 1097-1098. (5×4 ¹³/₁₆″) ADD. 28106, FOLIO 23 VERSO, BRITISH MUSEUM, LONDON.

observe the changes that gradually took place in the presentation of the scene of the Ascension of Elijah, which from the end of the 11th century on was customarily inserted in the large "P" at the beginning of the Second Book of the Kings. We can watch successive artists adapting it more and more boldly to the upward movement of the initial, so as to render with the utmost realism and dramatic effect the prophet's ascent in a chariot of fire; as when, in the bar of the letter, his discarded cloak is represented floating in the air below him and still retaining the form of the "translated" body.

Illustration page 176

In this scene the vertical development of the composition can be accounted for by the theme itself. But in other cases, the compression of narrative scenes into the relatively small field of an initial could make it necessary to change the whole presentation of the subject. When adjusted to an initial, a scene which had formerly been treated in breadth, frieze-wise, had to be squeezed into a narrow space, where it could only be developed in height—conditions which obviously favored the use of "acrobatic" figures. That most vertical of all letters, the capital "I", was especially well adapted to compositions in which a scene was divided up in registers one above the other. Thus in the initial at the beginning of the *Vita Sancti Martini* in the Morgan Library (M. 504) a medallion half way up the shaft of the letter shows St Martin tearing his cloak in two, while in another medallion nearer the bottom of the letter we see the beggar about to receive his share of it.

The practice of enclosing small narrative scenes in medallions was not wholly new; it had begun in the early Middle Ages but it reached its full fruition only in Romanesque art. When several scenes in medallions are superimposed, as is frequently the case with the initial "I" of the Book of Genesis, the general effect is much like that of the roundels in stained-glass windows and these may in fact have influenced the illuminators. The most elaborate composition of this kind figures in the Goderannus Bible from Stavelot Illustration page 180 (London, Brit. Mus., Add. 28106).

The wealth of motifs employed in Romanesque initials and the myriad decorative permutations and combinations permitted by their spirals and coils of foliage made it easy for the illuminators to fulfill a major requirement of medieval esthetic, that of *varietas*, or diversity. Even when a manuscript contains over a hundred ornamental letters, no two are ever quite alike. Moreover, though a few instances of this have been noted, it is extremely rare for the composition of an initial to be carried over unchanged from one manuscript to a copy of it. For the most part the designers and painters of ornamental letters were given a free hand; theirs was creative work, and each aspired to achieve a beauty of his own.

The predominance of decorative themes, while characteristic of Romanesque initials on the whole, did not meet with equal favor everywhere. In the earliest phase of the movement the makers of the large Italian Bibles showed a predilection for a form of initial leaving the interior of the letter empty, only the stem being enriched with ornament. Modeled on a well-defined type of ornamental letter—that of the Turonian Bibles of Carolingian times—the relative simplicity of these initials can be accounted for as being a deliberate reaction against the excessive sumptuousness of the Ottonian foliage initials done in gold; they were in keeping with the spirit of the age in which Pope Gregory VII launched his anathema against the German emperor.

For the second time the over-lavish ornamentation of Romanesque initials was combated by a vigorous reform movement when St Bernard of Clairvaux sought to impose on Christian art his ideal of moderation and simplicity. In the *Dialogus inter Cluniacensem Monachum et Cisterciensem*, believed to have been written by a German follower of St Bernard, we find the Cistercian reproaching the monks of Cluny for having

Illustration page 188

the ornamental letters of manuscripts produced in their monastery painted with gold —an obvious allusion to the Cluny foliage style imported from Germany. Such initials, he goes on to say, were exactly like golden chalices, golden paraments and the like: not called for by any practical purpose, but intended solely for the delectation of the eye. About the same time the general chapter of the Cistercian order pronounced an absolute veto on initials of this type: *Litterae unius coloris fiant et non depictae* (letters are to be made in a single color and to carry no pictures). Yet there are relatively few Cistercian manuscripts which fully comply with this injunction, and even when they do so the artist often succeeds in achieving no less sumptuous effects through the textural richness of the rinceaux, without the help of brush and body color.

Despite all the attacks made upon it, the painted initial never ceased to be one of the principal forms of Romanesque book illumination, and it was part of the heritage transmitted to the Gothic illuminators by their predecessors. And since a "reduced-size" type of initial had already been tentatively employed during the Romanesque period in certain manuscripts, the historiated initial could be adapted without much difficulty to the radical change of scale that became inevitable when the bulky Romanesque Bibles were superseded by the much smaller, more easily manipulated University Bibles of the Gothic age. But in the case of the overloaded foliage initials inhabited by hosts of grotesques, this reduction in scale raised problems of no little difficulty. Since there could be no question of abandoning entirely the accumulated wealth of decoration inherited from the past, a compromise solution was arrived at; the initials were relieved of a portion of their burden by shifting the decorative elements from the letter itself to the margin of the page, with the result that both the foliage and the zoomorphic forms inhabiting it enjoyed a new, less restricted field of action. This drastic change opened the way to a new development in the decoration of manuscripts and while, to begin with, the marginal rinceaux took the shape of short stems, little by little they proliferated, invading all the open space along the borders. This development, however, properly belongs to the Gothic period and lies outside the scope of the present volume.

Pictorial Styles in the Romanesque Miniature

Illustration page 185

Illustration page 187

How can we best define the qualities of Romanesque style in its different phases, as illustrated in the illuminated manuscripts? A comparison of two miniatures in the Municipal Library of Valenciennes will help to clarify the rather complex issues involved in this question. The earlier, from an 11th-century manuscript (MS 502), still keeps to the Carolingian tradition, even though showing signs of having been affected by that archaizing process of reduction of scale which was one of the distinctive characteristics of the early phase of Romanesque illumination in France. The later work (MS 501), dating from the second quarter of the 12th century, belongs to the period which followed, that of the mature Romanesque style. An interval of two or three generations separates the two pictures, and it is immediately obvious that in the meantime a radical change of style has taken place. Indeed at a hasty glance the two miniatures look so different that one can hardly believe they illustrate the same event. Yet such is the case. The subject is a vision which, an old legend has it, was granted to St Aldegundis as she was saying her prayers in the abbey church of Saint-Amand. An angel revealed to her how St Amandus, accompanied by the souls he had converted to the Christian faith, ascended into Heaven and there was given the crown of eternal life. The apotheosis of a great missionary is the theme of both miniatures.

In the earlier work the vision was treated on the epic scale. Twice as tall as his Illustration page 185 faithful companions, Amandus is shown walking in their midst between earth and heaven. Using a strip of ground adorned with foliage as a springboard, he is ascending with them towards the enormous crown which an angel leaning out of clouds holds ready for them. All the picture is in active movement—from the figures themselves, streaming past us like a flight of migrant birds, to the undulations of the clouds which, at the point where the angel has burst through them with the crown, are billowing out in all directions, like the water of a lake into which a rock has fallen.

Very different is the treatment of the scene in the later miniature. The artist has Illustration page 187 divided the picture surface into eight panels of equal size, in which tiny half-length figures are compactly grouped, and which are separated from each other by gold borders bearing inscriptions. The scene has lost what little landscape it had in the earlier version; the ground has disappeared and the swirling clouds that played so conspicuous a part in it have dwindled down to slender ripples behind which stand the followers of St Amandus and symmetrical pairs of censing angels.

Once again Amandus' stature far exceeds that of his associates and he literally stands out against the gilded framework, seeming to be levitated in mid-air, well in front of the picture plane. His ascent is mainly due to the efforts of two female figures personifying the virtues of *dilectio dei* (love of God) and *dilectio proximi* (love of one's neighbor) who, touching his arms and reaching forward, are propelling him aloft. No longer, as in the earlier miniature, does the saint remind us of a mountain-climber striding vigorously heavenwards; here he gives, rather, the impression of being carried up by an invisible mechanism—a sort of celestial elevator—whose motive power is supplied by the two Virtues and the large gold haloes behind them, which seem to act as wheels. His companions, too, play a less active part and though an inscription on the frame tells us that they "have taken the upward path in company with their father," actually they are mere passive spectators of the saint's ascension. Clad in his purple dalmatic and fiery red chasuble, he is the target of all eyes. "Behold the priceless, immaculate garment, twice steeped with purple, within and without," runs the versified inscription, alluding to the martyrdom of St Amandus and also perhaps to some sacred vestment preserved in the Abbey Treasure. Looking at the miniature, we are involuntarily reminded of the solemn presentation of such a relic. In fact the whole scene has been transposed on to a new plane, that of a religious ceremony.

At the same time (as our reproductions show) a remarkable change has come over the colors. Instead of the chalky, pastel tones of the earlier miniature, in which there still are traces of the "atmospheric" picture space of Carolingian painting, the pure, full-bodied colors of the later miniature produce a markedly heraldic effect, due to the alternating blue and green backgrounds and the strong concentration of reds in the central figure. Wholly absent in the earlier work, there now are many passages of gold —in the listels of the frames, in the haloes and on the borders of garments.

The 11th-century illuminator still had at his command a style allowing his brush a certain freedom both in his drawing and in his choice of colors. By the same token, it was a style directly appealing to the spectator's imagination, and this is why the older version of the Ascension of St Amandus retains all the glamour of an old fable or a medieval romance. The 12th-century miniature, on the other hand, with its inscriptions and personifications, appeals less to the imagination than to the intellect. Nor does the painter put his personality into his work to anything like the same degree. What before was sketchlike, unconstrained, has become formalized, governed by set rules. Already in the earlier work the arrangement of the figure groups had given rise to rhythmic repetitions, but now these repetitions wholly dominate the composition; hence the duplication of the angels and the virtues in the interests of symmetry. In fact the whole composition looks as if it derived from some preformulated schema, enacted by the Church, which the illuminator was obliged to follow.

Turning to the individual figures in the two Amandus miniatures, we notice no less striking differences of treatment. Things were easier for the 11th-century illuminator, in so far as he was more or less indifferent to the physical reality of his dramatis personae. The staff on which Amandus rests his somewhat ponderous bulk is no more than a thin black line; the factor of weight was not taken seriously by the artist. And obviously he had no concrete notion of the structure of the form beneath the clothes. Only the tensions produced by the stretching or bending of a human figure interested him; thus the most violent gestures and movements presented no problem, since beneath the drapery there was no solid body to offer any resistance. Hence the strikingly expressionist effects we so often find in Early Romanesque figure painting; effects no less forceful and unconstrained than those we met with in the Early Medieval miniatures.

By contrast, the High Romanesque style of figure painting seems much more sparing in the use of gestures. 12th-century artists aimed primarily at rendering the substantial, tactile qualities of the human figure; nor did they greatly care if, in so doing, they made it look stiff and wooden. In the later of the two miniatures from Saint-Amand the figures are built up along their vertical axes, almost as if they had been hewn in a block of wood or carved out of a treetrunk. Although the rigid garments of St Amandus convey little of the shape of the body beneath, we cannot doubt that the body actually exists, and that trunk and shoulders are organically connected with arms and neck. True, the saint's staff is still no thicker than a penstroke, but it now acts rather as a symbol of his high estate than a support for his body. In his depiction of the angels the artist shows that he is capable on occasion of giving his figures more vivacious attitudes, though their movements are far less spectacular than those of the angel cleaving the clouds like a shaft of lightning, in the earlier miniature. On the contrary, we get an impression that their gestures are euphonious developments of the natural forms of their bodies.

LIFE AND MIRACLES OF ST AMANDUS (I). THE ASCENSION OF ST AMANDUS.
SAINT-AMAND, SECOND HALF OF THE ELEVENTH CENTURY. $(6\frac{5}{8} \times 4\frac{5}{8}'')$
MS 502, FOLIO 119, BIBLIOTHÈQUE MUNICIPALE, VALENCIENNES.

What has been said of individual figures holds good also for their relation with each other. For the 11th-century painter a group is an aggregate of figures in which it matters very little whether, for example, the number of heads exactly tallies with that of bodies. Sometimes we can hardly tell where one figure leaves off and another begins—all the artist aims at is to represent collective movement. As for any individualization of figures, it is virtually non-existent. The High Romanesque painter, on the other hand, is fully conscious of the fact that a group is composed of a given number of people and even though he doubles the number of disciples, it is easy to tell them apart; indeed we have the feeling that we could give each man his name.

Fundamental to the High Romanesque style is a consistent effort to build up form by means of separate compartments or panels, like the pieces of a jigsaw puzzle. Just as the picture surface of the later miniature is divided into panels of the same size, so the drapery of the figures is divided into small separate units. Most of these are given the form of rounded-off triangles, circumscribed by soft "V" folds whose contours are duplicated on occasion. Here and there we find a group of nested "V" folds—a procedure characteristic of the High Romanesque style in general. This predilection for reiterated forms is sometimes carried over into the backgrounds, which may contain a central rectangle of a color different from that of the main ground, with the line of demarcation parallel to the frame around the picture. The earliest instance of this (if the date Illustration page 191 "before 1077" is correct) would seem to be the great "Creator" miniature in the Pommersfelden Bible. Other examples, illustrated here, are found in the Albani Psalter, the Illustrations pages 165, 171, 200, 204 Averbode Gospels, the Carmina Burana and the Bohemian Missal in Stockholm.

In the last analysis the Romanesque painters owed their new awareness of the anatomical structure of the human body to the traditional esthetic of antique art. The Carolingian Renaissance had strongly tinctured Northern miniature painting with the classical sense of form, whose effect at the outset of that movement was prepotent, though before long it was partly neutralized by the Northerners' instinctive urge to movement. In Germany, towards the end of the 10th century, the Master of the Registrum Gregorii had reverted to the plasticity and three-dimensional forms of antique art, thereby preparing the soil for the flowering of Romanesque. But the first fruits of his achievement were threatened with decay before the middle of the 11th century. The years that followed were a critical period in the evolution of the Romanesque style and the Ottonian formulae lost most of their force. Before the century was out, however, the leading artists had renewed contact with the classical tradition of plastic form by way of Byzantine art, and this time the lesson was assimilated under new, more durable conditions. The outworn, hackneyed forms of Carolingian and Ottonian art were gradually replaced by an entirely new repertory of type figures and drapery motifs, and it is these that give Romanesque art the stamp of a new humanism. This brings us to another fundamental difference between the two Saint-Amand miniatures which we have taken as the point of departure for our résumé of the stylistic changes that took place around 1100: whereas the earlier work shows no trace of Byzantine influence, the later would be inconceivable without it.

LIFE AND MIRACLES OF ST AMANDUS (II). THE ASCENSION OF ST AMANDUS. SAINT-AMAND, CA. 1140. (8 15/16 × 5 ¾ ")
MS 501, FOLIO 31, BIBLIOTHÈQUE MUNICIPALE, VALENCIENNES.

ST ILDEFONSUS: DE VIRGINITATE SANCTAE MARIAE.
ST ILDEFONSUS WRITING AND INITIAL D. CLUNY, SECOND HALF OF THE ELEVENTH CENTURY.
(EACH MINIATURE: 7 ¼ × 4 ⅝ ″) MS 1650, FOLIOS 4 VERSO AND 5, BIBLIOTECA PALATINA, PARMA.

It is in the treatment of drapery that the effects of Byzantine influence are most easily discernible. By employing what is known as the "damp fold," the artists of classical antiquity had invented a method of rendering garments in which the drapery carried on, as it were, a continuous dialectic with the body underneath, either adhering to it like wet clothes and thus exactly molding its form, or falling in loose folds having a fluid form of their own. In taking over the "damp fold" technique from antiquity, Byzantine art developed it into a systematic interplay of plastic folds forming well-marked ridges and drapery surfaces clinging closely to the body. The Romanesque illuminators in their turn took over this method of handling drapery, and though at first they tended to exploit its ornamental possibilities at the expense of functional values, it nevertheless taught them something about the organic structure of the human form.

Illustration page 168

From now on, more than in the past, artists are concerned with rendering the plastic values of the joints and bulging muscles of arms and legs, not only when these are naked but also when they are hidden under drapery. In the High Romanesque version of the Ascension of St Amandus, this is especially noticeable in the bodies of the personified Illustration page 187 Virtues, and also in those of the four angels, in the upper portion of the miniature.

Italian miniature painting was influenced by the Byzantine style at the close of the 10th century to begin with, though only sporadically and not always with real understanding; later, however, at Monte Cassino, steps were taken to establish direct contacts with the Byzantine capital. The line of development of Italian miniature painting is in many ways paralleled by that of the Southern French schools, which likewise made use of forms borrowed from Byzantine art at an early date and starting out from these achieved before 1100 the style described as High Romanesque. Unfortunately a detailed study of the evolution of these schools has not yet been published. At Cluny the transition—one is almost tempted to call it a complete *volte-face*—to the new Byzantinizing style is clearly evidenced in the famous Ildefonsus manuscript at Parma (Bibl. Pal., MS 1650) in which a uniform sequence of miniatures and initials closely related to Late Ottonian illumination is abruptly interrupted towards the end of the book by two scenes relating to the sending of the text to France, which reveal the hand of an artist with different aims and of a different caliber. On turning to these two

ST ILDEFONSUS: DE VIRGINITATE SANCTAE MARIAE. ABBOT GOMESANUS PRESENTING THE BOOK TO GODESCALC, ARCHBISHOP OF LE PUY. CLUNY, CA. 1100 (?). (6¾×4¹/₁₆″) MS 1650, FOLIO 102 VERSO, BIBLIOTECA PALATINA, PARMA.

Illustration page 189 miniatures we at once get that impression of plastic solidity which is basic to the High Romanesque style and which the other paintings in the manuscript, with their schematic linearism, still fail to convey. Faces have a new plenitude and dignity, and we are made aware of the density and volume of bodies under the garments. At the same time, notably in the throne and vestments of the bishop and the architecture of the building, purely ornamental motifs are more strongly emphasized. These two pictures could at first sight be taken for additions made at a later date, were it not for the fact that they are enclosed in Late Ottonian frames contemporary with those of the other miniatures in the manuscript. Obviously we have here the same characteristic style of figure painting Illustration page 187 as that of the High Romanesque version of the Ascension of St Amandus—so that this new trend would seem to be essentially of Cluniac origin. It is at Cluny, moreover, that we find this style again, in a somewhat more developed form, in the miniatures of a Lectionary in Paris (Bibl. Nat., Nouv. acq. lat. 2246) and in the Berzé-la-Ville frescos.

The Coblenz Bible at Pommersfelden (Schlossbibl., Cod. 333-334) is another instance of a manuscript in which two different styles of illumination are found side by side. The great majority of the illustrations were the work of an artist who also contributed to a second Bible from Coblenz (Staatsarchiv); his style is Early Romanesque and, to all appearances, owes nothing to Byzantine art. But for the large "Creator" picture at the Illustration page 191 beginning of the first volume another painter was called in, a man who had evidently kept abreast of the higher standards of Byzantine art in the field of figure painting. Quite possibly it was in Italy that he became acquainted with them, since the amply molded type of face, the "paneling" of drapery and the vivid reds and greens were something new in 11th-century miniature painting north of the Alps. Had more contemporary wall paintings come down to us, we should doubtless have been in a better position to trace the stylistic trend evidenced in this extremely impressive miniature. The only thing we can say for sure is that the style of the large effigy of God in the Pommersfelden Bible reappears to fine effect just before the year 1100 in the art of the famous goldsmith Roger of Helmarshausen.

In this Pommersfelden Bible, presented by Canon Hongarus to Coblenz Cathedral, we have the beginnings of a tendency leading up to the manuscripts signed by a Flemish calligrapher of the name of Goderannus. The oldest of these, the Lobbes Bible dated 1085 (Tournai, Grand Séminaire), whose decorations were made, it seems, by Goderannus alone, contains few if any indications that the artist had recourse to Byzantine models. But Illustration page 180 in the two-volume Stavelot Bible dating from the years 1097-1098 (London, Brit. Mus., Add. 28106/07) we find Goderannus working no longer single-handed but in an atelier including other artists, some more gifted than himself. Of one of these—Ernesto—he makes especial mention. K. H. Usener, to whom we owe a penetrating study of this Bible, sees in it the work of no less than three different hands besides that of Goderannus. One of them, known as the "Master of St Luke," is the most familiar with the Byzantine style, and the other two, the "Master of the Pentateuch" and the "Master of the Majestas" (perhaps not really two different artists but one and the same man working to different scales) are, like him, progressive-minded artists. Not only do these miniatures revive

BIBLE OF ST CASTOR'S OF COBLENZ. GOD THE CREATOR. WEST GERMANY, BEFORE 1077 (?). (17 $^{11}/_{16}$ × 13 $^{9}/_{16}$″)
COD. 333, FOLIO 2, GRÄFLICH SCHÖNBORNSCHE BIBLIOTHEK, POMMERSFELDEN.

the tradition of an Ottonian Stavelot miniature deriving from the Master of the Registrum Gregorii, but one of the artists, the Master of the Pentateuch, evidently drew fresh inspiration from some Late Antique model. These two men were the initiators of a stylistic trend which was soon to find its most accomplished exponent in the bronze-founder Renier de Huy, maker of the famous baptismal fonts in the Church of Saint-Barthélemy at Liége.

Whereas, north of the Alps, the lessons of Byzantine or Italo-Byzantine art had apparently been transmitted by a small number of exceptionally enlightened artists, after the turn of the century the influences began to flow in broader streams from east to west and from the south northwards. As Wilhelm Koehler has shown, the Byzantine technique of damp folds was adopted in almost every part of Europe in the course of the first half of the 12th century and did much to further that stylistic uniformity which is characteristic of High Romanesque illumination and in such striking contrast to the great diversity of styles we find in the early Middle Ages.

This Byzantine trend was now amalgamated with the dynamic tendencies inherited from Carolingian art, which had retained much of their potency. Not only in Spain but also in Italy and even in ateliers of the Holy Land, indigenous traditions were subjected to this influence, emanating chiefly from France. A characteristic feature of Western painting in general was that it tended to employ the damp fold as an ornamental device to a greater extent than the Byzantines had ever done and with more emphasis on its linear aspects. It was the English illuminators who went farthest in this direction. The practice of splitting up draperies into marked-off zones was carried to such a pitch that behind the tracery of folds bodies seem imprisoned in a net. And since its meshes are stretched into ovoid, bead-like shapes, a flickering overall vibration is imparted to the line and this purely decorative patterning adds to the dynamic effect of the composition as a whole. We cannot fail to be reminded of the "flamboyant" linework of Celtic fish-bladder ornaments—of the art forms, that is to say, of over a thousand years before, which had not been re-employed by the Irish and Anglo-Saxon illuminators of the pre-Carolingian period. Outstanding examples of this method of treating drapery are provided Illustrations pages 157, 166, 168, 176 by the Psalter of Henry of Blois (London, Brit. Mus., Nero c. IV), the Lambeth Bible and the early illuminators of the Winchester Bible, in particular the painter whom Walter Oakeshott has named the "Master of the Leaping Figures."

Thus once again England makes good its claim to be the chief country giving expression to the Northern feeling for movement and line. And when similar trends appear in Northern French illumination, their origin can practically always be traced to the other side of the Channel. In this context mention may be made of the sumptuous Gospel Book produced at the abbey of Liessies for Abbot Wedricus (1124-1147), which contained two magnificent Evangelist portraits now preserved at Avesnes, the rest of the manuscript—together with many other illuminated books—having perished in the destruction of the Metz library in 1944. It has been plausibly suggested that these are by the hand of the master responsible for some of the finest pages in the Lambeth Bible or by some other English artist.

In the conflict between abstractionism and naturalistic art, the latter steadily gained ground in the course of the 12th century. Forms became progressively more fully modeled, more convex. For a striking example of this new phase of the Romanesque style of miniature painting, we may turn to yet another miniature in the Valenciennes library representing the Ascension of St Amandus; this third version of the theme figures in a "new edition" of the *Vita et Miracula Sancti Amandi* (Bibl. Munic., MS 500), datable Illustration page 194 to ca. 1175. This time we have no difficulty in recognizing the subject since, as regards its content, the composition is an almost exact replica of the previous version dating Illustration page 187 to about 1140. The change that has come over the style is therefore all the more conspicuous. First to catch the eye is the fact that the personified Virtues on each side of the saint are no longer stretched full length along an ascending diagonal, but kneeling in a curiously hunched position, in such a way that only their toes project beyond the circular haloes in the background—they are doing their best in fact to conform to the new ideal of the "plastic sphere." Amandus himself is not only modeled in the round, but his figure is altogether more statuesque, indeed we hardly realize that he is supposed to be moving upwards. How superficial was the artist's interest in his thematic material is also evidenced by his omission of the explanatory verses on the frames. His one concern was for fully plastic sculptural effects and these he achieved by means of contour lines in sweeping curves and bulging folds of drapery. Notable, too, is the new emphasis given the rounded contours of chins, noses and eyes, and, in a general way, the volumes of the heads relieved against their blue and red haloes. Everything in this 12th-century miniature speaks for an emancipation from the constraints of that decorative surface patterning which still characterized the second version of the Ascension of St Amandus. Another factor contributing to this result is that the heraldic patternings of the blue and green backgrounds have now been replaced by a uniform ground of burnished gold whose luminosity floods the entire miniature—a change of technique which by and large is characteristic of this phase of Romanesque art.

The sculpturesque style appears for the first time in its fully developed form in Flemish miniature painting, in the works of the Mosan School, which also distinguished Illustration page 165 itself in the related fields of goldsmiths' and enamel work. These artists took their lead from the style sponsored by such men as Renier de Huy and the Master of the Pentateuch, Illustration page 180 and we may perhaps trace the ultimate source of this art tradition back to the Ottonian Master of the Registrum Gregorii. Hanns Swarzenski is of opinion that the set of Bible illustrations already mentioned, figuring on some loose leaves now in Liége (Wittert Collection), London (Victoria and Albert Museum) and Berlin (Kupferstichkabinett), may have some connection with the Ottonian choir-screen paintings in the church of Saint-Jacques at Liége. There is reliable authority for ascribing these paintings to "Johannes," the Italian court painter to Otto III who ended his days in that city. And if the theory be accepted that this painter and the Master of the Registrum Gregorii were really one and the same man—an hypothesis we tentatively put forward in our previous volume, *Early Medieval Painting*—it would throw new light on the problems confronting the art historian dealing with this period.

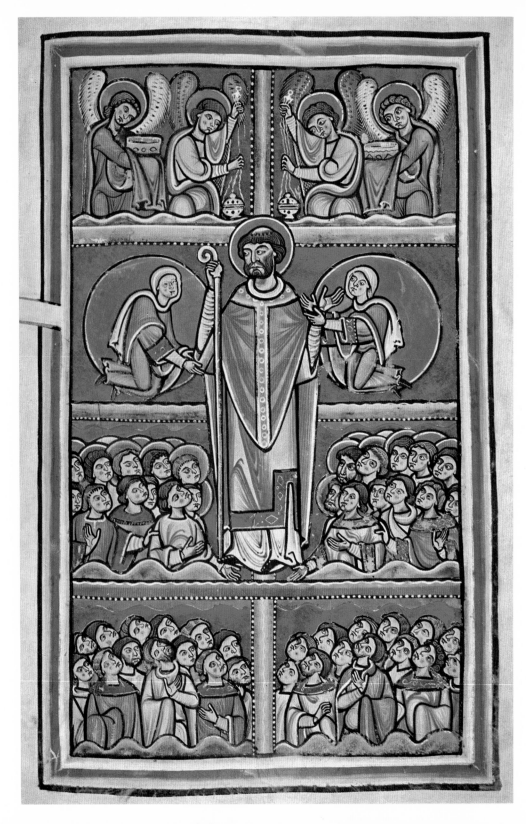

LIFE AND MIRACLES OF ST AMANDUS (III). THE ASCENSION OF ST AMANDUS. SAINT-AMAND, CA. 1175.
(9×5 ¹¹/₁₆″) MS 500, FOLIO 68, BIBLIOTHÈQUE MUNICIPALE, VALENCIENNES.

Be this as it may, the new predilection for fully modeled forms was reflected also in the contemporary statuary of the Ile-de-France, and by the end of the 12th century had affected all the pictorial and plastic arts of France. Its influence is basic to two great groups of illuminated Bibles: the "Burgundian" group centering on the Souvigny Bible and the Northern French group whose key work is the Manerius Bible. In England Illustration page 174 it superseded the "flamboyant" damp fold style, and there, as in Northern France, prepared the way for the naturalistic art of Early Gothic. The youngest of the artists collaborating in the Winchester Bible cultivated a style already lying on the borderline between Romanesque and Early Gothic.

In Italy, as a result of the relative proximity of Byzantium, the Romanesque style not only came to predominate earlier than elsewhere but also lasted longer than in other countries, and long remained impervious to the stylistic currents of Early Gothic. Purely Romanesque forms can still be found in, for example, the latest 13th-century Exultet Rolls of Southern Italy (Salerno, Biblioteca Capitolare) and in the oldest Bolognese Statutes (Bologna, Archivio di Stato, *Statuta Magistrorum lignaminis*), dated 1248. 13th-century miniatures of Sicily, Venice and Padua are painted in a *maniera greca* so pronounced that, were it not for the "western" initials, they might almost be situated, indifferently, in the domain of Byzantine or Italian art. I have in mind, *inter alia*, the magnificent manuscripts associated with the Venetian (?) calligrapher Giovanni da Gaibana, whose masterwork is an epistolary in the Cathedral Treasure of Padua, dated 1259.

The evolution of Late Romanesque miniature painting in Germany followed a more eventful course, for here the introduction of the sculptural style from France and Flanders led to a notable revival of creative activity. The scriptoria of the Rhineland were, it seems, the first to come in contact with the new style of the Mosan School. Miss Rosy Schilling has pointed out that a large Rhenish Bible from Arnstein (London, Brit. Mus., Harl. 2798-99) contains initials exactly reproducing those in the Floreffe Bible (Brit. Mus., Add. 17737-38). The so-called Prayer Book of St Hildegard of Bingen (Munich, Staatsbibl., Clm 935) also betrays western influences. But fresh, more fecund contacts were made with the West during the last decade of the 12th century, as is clearly evidenced by the sumptuous Gospel Book from the cathedral of Spires (Karlsruhe, Landesbibl., Bruchsal 1), commissioned by the—evidently wealthy— "Custos" Conrad von Danne, who seems to have originally intended it for a church in Worms. The master painter of this manuscript makes no secret of the fact that his source of inspiration was Lorrainese art of the type that had found expression in the work of the great goldsmith Nicholas of Verdun.

In Saxony the Gospel Book of Henry the Lion (formerly Gmunden, Collection of the Duke of Cumberland), produced about 1175, conforms in the main to the Romanesque stylistic tradition of the School of Helmarshausen. And even in a later Gospel Book at Trier (Cathedral Treasure, Cod. 142, olim 124, one page of which is now in the Cleveland Museum of Art), there still are miniatures very similar in style. But a younger artist, apparently schooled in the West, also collaborated on this manuscript and in the pictures by his hand we perceive a sudden break with ornamental surface patterning and a tendency to model figures and draperies in the round. Other North German artists aligned themselves to this trend in the early decades of the 13th century.

Much the same thing took place at Salzburg where, after the series of masterpieces in the pure Romanesque style, a new departure was made under Western influence in the beautiful Prayer Book of St Erentrude (Munich, Staatsbibl., Clm. 15 902), which dates to the last decade of the 12th century. With this manuscript, however, we come to the end of the golden age of the Salzburg School.

Illustration page 197

The sculptural style reached its apogee in German miniature painting after the turn of the century, in the remarkable manuscripts executed at Weingarten under Abbot Berthold (1200-1232): a Missal in a sumptuous binding (New York, Morgan Library, M. 710), part of a Bible, with the major and minor Prophets (now divided between Leningrad, Public Library, F. V. I. 133) and New York, Public Library, Spencer 1) and—all that has remained in Germany—a double page added to an 11th-century Gospel Book in Stuttgart (Landesbibl., H. B. II. 46). After the Ottonian Master of the Registrum Gregorii, German miniature painting had produced no other artist with a personality so distinctive as that of the creator of these works. The hallmark of his art is not only strongly plastic form, but also a vehement will to expression; in his way he almost might rank as a precursor of Claus Sluter and Michelangelo, whose majestic Prophets have more than a merely thematic affinity to those of this remarkable artist. The massive bodies of his figures seem charged with vibrant energy in every sinew; it is as if that passionate urge to movement which had given the Reichenau miniatures their well-nigh hypnotic instancy, had made its reappearance, two centuries later, in the world

Illustration page 197

of German art. Confronted by this master's interpretation of the Pentecost, the modern beholder might almost imagine he was in the engine-room of a power house, with the stalwart figures of the Apostles and the personified Rivers of Paradise in the corners playing the part of human turbines generating a high-tension current, whose vibrations can be sensed even in the tensely coiled foliage spirals of the initials.

Although this practice of painting "in the round" signified, up to a point, a release from the tutelage of Byzantium and a Declaration of Independence on the part of western art, it by no means follows that the West wholly lost contact with Byzantine art. On the contrary, thanks to their new and keener sense of three-dimensional form, western artists could now approach Byzantine models with a fuller understanding of their purport. Significantly enough we find biblical scenes in manuscripts conforming more strictly than ever to Byzantine iconography, and not only in the Latin schools of the Mediterranean lands but even north of the Alps, works were now produced giving the impression of being faithful paraphrases of Byzantine prototypes. The *Hortus Deliciarum* of Herrad of Landsberg is a case in point, and in German miniature painting of the 13th century we even find the slavish imitation of Byzantine models carried to the point of affectation. A sketchbook preserved in Brunswick illustrates the way in which the German painters anthologized these Byzantine motifs, which they then incorporated —as a writer might use quotations—in such manuscripts as the Gospels preserved in the

BERTHOLD MISSAL. THE PENTECOST. WEINGARTEN, EARLY THIRTEENTH CENTURY. $(8\frac{5}{8} \times 6\frac{1}{4}'')$
M. 710, FOLIO 64 VERSO, COURTESY THE PIERPONT MORGAN LIBRARY, NEW YORK.

Town Hall of Goslar and other works of the Saxonian school around 1250. That the style of the strongly Byzantinizing Gaibana miniatures (cf. p. 195) should have gained a foothold in Austria, too (e.g. the Seitenstetten Missal, New York, Morgan Library, M. 855), is easily accounted for when we remember how resolutely German illuminators of the end of the Romanesque period aligned their work to the Byzantine style.

Whichever way we turn, towards Germany, Italy, France or England, we find that all that is new and promising in the development of miniature painting after the end of the 12th century, derives from the artists' heightened powers of visualizing and rendering three-dimensional space. Hence, too, the increased vitality, the new aliveness of figures which, far more than ever before, look like creatures of flesh and blood. By way of the sculptural style they are now becoming emancipated from the limitations of the conception of space as a flat surface, existing solely on the picture plane. By the same token and to an extent hitherto unparalleled, drapery acquires a new freedom from the body underneath. Comparing yet again the last two versions of the Ascension of St Amandus (pp. 187 and 194), we cannot fail to see that in the later version the large, loose sleeves have real openings and that now the saint's broad, bell-shaped mantle falls in natural, graceful folds from his shoulders and the hems of his long white undergarment ripple fluently around his feet. Here drapery is treated as the cloth it really is, not as a mere pattern of folds. In the work of Nicholas of Verdun the process is carried a stage further, folds being rendered in fluent undulations of a silken softness. In France, from about 1200 on, this method of treating drapery had come to prevail even in large-scale statuary, and it also characterizes the Early Gothic miniatures of, for instance, the Ingeborg Psalter at Chantilly.

The same stylistic phase is illustrated in Germany by the Gospel Book of Great St Martin's church in Cologne (Brussels, Bibl. Roy., MS 466/9222). The other German schools, however, failed to follow the lead of Cologne. Unable to accept the new freedom in the rendering of drapery as a natural development whose desirability was self-evident, they obstinately persisted in the use of the schematized linear folds of Romanesque art. The result was the so-called "angular" or "jagged" style, which might be generically defined as a fusion of Byzantine and the new Early Gothic methods of rendering drapery, the former determining the linear details of garments, the latter their free plastic struc-

Illustration page 169

ture. Traceable from about 1215 in the Thuringian-Saxon school of painting, this style spread throughout Germany in the course of the following decade. The essence of the "jagged" style was a strangely agitated handling of drapery, which looks as if it had been first starched and then deliberately crumpled, a mannerism we meet with again in German sculpture of the 15th and 16th centuries, and an instance of that innate compulsion which periodically leads German art to treat form as a vortex of clashing lines and, thereby, as a means of emotional expression.

Thus Romanesque book illumination in Germany ended in a style which perpetuated that antinomy between the plastic and the ornamental which French Gothic had already resolved. To the last this tension between functional and formal elements remained a distinctive feature of the Romanesque style. The Romanesque painter, like all the

THE LETTERS OF ST GREGORY. PORTRAIT OF ST GREGORY AND HIS CORRESPONDENTS. ST MARTIN'S ABBEY, TOURNAI, MID-TWELFTH CENTURY. (14 5/16 × 9 3/4") MS LAT. 2288, FOLIO I, BIBLIOTHÈQUE NATIONALE, PARIS.

CARMINA BURANA. SUMMER LANDSCAPE. BAVARIA, EARLY THIRTEENTH CENTURY. (7×4⅞″)
CLM. 4660, FOLIO 64 VERSO, STAATSBIBLIOTHEK, MUNICH.

artists of the period, found a peculiar satisfaction in confining organic forms in the strait jacket of a strictly geometric and ornamental style—a strait jacket, however, that was never felt as such, but rather as a means of stripping the everyday world of all that is fugitive and perishable. This characteristic is particularly apparent in the stone carving of Romanesque churches, where it frequently leads to a happy combination of figural and architectonic forms. Similar tendencies are occasionally to be found in monumental painting, when directly associated with soffits, engaged columns and other architectural elements. The manuscript page, however, did not lend itself so easily to effects of this kind. Yet even so we can see how ingeniously the illuminators adopted figurative scenes and decorative motifs to the structural forms of initials and ornamental frames. But whether free or cramped, Romanesque figures always give more or less the impression of being subjected to a process of "hardening" which assimilates their natural forms to those of ornaments.

This impression gains strength when we find the ornamentalizing treatment of forms reinforced by representations of such purely decorative motifs as the adornments of costumes or furniture. Romanesque illuminators show a marked predilection for enriching the human figure and its surroundings in this way. These ornaments make their effect all the more strongly since they are less subjected than the forms that they embellish to the reduction of scale which is an inevitable result of the "miniature" dimensions of the picture, so that, as to their proportions, the ornaments seem out of scale with the figures or buildings supporting them and there is often something hard and metallic about the borders glittering with gems superimposed on garments to which they seem to be clamped. Another noteworthy point is that the ornamental motifs, whether woven in the material, embroidered or appliquéd, adapt themselves uneasily to folds and creases of the garments; often they seem to hover on the surface of the picture, as though intended to enrich the vellum page itself rather than the costumes of the figures. A *non plus ultra* of ornamental stylization, not merely of the costume but of the figure itself, is to be found in the portrait of Gregory the Great in a Tournai Illustration page 199 manuscript (Paris, Bibl. Nat., lat. 2288), which in its turn is based on one of St Augustine in a manuscript from Marchiennes (Douai, Bibl. Munic., MS 250); it is almost as if the pope were clad in a coat of mail composed of ornamental forms.

Nature herself was treated in much the same way. We have a veritable compendium of the stylized renderings of trees in the well-known landscape contained in the Munich *Carmina Burana* (Staatsbibl., Clm. 4660), which, as the text informs us, shows Nature Illustration page 200 in her summer finery:

> *Diu werlt fröut sich über all gegen sumerzîte*
> *aller slahte vogel schal horet man nu wîte...*
>
> (The world rejoices everywhere when summer is icumin in,
> All manner birdsong now is heard afield...)

The poet, we feel, is voicing a firsthand experience of nature, but the illuminator was unable to interpret the poet's vision in anything but unrealistic, ornamental forms and his trees might easily pass for the vine-tendrils of a Romanesque initial.

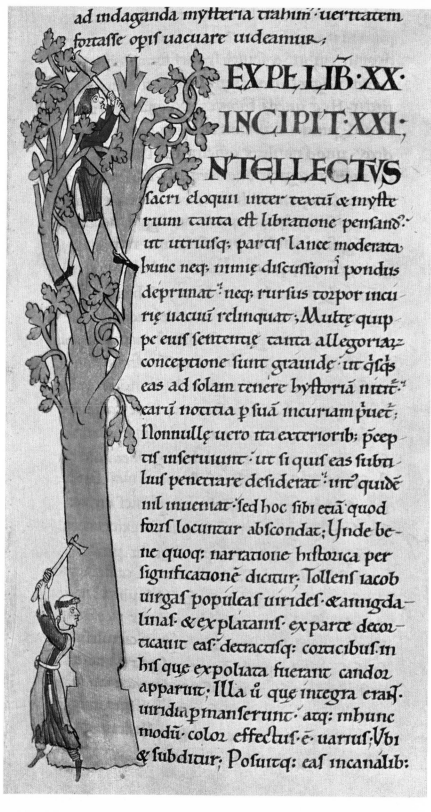

ad indaganda mysteria trahim' uertatem fortasse opis uacuare uideamur;

EXP̄ LIB·XX·
INCIPIT·XXI·
NTELLECTVS

sacri eloquii inter textū & myste rium tanta est libratione pensand'. ut utriusq; partis lance moderata hunc neq; nimiẹ discussioni pondus deprimat'. neq; rursus torpor incu riẹ uacuū relinquat; Multẹ quip pe eius sententiẹ tanta allegoriarꝝ conceptione sunt grauidẹ ut qscꝫ eas ad solam tenere hystoriā niteꝛ earū notitia p suā incuriam puet; Nonnullẹ uero ita exterioribꝫ ꝓcep tis inseruiunt· ut si quis eas subti lius penetrare desiderat'. int' quidẹ nil inueniat· sed hoc sibi etā quod foris locuntur abscondat; Unde be ne quoqꝫ narratione histoꝛica per significatione dicitur; Tollens iacob uirgas populeas uirides· & amigda linas· & ex platanis· ex parte decor ticauit eas detractisꝫ corticibus in his quẹ expoliata fuerant candor apparuit; Illa ū quẹ integra eraſ uiridiaꝑmanserunt· atꝗ; inhunc modū color effectus·ē· uaꝛius;Vbi & subditur; Posuitꝗ; eas incanalib:

ST GREGORY'S MORALIA IN JOB. MONK AND LAYMAN FELLING A TREE. CÎTEAUX, IIII. (8⅝×2⅜″)
MS 173, FOLIO 41, BIBLIOTHÈQUE MUNICIPALE, DIJON.

A connoisseur of oriental art, Kurt Erdmann, has drawn attention to the fact that exactly similar types of trees can be found in Sassanian works of art dating some nine centuries earlier. Needless to say, there was no direct borrowing on the Romanesque painter's part; we can only surmise that both derived from a common source—that is to say from the vast repository of art forms which, since Hellenistic times, had accumulated in the Mediterranean basin.

But there are also exceptions, all the more interesting for their rarity. At Cîteaux during the abbacy of Stephen Harding—almost a hundred years, that is, before the summer landscape in Munich—a painter decorated a four-volume edition of the *Moralia in Job* (Dijon, Bibl. Munic., MSS 168-170, 173) with figural initials whose themes Illustrations pages 202-203 were culled directly from the daily life of the monks and their environment. One initial shows a monk and a lay brother engaged in felling a tall tree whose trunk forms the letter "I". Here, in contrast to the schematic shrubs of the *Carmina Burana*, we have a real tree of almost normal stature, and in some other historiated initials of this Cistercian manuscript we find genre scenes of a no less realistic order. It is possible that the illuminator drew inspiration from Anglo-Saxon calendar pictures of about the year 1000, which in turn may go back to Late Antique prototypes. Yet, even if this view be accepted, it fails to account entirely for the precocious naturalism which here is so arresting. Whether consciously or unconsciously, the illuminator put his personal gifts of observation to the service of art with a boldness unusual in his day. It is certainly not due to chance that this remarkable picture should figure in a manuscript

ST GREGORY'S MORALIA IN JOB. MONKS CHOPPING WOOD.
CÎTEAUX, IIII. (2½×3½")
MS 170, FOLIO 19, BIBLIOTHÈQUE MUNICIPALE, DIJON.

MISSAL. ST GREGORY AND A GROUP OF BOHEMIAN NOTABLES; BELOW, MONASTIC SCRIBE AND LAY
PAINTERS HILDEBERT AND EVERWINUS. BOHEMIA, MID-TWELFTH CENTURY. (11 ⅛ × 8")
COD. A. 144, FOLIO 34, KUNGLIGA BIBLIOTHEKET, STOCKHOLM.

produced by the newly founded Burgundian monastery which then stood at the head of the reform movement; for one of the main points of the Cistercian program was the exploitation of natural resources by cultivation, clearing and tilling of the land.

Generally speaking, the realistic depiction of the tree in the Dijon *Moralia in Job*, no less than the decorative woodland in the Munich *Carmina Burana*, exemplifies a basic tendency of Romanesque art: its new worldly-mindedness. The trend towards realism makes itself also felt in the portraits of authors and scribes, with their often detailed and observant rendering of tools and furniture. Of special interest in this context is the drawing contained in a late 11th-century manuscript (Bergues, Bibl. Comm., MS 19) showing a scribe in his workshop. The furnishings of the room—shelves, tables and miscellaneous objects—are rendered with an unusual wealth of detail whose motifs, if not the forms, bring to mind the Master of Flémalle. The Romanesque illuminators were also the first to illustrate the various stages in the production of a manuscript, from the preparation of the vellum to the binding of the finished pages (Bamberg, Staatsbibl., Patr. 5 and Copenhagen, Gl. Kgl. Saml. 4, 2°).

Even the stock religious themes of Romanesque illumination were revitalized by direct contacts with real life; and in particular with the Mystery plays which now became one of the Church's means of appealing to the people. The explication of scenic action by means of realistic details is basic to the art of the theater and many such details in Romanesque miniatures were taken over from the Mysteries—much as the initial-painters' repertory of forms, as we have seen, was partly borrowed from the circus.

Also symptomatic of these new tendencies is the fact that now, more than before, artists personally claimed credit for their work. The richly illuminated manuscripts of the early Middle Ages had sometimes contained portraits of their donors or recipients, and it was only in company with these high dignitaries that scribes and illuminators occasionally figured on dedication pages. Even so great a man as the Master of the Registrum Gregorii failed to bequeath either his name or his portrait to posterity. In the Romanesque period, however, artists' portraits begin to appear more frequently in manuscripts. For the most part illuminators and calligraphers are represented humbly kneeling in the margin of a miniature or half hidden by the foliage of an initial. But they seldom forget to record their names. In a manuscript at Oxford (Bodleian Library, Bodl. 717), the work of a Norman named Hugo, the artist portrays himself at his writing-desk in the margin of the last page of text, where he explicitly describes himself as *pictor et illuminator*—"*pictor*" being probably intended to suggest his proficiency not only in illumination but in monumental painting too.

Still more realistic are the likenesses of an illuminator named Hildebert and his apprentice Everwinus, both of whom figure in a Bohemian Missal in Stockholm (Royal Illustration page 204 Library, A. 144) and in a *Civitas Dei* manuscript in Prague (Metropolitan Libr., A XXI/i). In the Stockholm Missal we see, in the lower margin of the miniature, two lay artists working on a scroll; on the left is seated a monk with a pen, the scribe with whom they are co-operating. The master painter is holding a brush and an inkwell, while his young assistant is running up with two pots of paint. Their portraits in the

Augustine manuscript are even more boldly conceived. Hildebert is seated at a desk whose foot is carved in the shape of a lion. At a lower level we see the apprentice trying his hand at sketching a rinceau. A meal stands ready on the table where, however, an uninvited guest has appeared—a mouse. In trying to pilfer a scrap of bread, it has upset a plateful of roast chicken which is falling to the floor. *"Pessime mus*—wretched mouse," we read in the open book in front of the master painter, "why are you always disturbing our work?" Here we have perhaps a faithful picture of what may well have been a fairly common incident of daily life in the scriptorium of a Romanesque monastery.

These scenes, like artists' portraits in general, properly fall into the class of marginalia, which, in the Romanesque period, comprised a range of subject matter that could scarcely be allowed to figure prominently. In the portrait of the English scribe Eadwine, however, at the end of the second copy of the Utrecht Psalter (Cambridge, Trinity College Library, MS R. 17.1), we have the likeness of a monastic craftsman which not only occupies a full page—a privilege normally reserved to saints alone— but even exceeds the normal size of saints' portraits in illuminated manuscripts. The truly monumental dimensions of this picture are all the more surprising since it comes immediately after the sequence of Psalter illustrations whose figures are scaled down to "miniature" size. The text in the border befits the large dimensions of the portrait:

Scriptor scriptorum princeps ego non obitura deinceps
Laus mea nec fama quis sim mea littera clama.

(Scribe, nay, Prince of Scribes, am I. Neither my praises nor my fame shall ever die. Let the letters traced by my pen declare the man I am.)

Though written by an obscure 12th-century monk, these lines ring with the proud assurance of some great master of the Italian Renaissance, rejoicing in his powers, and to whose thinking no words, however elogious, could overstate his merits.

Like the pure landscape in the *Carmina Burana* and the realistic genre scenes of the *Moralia in Job* from Cîteaux, this picture too must be regarded as a special case in Romanesque illumination. But exceptions of this kind are none the less instructive. True, there can be no question that book illumination in the Romanesque period was a religious art, sponsored by the Church, and that the Church was sustained by a faith whose roots lay neither in mundane reality nor in the human situation. Nevertheless the 12th and 13th centuries were the period in which Western Man entered, if timidly at first, on a new way of life which in the course of the succeeding centuries was to enrich and fructify the cultural heritage of mankind. And this, perhaps, is not the least of the lessons to be gleaned from an attentive study of Romanesque illumination.

APPENDIX

BIBLIOGRAPHY

INDEX OF MANUSCRIPTS

INDEX OF NAMES AND PLACES

LIST OF COLORPLATES

CONTENTS

APPENDIX

In the chapter dealing with Spanish wall painting (pp. 67-85) we mentioned, firstly, the marked affinities between a fresco in Piedmont (Fig. 1) and another in Catalonia (Fig. 2); and, secondly, we compared the type form of a face in a Mozarabic miniature (Fig. 3) with that in a Spanish fresco (Fig. 4), a schema which reappears under a more developed form in Figs. 1 and 2. Reproductions of all four works are given below.

FIG. 1. HEAD OF CHRIST. ELEVENTH CENTURY (?). FRAGMENT OF A FRESCO FROM THE MONASTERY OF SANT'ILARIO (DESTROYED). VILLA ROGGIERY, REVELLO (PIEDMONT).

FIG. 2. CHRIST PANTOCRATOR. 1123. DETAIL OF THE APSE FRESCO FROM SAN CLEMENTE DE TAHULL. MUSEUM OF CATALAN ART, BARCELONA.

FIG. 3. BIBLIA HISPALENSE. THE PROPHET NAHUM. DETAIL. MOZARABIC MINIATURE, 988. MS Vª 14-1, FOLIO 163, BIBLIOTECA NACIONAL, MADRID.

FIG. 4. CHRIST PANTOCRATOR. TWELFTH CENTURY. DETAIL OF THE APSE FRESCO FROM THE CHURCH OF ESTERRI DE CARDOS. MUSEUM OF CATALAN ART, BARCELONA.

BIBLIOGRAPHY

The following bibliography does not include works dealing with both the Early Medieval and the Romanesque periods which were listed in the bibliography of our previous volume, *Early Medieval Painting*, Geneva 1957.

MURAL PAINTING

GENERAL

J. VON SCHLOSSER, *Quellenbuch zur Kunstgeschichte des abendländischen Mittelalters*, Vienna 1896.

E. W. ANTHONY, *Romanesque Frescoes*, Princeton 1951.

ITALY

GENERAL

A. VENTURI, *Storia dell'arte italiana* III, Milan 1904.

E. BERTAUX, *L'art dans l'Italie méridionale*, Paris 1904.

J. WILPERT, *Die römischen Mosaiken und Malereien der kirchlichen Bauten vom 4. bis 13. Jahrhundert*, 4 vols., Freiburg-im-Breisgau 1916.

R. VAN MARLE, *The Development of the Italian Schools of Painting* I, The Hague 1923 et seq.

G. VITZTHUM and W. F. VOLBACH, *Die Malerei und Plastik des Mittelalters in Italien*, Potsdam 1924.

P. TOESCA, *Storia dell'arte italiana*, I. *Il Medioevo*, Turin 1927.

P. MURATOFF, *La Peinture Byzantine*, Paris 1928.

G. LADNER, *Die italienische Malerei im 11. Jahrhundert*, in *Jahrbuch der kunsthistorischen Sammlungen in Wien*, N.F., V, 1931, pp. 33-160.

E. B. GARRISON, *Italian Romanesque Panel Painting*, Florence 1949.

R. OERTEL, *Die Frühzeit der italienischen Malerei*, Stuttgart 1953.

SPECIAL PROBLEMS

C. R. MOREY, *Lost Mosaics and Frescos of Rome of the Mediaeval Period*, Princeton 1915.

R. VAN MARLE, *La peinture romane au moyen âge*, Strasbourg 1921.

F. HERMANIN, *L'arte in Roma dal secolo VIII al XIV*, Bologna 1945.

A. MUÑOZ, *Il restauro della chiesa e del chiostro dei SS. Quattro Coronati*, Rome 1914.

F. HERMANIN, *I monasteri di Subiaco* I, Rome 1904.

P. TOESCA, *Gli affreschi della cattedrale di Anagni*, in *Le Gallerie Nazionali Italiane* V, Rome 1902.

F. X. KRAUS, *Die Wandgemälde von S. Angelo in Formis*, in *Jahrbuch der preussischen Kunstsammlungen*, Berlin 1893, p. 3 ff. and p. 84 ff.

Ottavio MORISANI, *Bisanzio e la pittura cassinese*, Palermo 1955.

N. GABRIELLI, *Le pitture romaniche* (Repertorio delle cose d'arte del Piemonte), Turin 1944.

P. TOESCA, *La pittura e la miniatura nella Lombardia*, Milan 1912.

G. ANSALDI, *Gli affreschi della basilica di S. Vincenzo a Galliano*, Milan 1949.

Gianpiero BOGNETTI and Carlo MARCORA, *L'abbazia benedettina di Civate*, Civate 1957.

E. ARSLAN, *La pittura e la scultura veronese dal secolo VIII al secolo XIII*, Milan 1943.

A. MORASSI, *Storia della pittura nella Venezia Tridentina*, Rome 1934.

La basilica di Aquileia (articles by various hands), Bologna 1933.

SPAIN

GENERAL

C. R. POST, *A History of Spanish Painting* I, Cambridge, Mass. 1930.

Walter W. S. COOK and José GUDIOL RICART, *Pintura mural*, in *Ars Hispaniae* VI, Madrid 1950.

J. LASSAIGNE, *Spanish Painting, From the Catalan Frescos to El Greco*, Geneva 1952, pp. 11-30.

CATALAN PAINTING

J. PIJOAN, *Les pintures murals catalanes* 1-5, Barcelona n.d.

J. FOLCH Y TORRES, *Museo de la Ciudadela, Catálogo de la sección de arte románico*, Barcelona 1926.

Walter W. S. COOK, *The Earliest Painted Panels of Catalonia*, in *The Art Bulletin*, vol. V, No. 4; vol. VI, No. 2; vol. VIII, Nos. 2 and 4; vol. X, Nos. 2 and 4, 1922-1928.

J. GUDIOL Y CUNILL, *La pintura migeval catalana* (Els Primitius), Barcelona 1927-1929.

C. L. KUHN, *Romanesque Mural Painting of Catalonia*, Cambridge, Mass. 1930.

SPECIAL PROBLEMS

M. GOMEZ-MORENO, *Catálogo monumental de León*, Madrid 1925.

Walter W. S. COOK, *Romanesque Spanish Mural Painting, San Baudelio de Berlanga*, in *The Art Bulletin*, vol. XII, No. 1, 1930.

J. ANTONIO GAYA NUÑO, *La pintura románica en Castilla*, Madrid 1954.

FRANCE

GENERAL

GÉLIS-DIDOT and LAFFILÉE, *La peinture décorative en France*, Paris 1889.

H. LAFFILÉE, *La peinture murale en France avant la Renaissance*, Paris 1893.

Emile MÂLE, in André Michel, *Histoire de l'art* 1, 2. Paris 1905, pp. 756-781.

H. FOCILLON, *Peintures romanes des églises de France*, Paris 1938.

C. P. DUPRAT, *Enquête sur la peinture murale en France à l'époque romane*, in *Bulletin monumental* CI, 1943, pp. 165-223, and CII, 1944, pp. 5-90 and 161-223.

P. DESCHAMPS and Marc THIBOUT, *La peinture murale en France. Le haut moyen âge et l'époque romane*, Paris 1951.

SPECIAL PROBLEMS

L. BRÉHIER, *Peintures romanes d'Auvergne*, in *Gazette des Beaux-Arts*, XVI, 1927, pp. 121-140.

R. Crozet, *L'art roman en Berry*, Paris 1932, pp. 332-367.

Elisa Maillard, *L'église de Saint-Savin sur Gartempe*, Paris 1926.

Itsujé Yoshikawa, *L'Apocalypse de Saint-Savin*, Paris 1939.

G. Gaillard, *Les fresques de Saint-Savin* I, Paris 1944.

A. Humbert, *Les fresques romanes de Brinay*, in *Gazette des Beaux-Arts* XI, 1914, pp. 217-234.

J. Hubert, *Vic*, in *Congrès archéologiques* 1931.

M. Weber, *The Frescoes of Tavant*, in *Art Studies* III, 1925, pp. 83-92.

P. H. Michel, *Les fresques de Tavant*, Paris 1944.

F. Mercier, *Les Primitifs français, La Peinture clunisienne*, Paris 1931.

F. Mercier, *Berzé-la-Ville*, in *Congrès Archéologiques* XCVIII, 1935, pp. 485-502.

M. Varille and Dʳ Loiron, *L'abbaye de Saint-Chef en Dauphiné*, Lyon 1929.

L. Giron, *Les peintures murales du département de la Haute-Loire*, Paris 1911.

BELGIUM

P. Rolland, *La fresque tournaisienne*, Brussels 1948.

ENGLAND

C. E. Keyser, *A List of Buildings in Great Britain and Ireland having Mural and other Painted Decorations*, London 1883.

E. W. Tristram, *English Medieval Wall Painting* I. *The Twelfth Century*. II. *The Thirteenth Century*, 2 vols., Oxford 1944 and 1950.

M. Rickert, *Painting in Britain: The Middle Ages*, London 1954.

Clive Bell, *Twelfth Century Paintings at Hardham and Clayton*, with photographs by Helmut Gernsheim, Lewes, Sussex, 1947.

GERMANY AND AUSTRIA

R. Borrmann, *Aufnahmen mittelalterlicher Wand- und Deckenmalereien in Deutschland*, Berlin 1897 et seq.

SPECIAL PROBLEMS

P. Clemen, *Die romanische Monumentalmalerei in den Rheinländern*, Düsseldorf 1916.

H. Schmitz, *Die mittelalterliche Malerei in Soest*, Münster 1906.

A. Verbeek, *Schwarzrheindorf*, Düsseldorf 1953.

H. Karlinger, *Die hochromanische Wandmalerei in Regensburg*, Munich, Berlin, Leipzig 1920.

J. Garber, *Die romanischen Wandgemälde Tirols*, Vienna 1928.

P. Buberl, *Die romanischen Malereien im Kloster Nonnberg*, in *Kunstgeschichtliches Jahrbuch der k.k. Zentralkommission* III, 1909, pp. 25-46.

SWITZERLAND

GENERAL

K. Escher, *Untersuchungen zur Geschichte der Wand- und Deckenmalerei in der Schweiz*, Strasbourg 1906.

J. Gantner, *Histoire de l'art suisse*, Neuchâtel 1941, pp. 305-325.

SPECIAL PROBLEMS

J. Zemp and R. Durrer, *Le couvent de St. Jean à Münster*, Geneva 1906-1911.

J. R. Rahn, *Die Mittelalterlichen Wandgemälde in der italienischen Schweiz*, in *Mitteil. der antiquar. Gesellschaft in Zürich* XXI, 1881.

SWEDEN AND DENMARK

P. Norland and E. Lind, *Denmarks romanske Kalkmalerier*, Copenhagen 1944.

Andreas Lindlom, *Sveriges Konsthistoria* I, Stockholm 1944.

A. Borelius, *Romanesque Mural Painting in Östergötland*, Norrköping 1956.

BOOK ILLUMINATION

I. GENERAL WORKS

J. Baltrušaitis, *La stylistique ornementale dans la sculpture romane*, Paris 1931.

A. Haseloff, *Les miniatures*, in A. Michel, *Histoire de l'art* II: 1, Paris 1906, pp. 297-341 et 359-367.

W. Koehler, *Byzantine Art in the West* (Dumbarton Oaks Papers I, 1941, pp. 63-87).

K. Löffler, *Romanische Zierbuchstaben*, Stuttgart 1927.

J. Prochno, *Das Schreiber- und Dedikationsbild (Die Entwicklung des menschlichen Bildnisses*, edited by W. Goetz, vol. II), Leipzig 1929.

Meyer Schapiro, *On the Aesthetic Attitude in Romanesque Art (Art and Thought*, Febr. 1948, pp. 154-164).

R. W. Southern, *The Making of the Middle Ages*, London 1953.

S. H. Steinberg, *Die Bildnisse geistlicher und weltlicher Fürsten und Herren (Die Entwicklung des menschlichen Bildnisses*, vol. III), Leipzig 1931.

H. Swarzenski, *Monuments of Romanesque Art*, London 1954.

A. Watson, *The Early Iconography of the Tree of Jesse*, Oxford-London 1934.

II. STUDIES OF PARTICULAR SCHOOLS
AND THE MANUSCRIPTS PRODUCED BY THEM

CENTRAL EUROPE
(BOHEMIA, GERMANY, SWITZERLAND, AUSTRIA)

Ars Sacra, Kunst des frühen Mittelalters (Cat. A. Boeckler), Munich 1950.

S. Beissel, *Ein Missale aus Hildesheim und die Anfänge der Armenbibel* (Zeitschrift für christliche Kunst XV, 1902, p. 272 ff.).

A. Boeckler, *Das Stuttgarter Passionale*, Augsburg 1923.

A. Boeckler, *Die Regensburger-Prüfeninger Buchmalerei des 12. und 13. Jahrhunderts* (Miniaturen aus Handschriften der Bayerischen Staatsbibliothek VIII), Munich 1924.

A. Boeckler, *Beiträge zur romanischen Kölner Buchmalerei* (Mittelalterliche Handschriften. Festgabe zum 60. Geburtstag von Hermann Degering, Leipzig 1926, pp. 15-28).

A. Boeckler, *Corveyer Buchmalerei unter Einwirkung Wibalds von Stablo* (Westfälische Studien, Aloys Bömer zum 60. Geburtstage gewidmet, Leipzig 1928, pp. 133-147).

A. Boeckler, *Zur böhmischen Buchkunst des 12. Jahrhunderts* (Konsthistorisk tidskrift XXII, 1953, pp. 61-74).

P. Buberl, *Die Buchmalerei des 12. und 13. Jahrhunderts in Österreich* (Die bildende Kunst in Österreich II, Vienna 1937, p. 145 ff.).

O. Doering and G. Voss, *Meisterwerke der Kunst in Sachsen und Thüringen* (chapter on miniature painting by A. Haseloff), Magdeburg 1905.

R. Durrer, *Die Maler- und Schreibschule von Engelberg* (Anzeiger für Schweizerische Altertumskunde N.F. III, 1901, pp. 42-55, 122-178).

K. Erdmann, *Bemerkungen zu einer Miniatur der Carmina Burana* (Beiträge zur Kunst des Mittelalters, Berlin 1950, pp. 150-156).

A. Friedl, *Hildebert a Everwin*, Romansti Maliri, Prague 1927.

A. Friedl, *Kodex Gigas*, Prague 1929.

A. Goldschmidt, *Das Evangeliar im Rathause zu Goslar*, Berlin 1910.

A. Goldschmidt, *A German Psalter of the 12th Century written in Helmarshausen* (Journal of the Walters Art Gallery I, 1938, pp. 18-23).

H. R. Hahnloser and F. Ruecker, *Das Musterbuch von Wolfenbüttel* (Wiener Gesellschaft für vervielfältigende Kunst), Vienna 1929.

M. Harrsen, *Central European Manuscripts in the Pierpont Morgan Library*, New York 1958.

A. Haseloff, *Eine thüringisch-sächsische Malerschule des 13. Jahrhunderts* (Studien zur deutschen Kunstgeschichte IX), Strasbourg 1897.

F. Jansen, *Die Helmarshausener Buchmalerei zur Zeit Heinrichs des Löwen*, Hildesheim 1933.

F. Lehner, *Česká Skola Malirská XI. veku: I. Korunovačni Evangelistár Vratislava Krále, rečeny Kodex Vyšehradský*, Prague 1902.

K. Löffler, *Der Landgrafenpsalter*, Leipzig 1925.

K. Löffler, *Schwäbische Buchmalerei in romanischer Zeit*, Augsburg 1928.

E. Lutze, *Studien zur fränkischen Buchmalerei im 12. und 13. Jahrhundert*, Giessen 1931.

K. Preisendanz and O. Homburger, *Das Evangelistar des Speyerer Domes*, Leipzig 1930.

R. Schilling, *Studien zur deutschen Goldschmiedekunst des 12. und 13. Jahrhunderts* (Form und Inhalt, Kunstgeschichtl. Studien Otto Schmitt zum 60. Geburtstag), Stuttgart 1950, pp. 73-88, on the Arnstein Bible.

G. Swarzenski, *Aus dem Kunstkreis Heinrichs des Löwen* (Städeljahrbuch VII-VIII, 1932, pp. 241-397).

H. Swarzenski, *Die lateinischen illuminierten Handschriften des 13. Jahrhunderts in den Ländern am Rhein, Main und Donau*, vols. I-II, Berlin 1936.

H. Swarzenski, *The Berthold Missal—the Pierpont Morgan Library M.710—and the Scriptorium of Weingarten Abbey*, New York 1943.

E. Winkler, *Die Buchmalerei in Niederösterreich von 1150-1250* (Artes Austriae II), Vienna 1923.

ENGLAND

T. S. R. Boase, *English Romanesque Illumination* (Bodleian Picture Books), Oxford 1951.

T. S. R. Boase, *English Art 1100-1218*, Oxford 1953.

C. R. Dodwell, *The Canterbury School of Illumination 1066-1200*, Cambridge 1954.

A. Goldschmidt, *Der Albanipsalter in Hildesheim*, Berlin 1895.

M. R. James, *The Canterbury Psalter*, London 1934.

M. R. James, *Four Leaves of an English Psalter* (Walpole Society XXV, Oxford 1936-37, pp. 1-23).

N. Ker, *Medieval Libraries of Great Britain*, London 1941.

R. Mynors, *Durham Cathedral Manuscripts to the End of the 12th Century*, Oxford 1939.

W. Oakeshott, *The Artists of the Winchester Bible*, London 1945.

O. E. Saunders, *English Illumination* I, Munich and Florence 1928.

F. Wormald, *The Development of English Illumination in the Twelfth Century* (Journal of the British Archaeological Association VIII, 1943, pp. 31-49).

F. Wormald, *The Survival of Anglo-Saxon Illumination after the Norman Conquest* (Proceedings of the British Academy XXX, 1944, pp. 127-145).

F. Wormald, *The Sherborne "Chartulary"* (Fritz Saxl, A Volume of Memorial Essays, London 1956, pp. 101-119).

FLANDERS

Art mosan et arts anciens du pays de Liège (Notices by F. Masai), Liége 1951.

A. Boutemy, *La miniature* (in E. de Moreau, *Histoire de l'Eglise en Belgique*, II, 2nd edition, Brussels 1946, pp. 311-352).

J. Brassinne and M. Laurent, *Etude critique de deux miniatures de la collection Wittert* (Etudes liégeoises, Liége, 1919, pp. 113-129).

E. G. Millar, *The St. Trond Lectionary*, Roxburghe Club, Oxford 1949.

R. Schilling, *Two unknown Flemish Miniatures of the 11th Century* (Burlington Magazine, Nov. 1948, p. 312 ff.).

M. Schott, *Zwei Lütticher Sakramentare aus Bamberg und Paris und ihre Verwandten* (Studien zur deutschen Kunstgeschichte, vol. 284), Strasbourg 1931.

J. Stiennon, *Du Lectionnaire de Saint-Trond aux Evangiles d'Averbode* (Scriptorium VII, 1953, pp. 37-50).

J. Stiennon, *La Miniature dans le diocèse de Liège aux XIe et XIIe siècles* (L'Art mosan, articles edited by P. Francastel, Paris 1953, pp. 90-101).

K. H. Usener, *Das Breviar Clm. 23 261 der Bayrischen Staatsbibliothek und die Anfänge der romanischen Buchmalerei in Lüttich* (Münchener Jahrbuch der bildenden Kunst, Series III, vol. I, 1950, p. 78 ff.).

K. H. Usener, *Les débuts du style roman dans l'art mosan* (L'art mosan, Paris 1953, pp. 103-112).

P. Wescher, *Eine Miniaturenhandschrift des 12. Jahrhunderts aus der Maasgegend* (Amtliche Berichte aus d. Preuss. Kunstsamml., Berlin 1928, Heft 4, p. 9 ff.).

FRANCE

Les Manuscrits à Peintures en France du VII⁰ au XII⁰ siècle (Catalogue by J. PORCHER), Exhibition at the Bibliothèque Nationale, Paris 1954.

L'art du Moyen Age en Artois (Notices on the manuscripts by J. PORCHER), Arras 1951.

L'art roman à Saint-Martial de Limoges (Notices by J. PORCHER), Limoges 1950.

Exposition Scaldis (Notices by A. BOUTEMY), Tournai 1956.

Saint Bernard et l'art des Cisterciens, exhibition catalogue, Dijon 1953.

A. BOUTEMY, *Quelques aspects de l'œuvre de Sawalon* (Revue belge d'archéologie et d'histoire de l'art IX, 1939, pp. 299-316).

A. BOUTEMY, *L'illustration de la Vie de saint Amand* (Scriptorium X, 1940, pp. 231-249).

A. BOUTEMY, *Les enlumineurs de l'abbaye de Saint-Amand* (Scriptorium XII, 1942, pp. 131-167).

A. BOUTEMY, *Un grand enlumineur du X⁰ siècle : l'abbé Odbert de Saint-Bertin* (Annales de la Fédération archéologique et historique de la Belgique XXXII, 1947, p. 247 ff.).

A. BOUTEMY, *De quelques enlumineurs de manuscrits de l'abbaye de Corbie* (Scriptorium IV, 1950, pp. 246-252).

A. BOUTEMY, *Une Bible enluminée de Saint-Vaast d'Arras* (Scriptorium IV, 1950, pp. 67-81).

A. BOUTEMY, *La Bible de Saint-André-au-Bois* (Scriptorium V, 1951, pp. 222-237).

A. BOINET, *Vie de saint Omer* (Bulletin archéologique du Comité des travaux historiques 1904, p. 415 ff.).

A. BOINET, *Quelques œuvres de peintures exécutées à l'abbaye de Saint-Aubin d'Angers du IX⁰ au XII⁰ siècles* (Congrès archéologique de France, LXXVII⁰ session, Angers, 1910, vol. II, pp. 158-179).

Y. DESLANDES, *Les manuscrits décorés au XI⁰ siècle à Saint-Germain-des-Prés par Ingelard* (Scriptorium IX, 1955, pp. 3-16).

C. R. DODWELL, *Un manuscrit enluminé de Jumièges au British Museum* (Jumièges, Congrès scientifique du XIII⁰ centenaire, Rouen 1955, pp. 737-741).

E. A. ESCHALLIER, *L'abbaye d'Anchin*, Lille 1852.

E. GINOT, *Le manuscrit de Sainte Radegonde de Poitiers et ses peintures du XI⁰ siècle* (Bulletin de la Société française de reproduction de manuscrits à peintures IV, 1914-1920, pp. 9-80).

R. GREEN, *The Flabellum of Hohenburg* (Art Bulletin XXXIII, 1951, pp. 153-155).

P. LAUER, *Les enluminures romanes de la Bibliothèque Nationale*, Paris 1927.

J. LECLERCQ, *Les manuscrits de l'abbaye de Liessies* (Scriptorium VI, 1953, p. 51 ff.).

F. MERCIER, *Les primitifs français : La peinture clunisienne en Bourgogne à l'époque romane*, Paris 1931.

E. A. VAN MOÉ, *L'Apocalypse de Saint-Sever, Ms. lat. 8878 de la Bibliothèque Nationale*, Paris 1942.

L. MOREL-PAYEN, *Les plus beaux manuscrits et les plus belles reliures de la bibliothèque de Troyes*, Troyes 1935.

C. NIVER, *A Twelfth Century Sacramentary in the Walters Collection* (Speculum X, 1935, pp. 333-337).

C. NORDENFALK, *A Travelling Milanese Artist in France at the beginning of the 11th century* (Arte del primo millenio, Milan 1953, pp. 374-380).

C. OURSEL, *La Bibliothèque de l'abbaye de Saint-Bénigne et ses plus anciens manuscrits illuminés* (Mémoires de l'Académie de Dijon 1924).

C. OURSEL, *La Bible de Saint-Bénigne de Dijon* (Les Trésors des Bibliothèques de la France I, 1926, pp. 127-139).

C. OURSEL, *La miniature à l'Abbaye de Cîteaux*, Dijon 1926.

O. PÄCHT, *Hugo Pictor* (The Bodleian Library Record III, 1950, pp. 96-103).

M. SCHAPIRO, *New Documents on St. Gilles* (Art Bulletin XVII, 1935, pp. 415-430).

M. SCHAPIRO, *Two Romanesque Drawings in Auxerre and Some Iconographic Problems* (Studies in Art and Literature for Belle da Costa Greene, Princeton 1954, pp. 331-349).

S. SCHULTEN, *Die Buchmalerei des 11. Jahrhunderts im Kloster St. Vaast in Arras* (Münchener Jahrbuch der bildenden Kunst, Series III, vol. VII, 1956, pp. 49-90).

H. SWARZENSKI, *Der Stil der Bibel Carilefs von Durham* (Form und Inhalt. Festschrift für Otto Schmitt zum 60. Geburtstag, Stuttgart 1950, pp. 89-95).

A. WILMART, *Les livres de l'abbé Odbert* (Bulletin de la Société des Antiquaires de la Morinie XIV, 1924, pp. 169-188).

ITALY AND THE HOLY LAND

Mostra storico-nazionale della miniatura (Catalogue by M. SALMI and G. MUZZIOLI), Florence 1953.

M. AVERY, *The Exultet Rolls of South Italy* (Illuminated Manuscripts of the Middle Ages IV), Princeton 1936.

P. BALDASS, *Disegni della Scuola Cassinese del tempio di Desiderio* (Bollettino d'arte XXXVII, 1952, pp. 102-114).

P. BALDASS, *Die Miniaturen zweier Exultet-Rollen* (Scriptorium VIII, 1954, pp. 75-88).

E. BERTAUX, *L'art dans l'Italie méridionale*, Paris 1904.

H. BLOCH, *Monte Cassino, Byzantium and the West in the Earlier Middle Ages* (Dumbarton Oaks Papers III, 1946, p. 239).

H. BUCHTHAL, *A School of Miniature Painting in Norman Sicily* (Late Classical and Medieval Studies in honor of A. M. FRIEND, Princeton 1955, pp. 312-339).

H. BUCHTHAL, *The Beginnings of Manuscript Illumination in Norman Sicily* (Papers of the British School in Rome XXIV, 1956, pp. 78-85).

H. BUCHTHAL, *Miniature Painting in the Latin Kingdom of Jerusalem*, Oxford 1957.

P. D'ANCONA, *La miniature italienne du X⁰ au XVI⁰ siècle*, Paris 1925.

E. B. GARRISON, *Studies in the History of Mediaeval Italian Painting* I-III, Florence 1953 et seq.

E. B. GARRISON, *A Lucchese Passionary Related to the Sarzana Crucifix* (Art Bulletin XXXV, 1953, pp. 109-119).

M. INGUANEZ and M. AVERY, *Miniature Cassinesi del secolo XI illustranti la vita di S. Benedetto*, Montecassino 1934.

B. KATTERBACH, *Le miniature dell'Epistolario di Padova* (Codices ex ecclesiasticis Italiae bibliothecis V), Vatican City 1932.

G. LADNER, *Die italienische Malerei im 11. Jahrhundert* (Jahrbuch der kunsthistorischen Sammlungen in Wien, N.F. V, 1931, pp. 33-160).

G. LADNER, *The Portraits of Emperors in Southern Italian Exultet Rolls* (Speculum XVII, 1942, p. 181).

E. A. Lowe, *Scriptura Beneventana*, Oxford 1929.

L. Magnani, *Le miniature del Sacramentario d'Ivrea e di altri codici Warmondiani* (Codices ex ecclesiasticis bibliotecae Italiae praesertim selecti V), Vatican City 1934.

P. Pirri, *La Scuola miniaturistica dell'abbazia di S. Eutizio* (Scriptorium III, 1949, pp. 3-10).

M. Salmi, *Italian Miniatures*, New York 1954.

P. Toesca, *La Pittura e la Miniatura nella Lombardia*, Milan 1912.

P. Toesca, *Miniature romane dei sec. XI e XII. Bibbie miniate* (Rivista del R. Istituto d'Archeologia e Storia dell'Arte 1929, pp. 69-96).

G. F. Warner, *Gospels of Mathilda, Countess of Tuscany*. Roxburghe Club, New York 1917.

SCANDINAVIA

Greek and Latin Illuminated Manuscripts in Danish Collections, Copenhagen 1921.

L. Nielsen, *Danmarks Middelalderlige Haandskrifter*, Copenhagen 1937.

C. Nordenfalk, *Romanska bokmalningar i Skara Stiftsbibliothek* (Göteborgs Högskolas Arsskrift XLVII, 1941:20).

SPAIN

J. Dominguez Bordona, *Manuscritos con pinturas* I-II, Madrid 1933.

J. A. Marazuela, *Un scriptorium español desconocido* (Scriptorium II, 1948, pp. 3-27).

W. Neuss, *Die katalanische Bibelillustration*, Bonn-Leipzig 1922.

III. PRINCIPAL TYPES OF MANUSCRIPTS

A. BIBLES

S. Berger, *Histoire de la Vulgate pendant les premiers siècles du moyen âge*, Paris 1893.

H. Glunz, *Die Literarästhetik des europäischen Mittelalters* (Das Abendland II), Cologne 1937.

Dom H. Quentin, *Mémoire sur l'établissement du texte de la Vulgate* (Collectanea Biblica Latina VI), Rome-Paris 1922.

B. Smalley, *The Study of the Bible in the Middle Ages*, Oxford 1941.

B. PSALTERS

G. Haseloff, *Die Psalterillustration im 13. Jahrhundert*, Kiel 1938.

V. Leroquais, *Les psautiers manuscrits latins des Bibliothèques de France*, Paris 1940-1941.

C. EDIFYING WRITINGS

A. de Laborde, *Les manuscrits à peintures de la Cité de Dieu*, Paris 1909.

O. Pächt, *The Illustrations of St. Anselm's Prayers and Meditations* (Journal of the Warburg and Courtauld Institutes XIX: 1-2, 1956, pp. 68-83).

H. Swarzenski, *Eine Handschrift von Gregors Moralia in Job* (Wallraf-Richartz-Jahrbuch N.F. 1, 1930, p. 9).

A. Watson, *The Speculum Virginum with special reference to the Tree of Jesse* (Speculum III, 1928, pp. 445-469).

F. Wormald, *Some Illustrated Manuscripts of the Lives of the Saints* (Bulletin of the John Rylands Library XXXV, 1952, pp. 248-266).

D. ENCYCLOPEDIAS AND OTHER BOOKS OF LEARNING

Dom L. Baillet, *Les miniatures du Scivias de sainte Hildegarde conservé à la Bibliothèque de Wiesbaden* (Fondation E. Piot, Monuments et mémoires XIX, 1911, pp. 49-149).

O. Gillen, *Ikonographische Studien zum Hortus deliciarum* (Kunstwissenschaftliche Studien IX), Berlin 1931.

A. Goldschmidt, *Frühmittelalterliche illustrierte Encyclopädien* (Vorträge der Bibliothek Warburg 1923-1924, p. 220).

M. R. James, *The Bestiary*, Roxburghe Club, Oxford 1928.

H. Keller, *Mittelrheinische Buchmalereien in Handschriften aus dem Kreise der Hiltgart von Bingen*, Stuttgart 1933.

F. Saxl, *Illustrated Mediaeval Encyclopaedias* (Lectures I-II, London 1957, I pp. 228-254).

A. Straub and G. Keller, *Herrade de Landsberg, Hortus deliciarum*, Strasbourg 1879-1899; new edition 1901.

J. Walter, *Herrade de Landsberg, Hortus deliciarum*, Strasbourg 1925.

INDEX OF MANUSCRIPTS

Page numbers in italics refer to miniatures illustrated in the text

LENINGRAD, Public Library:
F.v.I.133 *Prophetical Books of the Bible* (see also New York, Public Library, Spencer 1), Weingarten, early 13th century, 196.

LEYDEN, University Library:
Bpl. 20 Manuscript from the monastery of Bec in Normandy (compilation of historical texts), 12th century 139.

LIÉGE, Bibliothèque de l'Université:
Cod. 3 *Averbode Gospel Book*, Mosan School, mid-12th century 162, *165*, 186.

LIÉGE, Wittert Collection:
Page from a Psalter (?) of Liége, Mosan School, mid-12th century 172, 193.

LONDON, British Museum:
Add. 17737/38 *Floreffe Bible*, Mosan School, third quarter of the 12th century 164, 195;
Add. 28106/07 *Stavelot Bible*, signed by Goderannus, Stavelot, 1097-1098 166, *180*, 181, 190;
Add. 39943 *The Venerable Bede, Vita Sancti Cuthberti*, Northern England, late 12th century 148;
Add. 42497 Strip of vellum, probably a flabellum, with Scenes from the Life of St John the Baptist, Hohenburg, second half of the 12th century 160;
Add. 46487 *Sherborne Lectionary*, with inventory of the Cathedral Treasure, Sherborne, mid-12th century 145, 146;
Arundel 44 *Conrad of Hirsau, Speculum Virginum*, Swabia, early 12th century 161;
Cotton MS Nero C.IV *Psalter of Henry of Blois*, Winchester, mid-12th century 114, 156, *157*, 192;
Egerton 1139 *Psalter of Queen Melisende of Jerusalem*, second quarter of the 12th century 138, 172;
Harl. 2798/99 *Arnstein Bible*, Rhineland, second half of the 12th century 143, 195;
Harl. Roll Y.6 Roll with Scenes of the Life of St Guthlac, Northern England, early 12th century 148;
Lansdowne 381 *Psalter of Queen Matilda* (?), fragment, Helmarshausen, 1167 (?) 172;
Lansdowne 383 *Shaftesbury Psalter*, Winchester (?), second quarter of the 12th century 170.

LONDON, Victoria and Albert Museum:
MS 413 Page from a Psalter (?) of Liége, Mosan School, mid-12th century 172, 193.

LONDON, Lambeth Palace Library:
MS 3 *Lambeth Bible* (see also Maidstone Museum, Kent, MS P.5), Canterbury, mid-12th century 167, *168*, 192.

LUCCA, Biblioteca Governamentale:
MS 1942 *St Hildegard of Bingen, Liber divinorum operum*, Rhineland, early 13th century 160, 161.

MAIDSTONE Museum, Kent:
MS P.5 *Lambeth Bible* (see also London, Lambeth Palace Library), Canterbury, mid-12th century 167, *168*, 192.

METZ, Bibliothèque Municipale (destroyed in 1944):
Salis 5 *Gospel Book of Wedricus* (destroyed, surviving fragment at Avesnes, Bibliothèque Municipale), Liessies or Canterbury, before 1147 192.

MICHELBEUERN, Stiftsbibliothek:
Cod. 1 *Walters Bible*, Salzburg, second quarter of the 12th century 167.

MONTPELLIER, Bibliothèque de l'Ecole de Médecine:
MS H.30 *Passional*, Cîteaux, ca. 1125 *155*, 156.

MOULINS, Bibliothèque Municipale:
MS 1 *Souvigny Bible*, Burgundy, second half of the 12th century 170, 195.

MUNICH, Staatsbibliothek:
Clm. 935 So-called *Prayer Book of St Hildegard of Bingen*, Rhineland, second quarter of the 12th century 195;
Clm. 4660 *Carmina burana*, Bavaria, early 13th century 186, *200*, 201, 203, 205, 206;
Clm. 15 902 *Prayer Book of St Erentrude*, Salzburg, late 12th century 196.

MÜNSTER, Staatsarchiv:
Cod. I.133 *Confraternity Book*, Korvei, second quarter of the 12th century 146.

NEW YORK, The Pierpont Morgan Library:
M. 504 *Vita Sancti Martini*, Tournai, third quarter of the 12th century 181;
M. 619 Page of the *Winchester Bible*, second half of the 12th century 168;
M. 710 *Berthold Missal*, Weingarten, early 13th century 196, *197*;
M. 736 *Vita et Miracula Sancti Edmundi*, Bury St Edmunds, ca. 1130 148;
M. 855 *Seitenstetten Missal*, School of Gaibana, second quarter of the 13th century 198;
M. 883 *Gospel Book of Saint-Trond*, Mosan School, mid-12th century 162.

NEW YORK, Public Library:
Spencer 1 *Prophetical Books of the Bible* (see also Leningrad, Public Library), Weingarten, early 13th century 196.

OXFORD, Bodleian Library:
Auct. D.2.6 *St Anselm, Meditationes*, Southern England, mid-12th century 152;
Auct. E. Infra I *Bible*, Winchester (?), mid-12th century 174, *175*, 177;
Bodl. 717 *Hieronymus in Isaiam*, illuminated by Hugo, *pictor et illuminator*, Normandy or England, ca. 1100 205.

OXFORD, University College Library:
MS 165 *The Venerable Bede, Vita Sancti Cuthberti*, Northern England, first half of the 12th century 148.

PADUA, Cathedral Treasure:
Epistolary, written by Giovanni da Gaibana, Padua or Venice, 1259 195.

PARIS, Bibliothèque Nationale:
Lat. 5 *First Bible of Limoges*, ca. 1000 166, 176;
Lat. 6 *Bible of Santa Maria de Ripoll*, Catalonia, first half of the 11th century 72, 166;
Lat. 8 *Second Bible of Limoges*, ca. 1100 167;
Lat. 254 *New Testament*, region of Agen-Moissac, ca. 1100 *179*;
Lat. 2288 *Letters of St Gregory*, St Martin's Abbey, Tournai, mid-12th century *199*, 201;
Lat. 2342 Anonymous writings on the Holy Scriptures and Monkhood, Bec (Normandy), ca. 1100 139;
Lat. 5058 *Flavius Josephus, De Bello Judaico*, Moissac, late 11th century 96;
Lat. 8846 *Psalter*, Winchester or Canterbury, ca. 1200 117;
Lat. 8878 *Beatus Apocalypse*, Saint-Sever, mid-11th century *132*, 138, 140;
Lat. 9865 *Cartularies of Saint-Pierre de Nevers*, second half of the 12th century 145;
Lat. 15176 *Bible of St Odilo*, written by Franco, Cluny, first third of the 11th century (finished in the second half of the 12th century) 166, 170;
Lat. 15675 *St Gregory, Moralia in Job*, region of Cambrai, ca. 1150 152;
Nouv. acq. lat. 1390 *Life and Miracles of St Aubin*, Angers, late 11th century 148;
Nouv. acq. lat. 2246 *Lectionary*, Cluny, first third of the 12th century 190.

INDEX OF NAMES AND PLACES

LIST OF COLORPLATES

ELEVENTH CENTURY

FRESCOS

MINIATURES

THIRTEENTH CENTURY

CONTENTS

THIS VOLUME OF THE COLLECTION

THE GREAT CENTURIES OF PAINTING

WAS PRODUCED BY THE TECHNICAL STAFF OF ÉDITIONS D'ART ALBERT SKIRA,
FINISHED THE FIRST DAY OF MARCH, NINETEEN HUNDRED AND FIFTY-EIGHT

TEXT AND COLORPLATES BY

COLOR STUDIO AT IMPRIMERIES RÉUNIES S.A., LAUSANNE

PLATES ENGRAVED BY
GUEZELLE ET RENOUARD, PARIS

The works reproduced in this volume were photographed by Claudio Emmer, Milan (pages 24, 26, 29, 31, 34, 35, 37, 38, 39, 40, 41, 44, 45, 47, 48, 50, 51, 52, 53, 54, 56, 57, 59, 60, 61, 62, 63, 64, 137, 147, 169, 188, 189), by Hans Hinz, Basel (pages 66, 70, 73, 74, 75, 76, 80, 81, 82, 83, 84, 119, 122, 123, 124, 150, 167, 171, 191), by Henry B. Beville, Washington (pages 77, 78, 79, 197), by Louis Laniepce, Paris (pages 86, 89, 90, 91, 92, 93, 96, 97, 99, 100, 101, 104, 105, 109, 149, 153, 155, 156, 162, 174, 185, 187, 194, 202, 203, 204), by Zoltan Wegner, London (pages 112, 115, 166, 168, 176), by Niels Elswing, Copenhagen (page 129), and by the photographic services of the Bibliothèque Nationale, Paris (pages 132, 179, 199), the British Museum, London (pages 157, 180), the Cambridge University Library (page 177), the Staatsbibliothek, Munich (page 200) and the Oxford University Press, Oxford (page 175).